Long-Range Planning
In American Industry

LONG-RANGE PLANNING
IN
AMERICAN INDUSTRY

By Brian W. Scott

American Management Association, Inc.

"It is always wise to look ahead, but difficult
to look further than you can see."

—Winston S. Churchill,
in a speech to the House of Commons,
July 23, 1952

Foreword

THE PRIMARY PURPOSE OF THIS BOOK IS TO CONTRIBUTE TO-ward an understanding of corporate long-range planning—an important area of managerial responsibility which so far has not received very much detailed analysis in business literature. The subject is examined from a general management standpoint, first by developing some insights about long-range planning as a unified concept and then by analyzing several important aspects in greater detail.

As the research basis for the study, executives in 12 companies were interviewed. The companies ranged in size from medium to very large, and each had spent a considerable amount of time, money, and energy in attempting to systematize its long-range planning activities. The interviews were conducted with senior executives who were intimately associated with planning activities. The executives were all willing to spend a good deal of time being interviewed, and return visits to some for follow-up interviews were made at a later date. This willingness to participate and the frankness with which these men were prepared to talk about the various facets of their job have been of enormous value and were indicative of the interest which they have in encouraging more research advancement in the study of long-range planning.

The executives interviewed typically discussed their companies' experiences chronologically, which provided an opportunity to review with them some of the insights they felt they had gained, some of the problems they had encountered, and, of course, some of the mistakes they had inevitably made along the way. In some cases internal company papers were made available, either for general background information or for direct or indirect inclusion in this book.

The information obtained during interviews is incorporated into the analysis of the book, but no attempt has been made to include an evaluation of the planning done by the different companies. The reasons for this exclusion will be fairly obvious to the reader. Any attempt at evaluation of long-range plans would quickly assume massive proportions. Not only are the results of long-range planning inevitably mixed in with many other company activities, but also the criteria developed for appraising results are not well defined. Thus, evaluation would only confuse the primary purpose of the study.

An extensive review of existing management literature pertaining to long-range planning reveals an anomaly. There are a vast number of articles written since World War II which deal with matters relating directly to long-range planning, though often they are disguised under titles which have little overt relationship to the subject. By contrast, books and monographs dealing *specifically* with long-range planning are rare prior to 1962. One of the few books published before this date which has the term "long-range planning" in its title is a collection of articles on the subject.[1]* Since 1962, however, there have been at least six full-length books published on various aspects of corporate long-range planning. It takes no great daring to predict that the literature on this subject will grow during the coming years.

Despite the paucity of books, a survey of the literature is extremely useful, both in discovering more about the way in which executives think and talk about long-range planning, and also in drawing together different ideas to sharpen and clarify various concepts. A select bibliography is printed at the end of the book.

The content of the book is focused upon three major areas of inquiry. The first is an examination of the subject and its background —including terminology, confusions, useful classifications, and historical development. Planning is a much misunderstood word, and it is essential at the outset to put the subject into clear and orderly perspective.

The second area of inquiry is strategic long-range planning, which is concerned with fundamental questions of corporate direction and purpose. It is, paradoxically, both the oldest and the newest form of long-range planning. It is the oldest, since it was employed informally by some of the early captains of industry (as is shown in Chapter 3). It is the newest, because only very recently have companies really become interested in its possibilities as a systematized, specialized area of study. Strategic planning can be of transcending im-

* All references in parentheses are listed in "Notes to the Text," which appears at the end of the book.

portance to a corporation, and Part II of this study is devoted to a detailed conceptual analysis of it.

The third area of inquiry is the organization of the long-range planning activity. One of the significant features of modern-day attention to the subject is the way in which companies have sought to formalize their approaches, and various organizational patterns and innovations are analyzed in Part III.

In summary, it is hoped that the results of this study will prove useful to practicing executives in clarifying a number of salient points and in providing insights facilitating a better conceptual understanding of the subject.

Acknowledgments

IT IS A GREAT PLEASURE TO BE ABLE TO ACKNOWLEDGE THE help which I have received from many different people while preparing the manuscript for this book.

The book began as a thesis written at the Harvard University Graduate School of Business Administration, and I want first to pay tribute to a trio of long-suffering thesis committee members—Professor Richard S. Meriam, Professor Charles A. Bliss, and Dr. Wilson Nolen. These men all assisted through their discerning criticisms, their invaluable suggestions, and their ready cooperation at all times. My debt to Professor Meriam is especially great. On countless occasions he helped to clarify ideas and to sharpen concepts. He spared no effort in giving counsel and assistance in this project, and I shall always be most grateful to him for his encouragement. It was a great privilege and a most rewarding learning experience to work closely with him.

Secondly, I want to pay a more general tribute to the two Business Schools I attended. As an Australian, I suppose it is natural that I should be especially appreciative of the opportunity to study at both Harvard and Stanford. This book incorporates many ideas stimulated by experiences and discussions held during the five years I spent at these two universities, and my thanks are due collectively to many fellow students and faculty members. May I just add that, like many another foreign student, I look back upon this period as a visitor in the United States with the greatest appreciation to the country and its people.

Next, I should like to express special thanks to members of my own family. My parents have always been a source of inspiration to me, and to them goes my heartfelt gratitude. I remember Dr. Lillian Gilbreth once talking about the importance of "choosing parents wisely"; and I am impelled to claim that in this matter I was a wise chooser. It gives me enormous pleasure now to be associated with my father in the management consulting firm which he founded some

11

26 years ago and which has now grown to the point where there are more than 100 consultants carrying out assignments on four continents.

And finally, I wish to thank my wife, who was cheerful, patient, and always encouraging during the slow and painful process of thesis writing. As she well knows, this acknowledgment is really the most important of all.

BRIAN W. SCOTT
Sydney, November 1964

Contents

Appendix

PART I

Long-Range Planning:
Introduction and Background

Chapter 1

The Nature of Business Planning

This is a study designed to inquire broadly into some aspects of corporate long-range planning. Its primary aims are three-fold: first, to achieve a better intrinsic understanding of long-range planning itself and of what the subject encompasses; second, to describe and analyze that type of long-range planning which will later be defined as "strategic"; and third, to describe and analyze various approaches to formalizing long-range planning activities.

The rationale for making such a study as this is readily explainable. Corporate long-range planning is a subject which has received the spotlight of managerial attention only in the years since World War II. In little over a decade and a half the subject has risen from relative obscurity to become one of the most illustrious bywords in management jargon today. Indeed, if the tone of recent literature is any indication, long-range planning has emerged as a pre-eminent symbol of executive excellence, the quintessence of achievement in professional management.

Yet despite the generally assumed importance and undoubted popularity of the subject, there is a notable dearth of systematic study relating to it. In colloquial terms, there is too much "fad" about long-range planning and too little "fact." Much more knowledge is needed about the "why," the "when," the "what," the "who," and the "how" of long-range planning activities. And it is toward this goal of greater understanding that the present book is directed.

HISTORY OF THE WORD "PLANNING"

Since today's long-range planning is essentially a modern scion of more traditional forms of business planning,[1]* we need to begin

* All references in parentheses are listed in "Notes to the Text," which appears at the end of the book.

this study with an examination of the nature of business planning. And at the outset it will be helpful if we consider some matters of terminology.

The word "planning" derives from the Latin *planus,* meaning "flat," and it first entered the English language in the 17th century. At that time it had a narrow and specific meaning, describing the act of drawing or sketching an object on a flat surface, such as the drawing of a blueprint.

While blueprint drawing is still recognized as one form of planning, the word has been applied to an ever-increasing number of other situations during its three centuries of English usage. Today it is popularly taken to refer to "any definite intention or undertaking," and as such it applies to almost everything people do. To cite a few representative examples, planning can relate to personal activities ("planning a career"); group or social activities ("planning an evening's entertainment"); military activities ("planning tactics"); and governmental activities ("planning a public works program").

Extensive use of the word "planning" in relation to business operations dates back less than 100 years. It became prominent during the late 19th century as a direct result of the growth of the scientific management movement. The pioneers of that movement sought to replace "rule of thumb practices" by "scientific methods," and to this end they introduced various techniques of "planning" factory performance and activity.

The ensuing years have seen an ever-widening range of managerial activities becoming "planned." They have also seen existing "planning" techniques become more refined as the result of continuing experience and experiment. The attention now being given to "long-range planning" represents a latter-day manifestation of this trend.

"PLANNING" AS A MANAGEMENT FUNCTION

Exponents of a so-called orthodox theory of management[2] have usually attempted to group the task requirements of a manager's job into a small number of functional elements. That is to say, they have sought to classify those characteristics which they consider to be the natural, normal, intrinsic parts of the job of managing a business, claiming that "managers perform the same functions regardless of their place in the organization structure or the type of activity in which they are engaged." [3]

The general pattern for this type of analysis was first set by the French industrialist Henri Fayol, who referred to five key functions of managing—planning, organizing, command, coordination, and control. [4] Since that time (1916) a considerable number of writers have formulated their own lists of functions, but there is still no general accord as to classification. [5] Some of the unresolved differences are primarily semantic in nature, while others relate to more basic differences in understanding the job of managing. [6] Here, however, we shall attempt no synthesis of varying viewpoints, but rather a description of the nature of these functions of management and in particular a clarification of the concept of "planning" as one such function.

Although differences exist regarding which functions, taken together, constitute an accurate picture of the job of managing, the inclusion of "planning" as one of these functions is nowhere disputed. This is not to imply that the function of "planning" will always convey the same meaning to each writer. [7] Nevertheless, it does mean that at the verbal level "planning" is universally accepted as one of the functions of managing.

We also need to view the concept of "planning" in two different perspectives or dimensions. In its broader perspective, "planning" is seen as only one part—albeit an important part—of the organic whole of managing. In other words, "planning" is an artificial abstraction from within the overall task of management, and it cannot exist meaningfully as an independent entity. Its usefulness ultimately derives from its interrelationship with other management functions.

Yet at the same time "planning" can also be seen in a narrower context as a separable concept upon which exclusive attention can be focused. It is conducive to specialization, and an attempt to view the subject through an analytic magnifying glass can be most helpful in identifying its important characteristics.

We will want to keep both these dimensions constantly in mind as we proceed with this analysis of long-range planning. They appear paradoxical, because "planning" is seen as both independent and interdependent, as separated and inseparable. Yet if both dimensions are not kept constantly in mind, one can easily lapse into the extremes of ivory-tower planning in the one case or arbitrary planning in the other. In theory as in practice, a manager continually has to balance planning needs with the problems of relating plans to other functional aspects of his managerial job.

DEFINITION OF THE WORD "PLANNING"

Henri Fayol's writings of 1916 again provide a convenient starting point when we seek to develop a definition of the word "planning" in the business context. Fayol captures the idea of planning as a process:

> The plan of action is, at one and the same time, the result envisaged, the line of action to be followed, the stages to go through, and the methods to use.[8]

For Fayol, therefore, planning meant "both to assess the future and make provision for it," [9] and writers on management since his time have accepted, by and large, these essential attributes of his definition. Two representative examples from recent management textbooks illustrate this point.

George R. Terry, in his *Principles of Management,* defines "planning" as:

> The selecting and relating of facts and the making and using of assumptions regarding the future in the visualization and formulation of proposed activities believed necessary to achieve desired results.[10]

Terry's definition is really an attempt to refine Fayol's concepts. Terry talks of "assessing the future" in terms of both desired results and assumptions; he talks of "making provision for the future" in terms of both fact finding and decision making; but he makes no basic departure from Fayol's approach.

The same conclusion applies to Harold Koontz and Cyril O'Donnell's *Principles of Management.* They describe "planning" as:

> An intellectual process, the conscious determination of courses of action, the basing of decision on purpose, facts, and considered estimates.[11]

They also leave Fayol's concepts of "assessing the future" and "making provision for the future" essentially intact. So, too, do most other attempts at formal definition. Some writers place prime emphasis upon the fact-finding aspects of the subject, while others stress the decision-making aspects. Most seem aware, however, that planning is a process which includes both of these concepts.

The definition of planning adopted for this study also relies, basically, upon these two concepts that Fayol formulated. Formally stated, the definition is as follows:

> Planning is an analytical process which encompasses an assessment of the future, the determination of desired objectives in the context of that future, the development of alternative courses of action to achieve such objectives, and the selection of a course (or courses) of action from among these alternatives.

IMPLICATIONS OF THE DEFINITION

A definition is only a starting point in any attempt to understand the meaning of a subject. This is especially true in the case of business planning, which is an abstract concept and therefore particularly prone to confusion. Consequently a number of important implications which stem from the definition should be noted.

The first implication is that business planning always has the mission of improvement—improvement, that is, from the standpoint of the interests of the company doing the planning. Such a mission can be traced through various evolutionary developments in business planning. The Gilbreths dramatized it for the early scientific management movement when they referred to "the search for the One Best Way." And much more recently (in 1960) one large company began a special corporate publication on business planning methods with these words: "Planning is based on man's assumption that even though the future is uncertain he can do something to make it better than it would be otherwise."

Of course there is no guarantee that a planned-for improvement will necessarily occur. In some cases it will not. However, the important point is that the planner is always concerned with visualizing changes which he thinks will improve the existing situation. It is in the context of this mission that the essential innovative role of business planning is seen most clearly. The mission also suggests one major reason why planning has become so integral a part of the manager's job in the mid-20th century.

A second implication of our definition of planning is that the plan must be accepted by the employees. Companies are made of people who have certain talents, hopes, and aspirations—both for themselves and for their companies—and a plan, if it is to prove successful, must take these human considerations into account. It is not enough for a plan to be technically sound; it also needs the additional virtues of being practical and intelligent.

While planners have a responsibility to make their plans acceptable to employees, a concurrent responsibility faces those employees. They have to recognize the fact that some changes in an organization are necessary and in the long run unavoidable and that they will facilitate successful planning if they adapt to reasonable changes willingly and cooperatively. Employee attitudes have a great deal to do with success—or the lack of it—in planning endeavors.

According to our definition, planning is concerned with the future. Yet, as has been well pointed out, "the overriding factor in business life is that the future is hidden." [12] Even the best of planners finds it impossible to anticipate all the opportunities and difficulties which may arise in the distant—or even, in many cases, the near—future. One result of this is that planning is often a process of groping forward, an uncertain attempt to cope with and anticipate circumstances as they *may* be at some future time. [13]

"Groping" is a matter of special importance for long-range planning. Later chapters give detailed attention to special aspects of this subject, such as uncertainty, risk, and the need for flexibility.

The definition refers to planning as a process. This means that it is composed of a series of conceptual phases, related to one another in an orderly fashion. There are, of course, a variety of possible ways in which these phases, or elements, may be classified. The approach outlined below is fairly typical, and it is a useful starting point in Part II of this study when we undertake a detailed analysis of strategic long-range planning as a process. The approach includes:

1. Establishing objectives.
2. Establishing planning assumptions.
3. Seeking the facts regarding possible courses of action.
4. Evaluating alternative courses of action.
5. Selecting a course (or courses) of action.

We have seen that the function of planning is really an artificial abstraction in the overall job of managing; in the same way, we need to think of these elements of the planning process as also being artificial abstractions. Although they are separable conceptually and, as such, are most valuable in phase-by-phase analysis, they are by their very nature interdependent and intertwined with the other phases of the process. The planning process, as observed in actual practice, requires a great deal of interaction among the various phases. For example, the objective of a plan is not always clear or obvious at the start, and it may be necessary to work through an entire subordinate planning process which has the objective of *finding* an appropriate objective. The objective in its final form may emerge only after a great deal of analysis has taken place in the main planning process.

Business plans are carried out at all levels of management, and most companies establish layers of plans which (in descending order) become progressively narrower and more detailed in their scope. They form, in other words, a hierarchy of plans whose various layers usually receive special designations, primarily to aid the administration of planning activities. These designations help clarify the scope of different plans, and they also help achieve consistency and harmony between the different plans.

Among the different types of plans commonly found in business firms are the following:

1. *Goals:* statements of the primary purposes for which the firm (or a component part of it) is being operated.
2. *Policies:* understandings (written, oral, or implicit) designed to set perimeters as guides to the thinking and action of subordinates within an organization.
3. *Budgets:* statements of expected quantitative results for some future period.
4. *Procedures:* statements which provide details of the way in which specific plans are to be accomplished.

From the standpoint of long-range planning, the need for consistency at these several levels assumes great importance. Most long-range plans fall into the category of either goals or policies, and their usefulness depends upon their being supported by accordant plans at lower levels of the hierarchy. One planning executive interviewed for this study stressed the same point in another way. "I have to see long-range planning," he said, "as being a part of total planning."

Finally, while the functions of "planning" and "control" may be conceptually separated, as a practical matter they should be seen as closely related and interdependent. Control is here considered to be measuring operating performance and seeing that it conforms to plans as closely as possible. Thus it is apparent that control is necessary if we are to receive any feedback regarding the progress of a plan.

We also have to recognize that many plans require not one but a series of decisions in order to achieve their desired objectives. These "sequential decisions" (as Spencer and Siegelman have termed them) are largely dependent upon control information for their effectiveness. They constitute—

> . . . a recognition that a multiplicity of changing factors may enter into the formulation of a plan, rather than a fixed set of circumstances to be reckoned with in a once-and-for-all or terminal manner. [14]

Long-range plans, by their very nature, require sequential decisions and subsequent readjustments more than most other kinds of plans. Interdependence is, therefore, very significant and will be stressed accordingly in this study.

CONFUSIONS ABOUT PLANNING

Broad agreement at the formal-definition level is one thing; agreement at the level of cognitive understanding is another. Unfortunately the situation at the second level is confused. As one man concluded some years ago, "It is doubtful whether any word in modern usage is more misunderstood than the word 'planning.' " [15]

This widespread confusion about the meaning of the word springs from several different, though overlapping, factors. First (as we have seen) the word "planning" is today used in many different contexts. In popular usage the word often has a much less specific meaning than that expressed in our formal definition, and it is difficult for businessmen to keep the popular usage completely separated from their business usage. As a result, there is some corruption of the

exact meaning given to "planning" in business. The word is sometimes used loosely in business to speak of anything which concerns
the future—whether or not there has been any attempt to assess the
future, and whether or not a decision has been based upon analysis
and considered judgment. In short, the word "planning" often trans-
mits only a blurry image of what is really meant.

A second factor adding to the confusion has also resulted from
the spillover of meaning from one context (politics) to another (business). At one stage the terms "planned economy" and "unplanned
economy" were confined to textbooks in economics and political
science. However, the growing attention focused upon the ideological
struggle between communism and free enterprise has given the word
"planning" a strong political connotation. While the word has a
utopian connotation for socialists and communists, it is often used
disparagingly by proponents of free enterprise.

This is an ironic situation, because the political point at issue is
not the desirability of planning, per se, but rather *who* should plan
and *how* planning should be organized. In this respect even the original textbook phrases were misnomers, and the confusion has been
compounded many times since the propaganda mills took over.

In actual fact the United States is not a country which spurns the
use of planning to direct its economic resources. Its demonstrated
ability to plan effectively at the individual business level has been a
vital contributing force in the country's economic progress. As a
prominent American once said: "Our history is one of planning, successfully, on an increasingly larger scale." [16]

Although these comments seem logical, politics is an emotional
subject, so logic does not always carry the day. Even casual observation reveals that many businessmen in the United States are still
wary of planning. They fail to keep the political and the business
contexts of the word separate, and they view the concept as "some
sort of infection exported by the Soviet Union." A national magazine
reported a few years ago that some companies were refusing to use
the term "five-year plan" because of its unfavorable political conno-
tations. [17]

These semantic difficulties need to be recognized by businessmen
if they are to understand the potential—and the limitations—of
long-range planning. The National Planning Association underscored the importance of this need in 1959 when it issued a statement

signed by many business and civic leaders. The statement says, in part:

> It would be one of the great tragedies of civilization if this country failed to realize the potentialities of long-range planning because it failed to distinguish between planning that is "made in USA" and planning that is "made in USSR." [18]

The psychological attitudes of businessmen toward business planning comprise another factor of the confusion. This factor is less easy to define than those based in semantic misunderstandings, but has perhaps the most significance. Universally acclaimed as a desirable activity, planning is "a dramatic new dimension in management" and is identifiable with the greatly admired quality of "farsightedness." Planning, however, necessitates dealing with uncertainty. The road ahead is not clear, but shrouded in fog, and the key landmarks are often not observable except at very short range. The problems of navigation are both difficult and unsettling.

These two orientations are clearly discordant. The pressures of each often result in the businessman's having ambivalent feelings toward planning, which, in turn, bring about degrees of obsessive thinking on the subject.

One reaction is to attempt to escape from the task of planning, to acknowledge the desirability of planning without really attempting it. Regret at the lack of time available for planning often accompanies this reaction.

Another reaction is to perceive planning as a means of controlling the future. In the realm of long-range planning, however, this is almost always unrealistic. The planner has to live with and deal with uncertainties which exist now and which will continue to exist. Most long-range planning partakes of "the art of associating yourself with the inevitable."

A third reaction is to conceive of planning as simply a means for minimizing risk. This is an orderly concept which has utility in certain quantitative approaches to planning. Nevertheless, it is not fruitful as a generalized way of thinking about planning. The planner often needs to be more concerned with being sure he is taking the *right* risks, even though this can be in many ways a more difficult task.

In short, business planning is still subject to a great deal of confused thinking. It has acute semantic problems, and also places the planner in an extremely uncertain and complex environment. Yet such is the nature of long-range planning.

REASONS FOR PLANNING

The answer to the fundamental question—"Why plan at all?"—is usually taken for granted; but planning, like everything else, requires justification of its existence. The underlying reasons for planning activities must, therefore, be defined.

The first justification stems from the fact that today's businessman operates in a system which is "by nature a form or method of economic change and not only never is but never can be stationary." [19] Planning is needed to help cope with this world of change. This kind of environment makes planning much more difficult, [20] but it also makes planning much more necessary. The businessman's choice is limited to two alternatives: Either he can try to grapple with these ever-changing conditions by means of planning techniques, or he can trust to luck by making no effort to plan. Business planning is predicated on the belief that, even though the future is uncertain, man can do something to make it better than would otherwise be possible.

A second justification of business planning may be stated in terms of the scientific order of things. As the late Professor Norbert Wiener observed, one of the most interesting aspects of the world is that it can be considered to be made up of patterns. A pattern, he writes, is essentially an arrangement characterized by the order of the elements of which it is made, rather than by the intrinsic nature of such elements. Such patterns may be spread out in space or distributed in time. [21]

Building upon these concepts, we can say that an essential aspect of business planning is to reveal and to use appropriate patterns, so that the job of managing in an increasingly complex world will remain manageable. The General Electric Company makes this point explicit:

> Our progress depends to a considerable extent on seeing to it that the simplifying processes move forward in approximate balance with the complicating processes. If this can be accomplished, then in-

dividuals with given ability can expect to go forward indefinitely without becoming casualties of their own competition. [22]

These, then, are the two major justifications usually offered for business planning. Together they make a powerful case for the importance of business planning, though they do not tell us how much planning is desirable. [23]

Chapter 2

The Meaning of Long-Range Planning

PLANNING HAS BECOME A PERVASIVE PART OF THE PRACTICE of management; it has steadily grown in scope, sophistication, and degree of specialization, and today there are many different classifications of business plans, each having distinctive characteristics and each requiring special investigation. "Long-range" planning is one such classification, and this chapter will seek to clarify its meaning and to explain the aims of the research upon which this present book rests.

CLASSIFICATION OF PLANS

While business plans may be classified in many possible ways, each classification is usually stated in terms peculiar to one of the following three major variables.[1]

1. *Subject area*. This variable is a low-level abstraction: Plans are simply described in the terms of observable specifications. One example of this kind of grouping is illustrated by the areas of functional specialization within an organization. Thus there are marketing plans, financial plans, production plans, and so on. Or there may be direct reference to the subject matter of the plan—as, for example, with product plans, manpower plans, and plans for international operations.

2. *Scope*. This second variable is a more complex abstraction: Plans are distinguished according to differing ranges of influence and differing amounts of detail.

One common example of classification by scope has already been mentioned: the hierarchical ranking of plans and the "layers of plans" within an organization which result. Goals, policies, budgets, and procedures are all examples of this type of classification. Another form of classification by scope relies on terminology borrowed from the military. Frequently one hears executives talking about their firm's strategic plans, tactical plans, and operational plans.

3. Time. The third variable, time, may be classified specifically (a one-year or a five-year plan) or vaguely (a short-range or a long-range plan). This is the variable by which "long-range" planning is distinguished from other forms of planning, even though the distinction is not nearly so precise as we should like.

This variable implies that there is something about the dimension of time which is significant and meaningful in the analysis of business plans, an implication which needs further exploration.

TIME AS A VARIABLE IN PLANNING

Classification by time is meaningful because time is one of the dimensions of our existence. The passage of time, proceeding as it does continuously and inexorably, is necessary for any action to take place. This symmetry in the passage of time makes it possible to utilize accepted units of time measurement—minutes, hours, days, weeks, months, years. This measurement gives a fundamental order to attempts to plan for the future.

The most common classification by the time variable differentiates "long-range plans" and "short-range plans." The distinction is imprecise and invites the questions, "How long is 'long-range'?" and "How short is 'short-range'?" These questions will be taken up subsequently, but their consideration is premature until the meaning of the terms is first clarified.

"Long-range" and "short-range" do *not* refer to any point of time at which planning decisions are made but to the futurity, or future actualization, of these decisions. Both long-range and short-range planning are concerned with decisions which need to be made in the present. As Peter F. Drucker has expressed it:

> The question that faces the long-range planner is not what we should do tomorrow. It is what do we have to do today to be ready for an uncertain tomorrow.[2]

If the time variable relates to the futurity of planning decisions, then how is this futurity to be measured? There are at least four different concepts of time measurement which concern us here.

The first of these is the *plan preparation time.* A plan which requires collaborative activity and the gathering of information which is not readily available may take months to complete; a simple plan with facts readily available may take only minutes.

Second, there is the necessary *lead time* which the plan requires for implementation. Lead time is a measure of the time which must elapse following one occurrence before a specified subsequent occurrence can take place.

The third concept measures the *direct impact time* of the planned activity, which is that period of time during which the activity now being planned will continue to operate or to have direct influence on operations.

Finally, there is the measurement of *epochal time*. This requires assessing historic trends and changes in order to determine the types of considerations which are likely to become of great importance to future business generations. It does not strive to measure futurity in any precise manner, but it suggests the kinds of momentous changes which may take place during coming decades.

DIFFERENT TYPES OF LONG-RANGE PLANNING

At a very general level, long-range planning is concerned with two separate questions:

1. Where are we going?
2. How do we get there?

In this study we shall describe the planning which deals with the first of these questions as being *strategic* and that which deals with the second as being *implementational.*[3]

Strategic long-range planning is a systematic approach by a given company to making decisions about issues which are of fundamental and crucial importance to its continuing long-term health and vitality. The fundamental and crucial importance of the issues is derived from the fact that they provide an underlying and unifying basis for all other plans to be developed within the company over a determinate period of time. Thus a long-range strategy is designed to provide information about a company's basic direction and purpose, which will serve as a guide for all the operational activities of that company.

Strategic long-range planning is a complex subject and not an easy one to analyze. It requires a great deal of subjective judgment and evaluation, and company planners sometimes have great difficulty in determining the issues upon which they should concentrate. Notwithstanding these difficulties, however, the subject is today receiving increasing attention in many companies, especially in large, well-financed corporations. It receives the primary focus of attention in this study, and Part II is devoted entirely to a detailed conceptual examination of it.

Implementational long-range planning is concerned with details of accomplishment: "How do we get there?" Implementational planning takes the guidelines for the future which are set forth in the company strategy. It seeks to spell out the details of those policies and procedures needed to accomplish the strategies in an effective manner.

Implementational long-range plans vary widely both in subject areas and in degrees of detail. Among the subjects frequently included under this heading are the following:

- Product development.
- Market development.
- Capital budgeting.
- Facilities development.
- Resource development.
- Manager development.

Since implementational long-range planning is closer to traditional planning activity and deals with more tangible concepts than strategic long-range planning, we should not be surprised to find that it currently appears to be the better understood and the more widely practiced form. [4]

AN ILLUSTRATIVE EXAMPLE

The distinction between strategic and implementational long-range planning is seen in the following hypothetical illustration which shows the relation of each type to the various concepts of time measurement.

Consider a large manufacturing company which has undertaken a major long-range planning project in January 1965 and expects to have definitive planning recommendations ready by July of that year. The company, let us say, is a manufacturer of a variety of different metal products and has been active in the production of assorted steel products.

One of the possible expansionary moves being considered is the construction and eventual operation of a large new mill for producing basic steel. Construction of such a mill could begin in early 1966, and indications are that the mill could reach operational readiness by the beginning of 1971. Industry information suggest that, judging by past performance, a mill of this kind will need to operate at least through 1990 if a satisfactory long-term return on the original investment is to be assured.

Even with such limited information, there are several conclusions regarding the various time measurements which can be drawn immediately.

First, the plan preparation time is expected to be six months. This is self-evident and requires no explanation.

Second, we can deduce that the suggested plan would require a lead time of five years. It will take this much time to construct the mill, purchase and install the necessary equipment and machinery, hire and train a workforce, and develop the various networks of suppliers, distributors, and shippers.

Third, it is apparent that the suggested plan would have a direct impact time extending well beyond this five years of preparatory activity. In fact, its direct impact would extend for at least the following 20 years—the period during which the investment should be paying for itself and earning a satisfactory profit. Thus the direct impact time in this plan would be about 25 years.

Fourth, the epochal time would have no precise measurement in such a plan as this, but its effect is apparent. The position of a company of this type in (let us say) the year 2000 will obviously be affected significantly by the various major planning activities it undertakes in the intervening years. A plan of the sort contemplated would have a major impact in helping to develop the traits which the company will have in coming decades.

This illustration can also be interpreted in the special considerations of strategic and implementational long-range planning activities. Strategic long-range planning is concerned with the wisdom of building the new steel mill. It raises such questions as: (a) Is this the direction in which the company should be expanding? (*b*) What implications does the plan carry for subsequent long-range plans? (*c*) What alternative possibilities are forgone if the plan is adopted?

Strategic long-range planning is concerned with the perspective suggested by the time measurement concepts of "direct impact time" and "epochal time." To illustrate, there are three different types of considerations which often are important in strategic long-range planning.

First, the person who is engaged in this kind of planning thoroughly examines the underlying assumptions which a proposed plan implies. Thus in the case of the plan calling for construction of a new steel mill there is apparently an assumption that demand for basic steel will remain strong at least through the 1980's. This means, in other words, an assumption that the market will not be badly harmed by interindustry competition (for instance, by aluminum, plastics, or exotic metals) during the next quarter of a century. Further, there is also the assumption that a plant built during the next five years would be able to compete satisfactorily with other American and foreign plants built in later years and incorporating more recent technological advances. These questions clearly require a consideration of problems in the context of their direct impact time.

Second, a strategic long-range planner considers the costs of making such commitments. The proposed investment in a large steel mill can be seen as a choice to invest in steel rather than (say) aluminum, plastics, oil, or electronics. There are many investment alternatives available, and the strategic long-range planner examines the major ones in the light of a corporate self-appraisal, an environmental assessment, and a competitor assessment. This requires review in the light of both direct impact time and the epochal time implications.

Third, the strategic long-range planner looks for hidden time commitments. Herbert Simon points out that a man who has spent seven years of his life preparing to be a physician and ten more practicing that profession does not ordinarily spend any more time deciding whether medicine should be his chosen career. "Alternative occupations," says Simon, "are practically closed to him by virtue of the investment he has already made in the strategy pursued thus far." [5] Analogously, an organization also "can be committed to a particular line of action from the fact that, having once initiated it, it appears preferable to continue with it rather than to relinquish completely the portion which has already been carried out." [6] This means that a commitment such as the one comtemplated will take the steel mill in a certain direction and therefore may influence many future decisions relating to other company plans. This aspect of strategic long-range planning, which is very important indeed, is closely associated with the concept of epochal time.

Implementational long-range planning, by contrast, starts with the premise that construction of the new steel mill seems, *prima facie*, to be a sound idea. It is concerned with more detailed, more specific, and more tangible considerations—the requirements and the financial soundness of the particular project and the steps needed for actual construction. Thus its main concern is with lead time.

HOW LONG IS "LONG-RANGE"?

The question, "How long is 'long-range'?" is usually raised with one of the following thoughts in mind:

1. What is the minimum lead time necessary to qualify a plan as "long-range"?
2. What is the most desirable lead time for long-range plans? [7]

Minimum lead time necessary for "long-range." The first question takes for granted that there is such a thing as a minimum lead time. As a result, further questions arise. At what point in the future does the planning activity split itself into "long-range planning" and "short-range planning"? If x denotes the time span, how long is x?

There are some immediate difficulties in trying to provide a quantitative answer. First, while the distinction between "long-range" and "short-range" is useful for analytical purposes, it has no necessary counterpart in organizational practice. A number of executives who were interviewed for this study disclaimed any formal separation of short- and long-range planning activities within their companies. They usually said that the two were "intertwined."

A second difficulty arises because the time span (x) does not have a constant value for all industries and all firms. In the fashion industry three months may seem long-range; in the electrical utility field three years may seem short-range. In other words, different industrial conditions may result in vastly different views about the time span.

Any attempt to provide a quick, neat, numerical answer to the question which will satisfy everyone seems bound to fail. In view of this the next step is an examination of possible nonquantitative criteria for the measurement of x.

One criterion states that every kind of plan which envisages a lead time extending beyond the length of a cycle of production should be considered long-range. This standard recognizes the time variations between different firms, but the term "cycle of production" is not clearly defined. If the period from the point when raw materials come in until the point when the end product goes out is meant, the time considered is often no more than several weeks and sometimes much less. This possibility is rejected because such a short period of time is inconsistent with all empirical observations of what is currently known as "long-term planning." If, on the other hand, "cycle of production" implies the time between introduction of new products or new models of products, the problem of measurement is oversimplified by the implication that product change is the only significant variable requiring consideration. Since there are instances in which product change is unimportant but long-range planning is very important, as in the electrical utility industry, this definition must also be rejected as inadequate.

Another possible nonquantitative criterion denies the existence of x as a measurable time span. This view says, in effect, that the question being discussed has no generally useful answer. The critical importance of long-range planning stems not from the three or five or ten years of future time it happens to cover but from the types of problems it encompasses and the decisions it is charged with making.

This is the more intelligent approach. We have seen that there is no point (x) which has general applicability. We have also seen that there are many different subjects which come under the umbrella of long-range planning, and each may require different lead times for effective usage. In these circumstances it makes little sense to try to impart a conformity and uniformity which do not really exist. The important consideration is not the definitional point of time at which long-range planning begins, but rather what long-range planning is being done, can be done, and should be done.

Before leaving this question altogether, however, there is one impression stemming from empirical observation which should receive attention. Some companies feel that there is a void between their "short-range planning" and their "long-range planning." They may, for example, have one-year plans which are designated "short-range" and five-year plans which are designated "long-range" and nothing between. Recognizing this gap, they have introduced the notion of an "intermediate-range" category of plans. Their purpose in so doing is to allow a clearer and more inclusive pattern of planning activities within the company and also to focus attention upon the need for balance and consistency between the various plans. International Business Machines Corporation, for example, recently introduced a two-year planning procedure which was required at all divisional levels in the belief that it would bridge its existing one-year and five-year plans.

A gap between short- and long-range frequently does exist, and, conceptually, intermediate-range planning is a sound way to draw the two into closer harmony. Its importance is well expressed by Martin Gainsbrugh, Chief Economist for the National Industrial Conference Board:

> If I were to single out the largest blind spot as I see it in the planning process of the past decade, it wouldn't be in terms of the short-run outlook, nor would it be in terms of the long-run outlook. I think where we fell short was in lack of attention to the middle-term.[8]

Desirable lead time. The second question is concerned with the desirable lead time for long-range planning. How far ahead *should* a company plan? Again it is difficult to formulate a quick answer which will be generally acceptable. A useful first step, however, is to determine the lead times required for existing functional plans. It is at least a starting point to say that a company's long-range planning should cover at the minimum a period as long as the longest of these required lead times.

There is much more to it than this, however. The estimated lead times for functional plans are only conditional, and sometimes they will be radically altered by changed circumstances. For example, the company itself may make decisions which affect the lead times. A decision to produce a new product may change the lead times relating to resource development and capital budgeting. Then, too, competitors' actions may affect the lead times. A technological advance by its competitor may cause a reassessment of a company's plans and may require longer lead times for its research activities. Yet another possibility is that environmental changes may cause lead times to change. An alteration in government policy can often dictate a sudden readjustment in required lead times.

Thus, while it is useful to say that the longest of the required lead times in functional plans gives a first approximation to the minimum desirable lead time requirement in long-range planning, we must also note that this lead time is a moving target, influenced by many changing factors in the economy. Management's decisions and actions must be based, as Wallace Clark once said, "not only on carefully proved facts but also on a full appreciation of the importance of the momentum of those facts." [9] The momentum of changing circumstances prevents us from being more precise, but this same momentum helps create the dynamic conditions which make long-range planning so necessary and potentially so valuable.

Although the minimum desirable lead time cannot be exactly determined, there are criteria which we may suggest in seeking to determine the maximum desirable lead times in long-range plans.

First, there is no value in making planning commitments on matters which can be left until later without any disadvantage. That is to say, planning commitments should be made only if they have an impact upon present policy making. [10]

Second, plans are justifiable only if they provide better than chance insights about the future. As lead time increases, however, a point is reached sooner or later where there are so many variables and the outlook is so obscure that planning can offer no more than chance insights. The maximum desirable lead time for any plan will stop short of such a point, but how far short depends upon each individual situation. Observation of business practice suggests that many companies find five years a desirable lead time in their implementational long-range planning activities. The advantage of a five-year span is that management, while able to plan this period in some detail, has enough elbowroom to catch the pieces if the plans collapse. [11]

The fact is, however, that this whole question of "How long is 'long-range'?" cannot be answered specifically. Circumstances vary from case to case, and the significance of the time variable becomes apparent only when it is associated with the scope and the subject matter of the plans being contemplated. There is a good deal of wisdom in the reported response of a no-nonsense executive who, when asked how far ahead his company planned, promptly snapped: "As far as is necessary."

Chapter 3

Historical Evolution
Of Long-Range Planning

IT IS EASY TO THINK OF LONG-RANGE PLANNING EXCLUSIVELY
in its corporate context and to conclude that it is a new phenomenon,
a child of the 20th century. But examples of significant and skillful
long-range planning can be found throughout recorded history.
Moses is described as "the first long-range planner" because his
scheme to deliver the Jewish people out of Egypt and into the Prom-
ised Land took 40 years to implement. Or, to cite another Biblical
example, Noah and his family survived the flood because he planned
the construction of an ark sufficiently far in advance. Although the
lead time required for this task is not known, the consequences of the
plan remain significant for the world.

A relatively more modern example is furnished by the explorers
and traders who began sailing to distant lands during the latter part
of the Middle Ages. They were forced to lay long-range plans in the
interests of their own survival, even though the risks and uncertainties in these plans were very great. Still later, the founding of the
American nation was marked by a long-range planning task of vast
magnitude. Today the Federal Constitution remains "perhaps the
most famous and most copied example of American long-range planning." [1]

These examples are useful reminders that long-range planning is
not a brand-new discovery nor a newly acquired gift of divine guidance. It is well to remember this at a time when long-range planning
is often hailed as "a dramatic new revelation" in some management
circles.

THE CHANGES OF 65 YEARS

The growth of interest in corporate long-range planning is, however, mainly a phenomenon of the 20th century. It therefore is ap-

propriate to take the year 1900 as a convenient starting point for our analysis.[2] By so doing we are able to see some striking differences between the long-range planning techniques of 1900 and those of the 1960's.

Two major differences stand out. First, such long-range planning as was done in 1900 was characterized by informal organizational arrangements—in contrast with the formal organization for planning frequently found in the 1960's. Second, whereas the long-range planning of 1900 relied in large measure upon intuitive judgment, that of today relies much more upon systematic (though not necessarily quantitative) analysis.

The long-range planning of around 1900 was strategic rather than implementational; basic directional planning was undertaken by some companies, but few, if any, had reached the stage of planning the details of their functional activities over a long-range period. The strategic planning was of two major forms:

1. Aggressive personalized planning for growth, which was undertaken by the business tycoons and empire builders of the period.
2. An intuitive "long think ahead" type of planning, whereby a manager attempted to assess the long-range future and to determine what opportunities could be exploited by the company in the context of that future.

The first kind was flamboyant and freewheeling, characterized by aggressiveness, personal drive, and opportunism. It was long-range planning in the sense that it was concerned with "direct impact time" and could, in fact, be measured in the context of "epochal time." It included such strategies as (1) rapid expansion of existing resources and capabilities (market penetration) to meet the opportunities of rapid population growth and urbanization; (2) vertical integration, by which manufacturing companies expanded to assure themselves of adequate raw materials and competent marketing outlets; and (3) consolidations, whereby several companies would pool resources to emerge a single unit with greater size and power. (General Electric Company, United States Steel Corporation, and General Motors Corporation all came into being in this manner.)

While this type of long-range planning had great impact upon the industrial development of the United States, it was not truly formalized or systemized. Furthermore, few of the period's captains of industry had any interest in encouraging this kind of development. Today the attitude taken toward long-range planning activities is for the most part vastly different, and as Edith Penrose states, "certainly today the role of the empire-builder is of marginal importance for the understanding of business growth." [3]

The second kind of strategic long-range planning, *circa* 1900, was also intuitive, but it was much less freewheeling than the first. This kind of planning can best be explained by means of an illustration.

In the early 1900's, General Electric Company was concluding an agreement valued at $1.5 million for patent rights on a new turbine engine. However, before the agreement was signed, the then president of General Electric, Edwin W. Rice, insisted on a clause which permitted the company to use these turbines on ships—that is, if ships should ever be electrically run. There was no formal blueprint drawn up which showed General Electric's intention to build turbines for ships. As a matter of fact, most electrical engineers at this time were dismissing as impossible the idea of driving an ocean liner by electricity. The generating plant needed would be so large as to sink the ship, they said. Fifteen years later, however, the value of the clause became apparent, and in fact it played a leading part in the subsequent future growth of General Electric. [4]

This example is representative of the period, in that the planning is characterized both by informality and by intuitive judgment. It demonstrates as well that such planning can prove shrewd and farsighted.

Now let us suppose that a comparable situation had arisen in 1965. [5] Some aspects would still remain the same; for example, a company would certainly want to take full advantage of the bargaining strength it possessed. Chances are, however, that a company in the 1960's would adopt a more formalized approach to the question of turbines for ships. It probably would conduct some sort of corporate self-appraisal to determine what opportunities for exploitation this kind of market offers. Then very likely the company would also establish task forces to analyze the potential of such turbines in terms of (a) technological feasibility, (b) market prospects, (c) financial investment, and (d) attractiveness of the prospective return on that investment. The company might also institute a study to determine the chances of such a turbine's becoming obsolete before it had a chance to recoup its investment. In short, the 1965 treatment would probably be much more formalized and much more analytic in nature.[6]

A "TROIKA" OF PROGRESS

The growth of formalized long-range planning in this country may be ascribed to a "troika" of continuing progress and change. Management itself has become a much more highly skilled practice than it was 65 years ago. It has built upon the foundations of scientific management, the insights of human relations, and the analytic skills of business mathematics, so that today it reflects a much more substantive body of knowledge than previously. Evidence of this development is seen in many directions. One example is the advent of collegiate schools of business. At the turn of the century, business education was undertaken on a very small scale, and its outstanding characteristic was the sentiment that "there wasn't much to be taught." Professor C. R. Christensen of the Harvard Business School has observed that the teaching of business management in 1908 (the year in which the Harvard Business School was founded) was "roughly at the same state of development as was the medical profession when medicine show men traveled the West dispensing elixirs from the tail gates of their wagons." [7] Today there are hundreds of business schools in the United States, and, while the individual schools continue to have their critics, the wisdom of teaching management is no longer questioned.

Many other examples might also be cited. The number of management books and journals published has increased greatly; business societies have sprung up and expanded; and everywhere there has been an increasing awareness of advances in the field. In addition, more enlightened managerial practices have focused attention on the problem of developing better managers for the future. For instance, such activities as coaching subordinates have helped to raise the level of managerial skill. In sum, management has now become sufficiently skilled and sophisticated to recognize and employ usefully the techniques of long-range planning.[8]

A second facet of progress is seen in the internal growth of companies, both in size and in complexity of operation. During the last quarter-century many companies have grown to a size which they could not have imagined possible during the 1930's. They now produce much wider ranges of products than before; they distribute them over much wider areas; and they have many more skilled employees to manage. All of these changes have underscored a great and growing need for better communication and clearer policy formulation. The challenge of attempting to meet these needs has also encouraged the growth of corporate long-range planning.

Third, the economic environment in which companies operate has itself become much more complex. It has also been characterized by accelerating change in technology, especially since the start of World War II. Later in this chapter the reasons why these changes have promoted the growth of formalized long-range planning activities are examined.

These several features of progress and change are not isolated forces, but overlap and are influenced by one another. The clearest and most convenient way of reviewing the development of corporate long-range planning during this 65 year period is to divide the analysis into four major time phases:

1. Pre-depression (1900-1929).
2. The depression years (1930-1939).
3. World War II (1940-1945).
4. The postwar era (1946-1965).

PRE-DEPRESSION (1900-1929)

It is difficult to estimate how widespread was the practice of long-range planning prior to 1930, because the subject received almost no direct attention in the business literature of the period. However, there is evidence of some planning corresponding to our term "strategic" but little corresponding to our term "implementational." The planning that was done was informal and relied heavily upon intuitive judgment.

Why was there so little attention to the formalizing and systematizing of long-range planning activities during this period? Using hindsight, we can discern several contributing reasons.

The environment of the business economy of the time was (by current standards) comparatively simple. It was a younger economy, with a large proportion of the country's productive capacity still being devoted to basic needs: food, clothing, and shelter. Competition was still mainly concentrated in the realm of operating management techniques: for example, more efficient factory operations. It was not until later that competition developed in areas which require long lead times—such as the continuous pressure for new products which exists in many industries today.

Another reason stems from the fact that many business firms exhibit common characteristics in the evolution of their attitudes toward business planning methods. The importance of this will become clearer after several points of progression are identified:

- *Phase I:* In the early history of a firm, whatever planning is done is the personal responsibility either of one man or perhaps of several men at its head. The firm is so small that it does not as a rule require much planning activity. Consequently, interest in formalizing any sort of planning is negligible.
- *Phase II:* As the firm becomes more solidly established and grows larger, typically there emerges a movement toward the most easily measurable forms of functional planning. Among these are budgeting, production scheduling, and methods analysis, all of which have the primary aim of assisting the firm in its short-term operating effectiveness.
- *Phase III:* In the third phase the firm continues to grow and begins to make use of more refined and more detailed techniques of functional planning. Market forecasting and research become established as parts of the firm's planning activities. Financial planning becomes more sophisticated, and corresponding refinements take place in other existing planning methods as well.
- *Phase IV:* Here the firm grows to a stage of development where internal pressures are demanding (1) better coordination of planning activities, and (2) clarification of long-range objectives. This stage often comes as a result of increased attention to product planning, which typically requires a good deal of information to be supplied by other departments. It is generally only in this fourth phase that formalized long-range planning becomes a reality.

The historical background of International Business Machines

Corporation provides an example of this kind of progression. In its early years (Phase I) IBM was run personally by its president, Thomas J. Watson, Sr. Watson was at this time the corporation's "master planner." Then during the 1930's additional attention was given to the more measurable types of functional planning (Phase II). During this time IBM's sales volume was still comparatively small (in 1938 it amounted to $34.7 million), and the corporation remained organized as a single operating unit.

During World War II, IBM grew rapidly and began formalizing and streamlining a widening number of functional planning activities (Phase III). This development was demanded both by the corporation's rapid growth in size and by the importance of meeting wartime schedules.

In 1950 IBM formed a product planning department, and in 1959 its organization structure was divided into nine decentralized divisions. Also in 1959 a long-range planning department was established at the corporate level, with responsibilities for guiding and coordinating activities in each division (Phase IV).

Having observed these phases of progression in a firm's planning activities, we can now return to the original point. It is clear from the example above that IBM was not even approaching Phase IV in 1929, and there were exceedingly few firms which had reached Phase IV in their planning progression prior to 1930. In attempting to explain why this was so, we should first note how much smaller the U.S. economy was in 1929 than it is today. The gross national product for that year (a boom year) amounted to $104 billion. Even when the 100 per cent price level increase over the subsequent 30 years is taken into account, this still represents in real terms only two-fifths of the gross national product for 1960.

The comparison for individual firms is even more revealing. The "big" companies of 1929 were not "big" by modern standards of dollar sales volume. The dollar sales volume of General Electric Company in 1929 was substantially less than one-fifth of the volume achieved in 1963 by the same company, the comparison being in constant dollars. Similarly Eastman Kodak Company, the country's photographic leader in 1929 as it is today, boasted a sales volume of $90 million in 1929. By 1963 its sales volume passed the $1 billion mark, and its net profits amounted to more than $140 million.

Very few companies had reached such size and complexity prior to

1929 as to realize the necessity for formal long-range planning activities. There were, however, some scattered exceptions. These were the real pioneers. There were some companies which sought to make a clear distinction in their formal organization between top management positions with responsibilities for day-to-day operations and those with responsibilities for basic entrepreneurial policies—or, in our terminology, long-range planning. "One of the very first" [9] to attempt such a formal distinction was the Pennsylvania Railroad. During the final years of the 19th century, the Pennsylvania's management specified that vice presidents were to concentrate on broad, long-term entrepreneurial activities, while general managers were to attend to day-to-day operations in the respective departments under their control. This development, to be copied later by many other companies, foreshadows the increase in formal attention to long-range planning activities. In particular, it was a step toward the full-time staff planning units which are to be found in a substantial number of large corporations today.

There were also some companies which established a central office of general executives and staff specialists to attend to "forward planning and policy formulation"—again, in our terminology, activities resembling long-range planning. One outstanding example is General Motors after its organization structure was revised in 1920. Alfred P. Sloan, Jr., who designed the new structure, established a general office which included four group vice presidents (the manufacturing activities of the company were divided into four "groups"), none of whom had any specific day-to-day operating responsibilities. Collectively they were to help set the overall policies of the corporation. The advisory group of specialists in the central office was composed primarily of functional specialists in accounting and finance. They were to provide all kinds of information to assist both in control and performance measurement of company activities and also to facilitate planning for the future for the entire company. [10] This approach anticipated the staff unit which devotes its full time to problems of long-range planning.

Finally, some few companies demonstrated a systematized and detailed approach to major problems of long-range planning. One early and significant example of this kind of planning comes from American Telephone and Telegraph Company. Again, this example is a forerunner of later developments in long-range planning techniques. In 1910 engineers in the company's Bell Telephone Laboratories were examining the future potential of two alternative telephone systems: the use-of-operator system and a new, seemingly visionary, device allowing automatic dialing. These engineers looked at the data showing expected growth in demand for telephones, and they speculated that perhaps one day every family in the United States would have a home telephone. They studied the implications of this surmise and came up with a definitive conclusion. "Unless we put in dialing by the customers themselves," they told the vice presidents, "the telephone system will someday collapse of its own growth. Within a generation you won't be able to hire enough girls to run the phone system even if you could get every eligible girl of the right age and education in the whole country."

As a result of their recommendations, immediate attention was given to perfecting the automatic dial telephone. Within ten years automatic exchange equipment and dial phones were being installed throughout the country. The wisdom of the engineers' conclusion is revealed by the fact that, in 1954, the use-of-operator system would have required 1,500,000 full-time operators to handle the volume of telephone calls. Instead, there were only 250,000 operators on the company's payroll in 1954.[11]

We may ask why such companies as these were so far advanced in their approaches to long-range planning. Several reasons may be suggested. First, they possessed forward-looking managements—and effective long-range planning needs to become part of an attitude of mind. Second, they were already large enough to sustain the expenditures of planning and subsequent research needed to render the work effective. Third, each was operating in growth areas where the potential of the future looked bright and appeared to justify careful planning activities.

However, while these are notable examples, they remain exceptions to the rule. Most of the long-range planning carried out prior to 1930 was intuitive and informal. Very few companies had yet reached a stage of development where they felt the need to approach the subject of long-range planning systematically and analytically. J. O. McKinsey reflects the general tenor of the times in the introduction to his *Budgetary Control* (1922):

Although much has been written of budgetary control as applied to particular phases of a business, this is the first attempt, so far as the author is aware, to present the subject as a whole and cover the entire budgetary program. [12]

Henri Fayol correctly evaluates the period as follows:

It has not yet become established custom to regard the staff as an organ of thinking, studying, and observation, whose chief function consists, under managerial impetus, in preparing for the future and seeking out all possible improvements. [13]

THE DEPRESSION YEARS (1930-1939)

Paradoxically, the advent of the Great Depression appears both to have hastened and delayed the advance of corporate long-range planning activities. It forced many companies to devote all their energy to fighting off impending disaster, leaving no time for consideration of such abstractions as long-range planning. But, at the same time, the depression forced business and social leaders to do much hard thinking about the role of planning in business.

Some delaying effects of the depression are seen in an example from the history of General Electric Company. Between 1920 and 1930 General Electric's dollar sales volume grew by 30 per cent, reaching $376 million in 1930. At this time General Electric was predominantly an organization with centralized management responsibilities, although certain divisions had received increased independence with the passage of time.

In 1929 a special meeting was held, attended by approximately 200 of General Electric's top managers, whose purpose was to consider a long-term organization plan in view of the size and character of General Electric as foreseen at that time. The dominant theme of the meeting was decentralization, and the consensus was expressed by one speaker:

The multiplicity of problems attendant upon the rapid and widely diversified expansion of the company's business makes it impossible for those heading the functional form of organization to know, as they should know, the distinctive and special problems which are inevitably involved in the many different lines of our endeavor.

However, the move toward decentralization in General Electric did not really get under way until the years following World War II. Shortly after the meeting took place, the depression took charge of the economy and in the process reversed General Electric's pattern of growth for a full decade. By 1933 the company's sales volume had shrunk to $136 million, and even in 1939 the sales figure ($342 million) was still below the peak of 1930.

This example is suggestive of the experience of a great many other companies during the 1930's. Rapid growth during this period was very much the exception. As one indication, the 1939 gross national product was only a scant 4 per cent above the 1929 level when compared in terms of constant dollar values. Very few companies tended to progress into Phase IV of planning activities during the period under review. The depressed economic conditions meant that the majority of firms were hungry, and hungry firms, like hungry people, are most interested in immediate action to relieve their hunger. Then, too, there was a good deal of confusion and apprehensiveness about economic prospects for the future.

The continued absence of widespread formal long-range planning activities is also demonstrated by an empirical study carried out in the late 1930's. Professor Paul Holden and two associates from the Stanford Business School made a study of 31 large organizations, concentrating their attention upon practices in top management. Of these 31 companies, only two had laid formal plans for a five-year period ahead, while half of them had laid plans for some or all of their operations up to a year in advance. The authors concluded, "One of the greatest needs observed during the course of this study is for more adequate planning and clarification of future objectives, both near-term and long-range." [14]

Yet if there was not much progress in implementing formal long-range planning during this period, there was a great deal of talk about it. Speakers on the subject ranged from Socialists to representatives of the National Association of Manufacturers, and their ideas, predictably, differed widely. A lot of the discussion concerned the relative merits of business planning versus politically centralized planning, and so it is not surprising that much of it is distinguished more by rhetoric than by logic. [15]

In the later 1930's there were several Federal Government projects which utilized some of the approaches of business long-range planning, the most notable being the Tennessee Valley Authority. The chairman of that Authority, David E. Lilienthal, points out that the individual tasks executed by the TVA were not unusual. Public power systems were not new, while Government activity in flood control and navigation, in forestry and agriculture, and in research were all time honored. What was new, says Lilienthal, was that one agency should " 'envision in its entirety' the potentialities of the whole river system, for navigation, for power, for flood control, and for recreation." [16] Lilienthal describes this "unified development" as the TVA's synonym for "planning," and he relates it to existing concepts of corporate long-range planning.

A significant analytic contribution to the development of corporate long-range planning was made during this period by Wallace B. Donham, then dean of the Harvard Business School. In his book *Business Adrift*, published in 1931, Donham was able to anticipate some of the developments in business planning which were later to take place in the 1950's. Particularly of note are his comments on foresight.

> The time seems ripe for developing as a larger aspect of economic thought the whole subject of foresight and its limitations, including both political and business judgment as to the future. . . . I believe it possible to construct a theory of foresight, which might well in the hands of able men have a marked effect on both business and politics. Any such theory must approach the subject from a scientific point of view and must therefore start with an effort to define the rational limits of foresight. Such limits in every particular case will depend on the ability to reduce the variables involved in the special problem to a manageable number and to well defined characteristics. . . .
>
> Because of this new element of rapid change, any theory of foresight must recognize time as the major element and must provide for the determination as to each problem of the time zone within which rationalization is possible. [17]

This work by Donham and a formal economics study by A. G. Hart [18] are indicative of the attempts made during the 1930's to grapple with problems of business planning. Probably the greatest value of such efforts was the intellectual challenge which they provided; certainly this has helped to encourage subsequent advances in the practice of long-range planning.

WORLD WAR II (1940-1945)

World War II is the greatest single factor contributing to the development of formalized corporate long-rang planning. This statement may appear overly dogmatic and may be disconcerting. However, the following four contributing factors establish its validity.

1. Build-up in arms. The first of these factors is the dramatic and urgent build-up in arms brought about by the threat of war and then by the start of the war itself. Again an example from the history of General Electric Company serves to illustrate the significance of this. General Electric was one of many firms upon which the country depended when it called for great increases in arms production. As a result the company's sales volume went from $342 million in 1939 to $1.37 billion in 1943—representing a fourfold increase in four years. This tremendous rate of growth caused General Electric's management to re-examine the company's existing organization methods, and in 1943 it inaugurated a major study of the "new problems of organizing and managing such a large and rapidly growing enterprise." The head of this project was R. J. Cordiner, who was later to become the president and chairman of the board. In *New Frontiers for Professional Managers,* Mr. Cordiner observes that—

> From the beginning of the study, it was apparent that the Company was going to require increasingly better planning, greater flexibility, and faster, more informed decisions than was possible under the highly centralized organization structure, which was suited for earlier and different conditions.[19]

This example shows that General Electric suddenly grew to a size far beyond all its previous expectations. It needed to streamline its planning activities to meet the managerial challenges of its increased size and scope. This was an experience common to many other firms, and one consequence was a growing awareness of the need for long-range planning in business corporations.

2. Scarcity of resources. World War II was the first real mass-production war, and those companies committed to mass production were obliged to try to reduce bottlenecks on their production lines wherever and however possible. This meant added pressure for forward planning of both physical and human resources. A wartime economy inevitably brings with it acute scarcities in certain resources. World War II, with its chronic shortages in certain strategic resources, provided situations in which the difficulties of planning were tolerated only because of the demonstrated necessity of planning.[20]

The scarcity of skilled labor had special significance for larger companies. In his study of General Motors Corporation, Peter Drucker gives an interesting account of the way in which that company employed long-range planning techniques to forestall potential labor shortage crises:

> A considerable time before Pearl Harbor central management had decided that labor supplies would be the critical and controlling factor in the war program, and that the extent to which General Motors could produce for the war effort would depend on its ability to avoid labor shortages. Hence in the spring of 1941 central management made case studies of the future labor situation in each of the geographic areas in which the company operates. The magnitude of this task can be seen from the fact that General Motors operates important plants in twenty industrial districts distributed over ten states; in some of these areas its plants are the major employers, while in others General Motors is only one of a number of employers, so that the labor needs of other companies had to be taken into account as well. By the fall of 1941 the employment limits had been worked out for each major plant-city, and it was possible to plan to throw the maximum expansion into the areas where industrial workers would be obtainable most easily. On this basis alone the divisions were allocated the maximum war business they could accept; neither finance, plant equipment, available floor-space, nor type of production usually handled by the plant were considered decisive wherever labor could be obtained. This policy in all its details was completed three weeks after Pearl Harbor, that is, even before the Government was ready to give out armament orders. And though the armaments program underwent great changes, actual experience proved these forecasts of possible maximum production in each area to be correct within a margin of ten per cent.

> As a result of this planning, divisional managers knew from the start precisely how far they could commit the company and how much work they could and should accept. From the start, the divisional managers knew that they had to plan on a war production job scheduled to average twice the annual peacetime peak load. This made it possible for them to plan for maximum expansion at a time when many other corporations were still thinking and working in terms of much lower goals. Therefore, much of the job of

building plants, of designing and buying new equipment, could be done at a time when there were as yet no major shortages of building materials and machines. Finally, General Motors never had a serious labor supply or housing problem, and never had to go to the Government for housing or transportation. Nothing is considered by General Motors management as much a proof of the soundness of its organization as the fact that it succeeded in foreseeing and forestalling wartime labor and transportation shortages.[21]

Few companies, of course, carried out planning activities comparable in depth, breadth, or competence with the one just described. Nevertheless, the case is a significant illustration of the more formalized and analytic character of planning during the war period. The circumstances of war forced many companies to determine their resource requirements and to plan their schedules in much greater detail and for much longer time periods than had been done previously.

3. Technological advance. During World War II Government expenditures on research and development for defense made industry the indirect beneficiary of many new discoveries—for example, the adaptation of advances in military aircraft design has helped develop more modern commercial airplanes. These expenditures had several important effects on corporate long-range planning. They accelerated the economy's rate of technological advance, which made long-range planning both more difficult and more necessary than before. Next, they helped to establish industrial research as a commercial proposition by offering the practical proofs of achievement. And, finally, these expenditures focused the businessman's attention on product competition and product obsolescence—and consequently on product planning. In each of these ways the wartime attention to research and development encouraged businessmen to take greater account of lead times and direct impact times in their planning activities.

4. Government experience. Large numbers of private businessmen were exposed to military and civilian government methods of organization during the war years, and sometimes this experience affected the way in which they later viewed their own jobs. In a research study Ginzberg and Reilley draw attention to this fact:

> Among the present generation of managers, many have had considerable experience in government service, civilian and military.

. . . Although some businessmen responded negatively to their Washington experiences, others were favorably impressed with the reliance that many government departments, particularly the Armed Forces, place on long-range planning, the use of staff, and the development of objective measures of performance. This experience led some to try to adapt what they had learned.[22]

THE POSTWAR ERA (1946-1965)

If World War II brought about conditions which demonstrated the need for long-range planning, the postwar era saw the ensuing popularizing of the subject. Since 1946, and especially since 1950, long-range planning has received almost constant attention at management conferences, and large numbers of firms have established activities which they designate long-range planning.

Long-range planning has thus become fashionable, and as with most fashions there is wide variation in its quality and scope. However, it is worth noting how widespread the practice has become in industry today. *Nation's Business* carried an article in 1958 which observes that—

> Management authorities say more than 50 per cent of today's businesses have some kind of long-range planning. Five years ago the figure was scarcely 20 per cent.[23]

A 1959 industry survey gave more specific information about the chemical industry. Sixty out of 240 chemical companies responded to a questionnaire on long-range planning; these 60 accounted for about 60 per cent of the industry's dollar sales volume. The survey indicated that 93 per cent of the responding companies had "definite long-range planning programs." Of these, 65 per cent had initiated their present programs between 1954 and 1958, with about half of them giving 1956 as their starting date.[24]

A number of developments, both internal and external to the firm, have facilitated and encouraged this rapid growth.

1. Greater economic stability. The postwar economy has succeeded in avoiding the violent economic gyrations of earlier times. Economists have gained confidence in man's ability to control the business cycle within moderate oscillations, and they have proceeded to develop techniques of long-range trend forecasting not previously deemed feasible. There have been some remarkably accurate achievements through this type of forecasting.[25] This greater economic stability has encouraged many companies to undertake the kinds of long-range planning studies which rely upon the use of future economy projections as bench marks.[26] These companies have been further fortified by the knowledge that any future depression would spell political disaster to the Administration in office and therefore would be avoided at all costs.

2. *Increased importance of government.* The increased importance of governmental policies and expenditures has promoted the development of long-range planning. This is partly the result of policies designed to aid economic stability, but there are other factors to be noted. One is the much greater proportion of total expenditures in the economy that government expenditures (Federal, state, and local) now account for than in the prewar years. In 1929 governmental expenses amounted to about 8 per cent of the gross national product. By the late 1950's this figure had reached approximately 20 per cent, and it still (1964) maintains that level. This has meant an increased reliance by many companies upon government policies, and in turn it has encouraged such companies to try to anticipate trends in governmental activity.

Another factor is the vast expenditure for national defense made necessary by the Cold War. The demands of the military during the 1950's and 1960's have led to the development of control systems, ballistic missiles, satellites, and supersonic aircraft (to mention but a few defense budget items), all of which require not only precision engineering but long-range production and financial planning as well. The problems of coordinating the efforts and activities of a vast array of subcontractors have frequently proved enormously complex and monstrously expensive. Coordination has demanded a high degree of planning skill. It is likely that these factors will continue to apply so long as the Cold War continues.

The Federal Government also utilizes the techniques of long-range planning. On May 1, 1964, Douglass Cater was appointed special assistant to President Johnson. In this capacity Mr. Cater is under orders to "think ahead," and he said that his main goal would be "to think beyond tomorrow" on both domestic and foreign issues.[27]

3. *More statistics available.* In recent years there has been rapid growth in the availability and the usefulness and accuracy of business

statistics. Economic indicators and industry information have been published both by governmental agencies and by private service and consulting organizations. This information has helped companies in examining trends for the future and has aided in the replacement of guesswork judgments by systematic, more factual, analyses.

4. Rapidity of technological change. The governmental research expenditures of World War II set the stage for greater attention to industrial research once peace was restored. The postwar years have seen industrial research expenditures rise at a near-exponential rate, reaching an estimated $17 billion in 1964. In large measure this emphasis upon research has brought greater attention to new products in many industries. To cite one example, Eastman Kodak Company reported that about 40 per cent of its total sales volume in cameras and projectors for the year 1960 came from new products introduced during that year.[28]

All this has meant an accelerated rate of technological change in the economy as a whole and has placed management in a very difficult situation. The fast-changing technology has made it more difficult than ever to forecast the future with accuracy, but it has also made such forecasts imperative, for whatever the techniques and processes of 1970 may be, it is certain that they will improve significantly the techniques and processes of 1965. Thus, to repeat, the rapidity of technological advance makes long-range planning at once both more difficult and more necessary than before.

5. Large incremental changes in the economy. In February 1965 the population of the United States reached 193.5 million, and Bureau of the Census projections suggested that by 1970 it would reach 205.8 million and by 1975 218.8 million. In 1964 the gross national product was $633.5 billion, and projections suggested that by 1970 it would reach the order of $750 to $790 billion (in constant dollar terms). In the postwar period America's economy has reached an absolute size large enough so that even the marginal changes of each year constitute substantial increases in absolute terms. These marginal changes will often be of a size sufficient to represent large-scale opportunities for individual firms.

We can illustrate this point by referring to the expected increase in population during the 1960's in the 15-to-19-year age group. The projected growth of this group is from 15 million in 1962 to 19.3 million in 1970. The trend toward higher education is expected to continue, and many educators claim that America needs to double its 1960 school capacity by 1970 if it is to keep pace with expected educational demands. Increases of this magnitude mean large markets in many fields, and the expected growth is bound to have an impact upon all kinds of industries: school construction, student textbooks, stationery, classroom equipment, and so on.

The postwar era has seen many instances of incremental increases being large enough in absolute terms to present important opportunities to business firms both large and small. As a consequence, firms have given more explicit attention to trends in the economy and to tracing their impact upon the future prospects for an industry.

6. Growth in international trade. Since about 1949 there has been a rapid expansion in the volume of world trade, and in the mid-1960's it represented for most countries of the world (including the United States) an important and growing segment of gross industrial output. This has had an effect on corporate long-range planning in at least two major ways. First, because international trade opens up possibilities for a volume of output often much larger than is possible for a purely national market, it motivates the expansion of national income and increases the potential market opportunity for the individual firm.[29] Second, international trade affects long-range planning because, in dealing with a foreign country, many environmental factors can no longer be taken for granted. The laws of the land, the political prospects for stability, the social customs and conventions, the people's attitudes, as well as the people's ability to buy must be analyzed systematically. The problems of forecasting and implementational planning must be carried out without the intuitive sense of understanding that characterizes domestic business activities.

7. Interindustry competition. Another tendency in the postwar period is increasing interindustry competition. Nowadays the purchase of a new car may compete directly with the "purchase" of a trip abroad; television may compete with gardening utensils or power tools. In competition the crucial factor is often time, rather than product line. It is not hard to find a reason for this development. Today discretionary income represents an ever-increasing proportion of total consumer buying power. In other words, a progressively smaller proportion of the consumer's spending money is now being used for the more predictable purchases of food, clothing, and shelter.

Another trend suggestive of the development toward interindustry competition is the increasingly heavy emphasis upon performance of services. According to one estimate, there were some 33 million persons employed in the performance of services in the United States in 1960, compared with only 27 million employed in the production of goods.[30] The emergence of these trends has resulted in greater emphasis on the marketing function. Since companies have had to consider potential competition from quite dissimilar types of products, many have sought to look further ahead and farther afield in their efforts to anticipate future market developments.

8. Increasing size and complexity of firms. The postwar era has been a period of almost continuous expansion, and the continuing trend of most established companies to grow both in size and complexity is implicit in most of the foregoing analysis.

The significance of larger firms can be stated in terms of the four phases in which long-range planning becomes an explicit, formally recognized part of the management task only in Phase IV. It is obvious that during the postwar era many more companies have reached Phase IV than ever before. Greater complexity has already been suggested by the rapidity of technological advance. One result has been the need for longer lead times in implementing a predetermined plan of action. The advent of automation has also been an especially important factor. Both factory and office automation have had many effects upon planning activities. It has, for instance, dictated the need for larger units of capital expenditures. It has also resulted in the need for better scheduling and coordination of activities. And, perhaps most important of all, the computer has offered the mechanical means of making a much greater supply of data available for planning purposes than was ever previously possible.

CONCLUSION

The major conclusion of this historical review is that long-range planning has emerged in the past 25 years to become widely recognized as a very important part of the top management job. Looking ahead, it seems certain that long-range planning will become even more important as a management technique; managerial skills will advance still further; firms will become larger and more complex; and the pressures of the external environment will demand more, not less, long-range planning activity. All this will become clearer as we discuss the major characteristics and place of strategic long-range planning in the modern corporation. It is to this subject that we now turn our attention.

PART II

The Mission of Strategic Long-Range Planning

Chapter 4

Some Basic Tenets
Of Strategic Long-Range Planning

STRATEGIC LONG-RANGE PLANNING IS A SYSTEMATIC APPROACH
by a given company to making decisions about issues which are of
fundamental and crucial importance to its continuing long-term
health and vitality. These issues provide an underlying and unifying
basis for all the other plans to be developed within the company over
a determinate period of time. Thus a long-range strategy is designed
to provide information about a company's basic direction and purpose, information which will guide all its operational activities.

ELABORATION OF MEANING

1. Military derivation. The word "strategy" is derived from two
Greek words meaning "army" and "lead." In military usage it has
long been associated with generalship—determining basic plans of
action regarding matters considered to be of critical, even decisive,
importance. Military strategies include battlefield maneuvers such
as "attrition" and "breakthrough" and also preparedness policies
such as "massive retaliation" and "preparedness for nonnuclear warfare." Strategic planning in the military, concerned as it is with
assuring the long-term well-being of a nation, usually requires several different kinds of assessments preparatory to making commitments. First, it demands a rigidly accurate appraisal of the strengths
and weaknesses of the nation's own military resources. The military
must assess its ability to strike, to maneuver, to retaliate, and to de-
fend. Second, strategic planning in the military requires consideration of environmental factors—for example, the types of terrain,
the climatic conditions, and the transportation routes available. And,
third, this kind of planning requires a realistic assessment of the

antagonist or potential antagonist, including his numbers, his skills, his capabilities, and his likely strategies and tactics.

There are admittedly some difficulties in transferring the word "strategic" from a military to a business environment. Past experience indicates that whenever a military term has been applied to business, there have been attendant problems. Some major hindrances to progress in understanding business organizations have arisen from the use of military terminology. Too often it has been erroneously assumed that business closely resembles a civilian form of military organization. Think of the confusion over "line" and "staff"!

Despite such problems, the word "strategic" conveys most accurately the sense of the kind of planning with which we are concerned.[1] At the same time, the difficulties in transposing "strategic" from military to civilian usage make it especially important that its meaning in the business context be cleary defined. In broad terms, the required assessments needed in strategic planning for business parallel those required for military strategy. There is the need for a self-appraisal of the company's own strengths and weaknesses. There is the need to assess likely changes in the environment: economic, political, technological, and social. And there is a need to assess the competitors' capabilities and their likely strategies.

There are also important variations between the military and business concepts of strategy which must be noted. There are, for instance, major differences in the characteristics of the competitive environment. In the military there are usually clear-cut alignments and few protagonists. In industry, by contrast, there are frequently scores of competitors within an industry grouping, and often competition extends to an interindustry basis as well. In the military any conflict is likely to take the form of direct action against a foe, whereas in business the conflict is indirect (that is, vying for customer patronage). And the military has an end result to the conflict (victory, defeat, stalemate), whereas one company does not necessarily triumph over others. A company's primary aim is to achieve continuing health and vitality over the long run, not to bring about the capitulation of its competitors.

There are likewise major differences between the military and business in regard to the availability of primary resources, and this again is reflected in their respective concepts of strategy. The military can readily call for additional resources when necessary. Additional finance is made available, and plant capacity and manpower is quickly transferred from nonmilitary to military activities when required. Thus there is great flexibility when different contingencies arise. By contrast, a business firm has to develop its strategies on the assumption that resources are relatively fixed. It is unable to call upon unlimited extra supplies of men, money, or machines, no matter how great the crisis or how promising the opportunities. As a consequence, business strategic planning needs to be much more concerned with problems of adapting to environmental considerations than does military strategic planning. Strategies in business are thus obviously not identical in nature with strategies in the military, although there are common elements in the types of analysis required. We need, therefore, to be wary about making analogies with the military concept of strategy, because they will not always prove valid.

2. *Plural strategies.* A company may have, and usually does have, more than one long-range strategy. The activities of most companies are guided by some sort of grand strategy (expressed or unexpressed), but usually they will also have other supporting strategies, which are not universal in their application but which are nevertheless comprehensive within their given scope. While the discussion in Part II concentrates primarily upon the development of grand strategies, much of it applies with minor modifications to the development of supporting long-range strategies as well.

The concept of supporting strategies is very significant. It is not always possible for a grand strategy to provide the needed specificity for unifying the implementational plans of a company—especially if that company is large and diversified. Supporting strategies fill the gap by concentrating on one part of a company's operations: for example, a division, a functional area, or a product line.

3. *Subject matter.* A third observation about the definition of strategic long-range planning is that its subject matter can vary widely. Strategic long-range plans are concerned with those factors in a given situation which Chester I. Barnard defines as "strategic or limiting": those which constitute the crucial or decisive elements in that situation.[2] It is not possible to state that all strategic plans have one predominating subject area. The essence of one strategy may be concentration upon a certain area of research. Another strat-

egy may state that wise selection of retail store locations appears to be a controlling factor in the financial success of the company. Still another strategy may emphasize the need for international expansion of plant operations.

While it is not possible to become specific about the subject matter of strategic long-range plans, the subjects of finance and product line deserve special attention because they are always involved to some extent in the development of long-range strategies. Financial considerations affect the aspirations and ambitions of any company by indicating, in general terms, what strategies are or are not feasible. In addition, financial comparisons also furnish bench marks in judging possible alternative strategies. While detailed financial analysis is sometimes necessary in developing strategic long-range plans, however, it is usually more closely associated with implementational planning.[3] It is usually not crucial for grand strategy, because most systematic approaches to strategic long-range planning are the work of companies which have considerable financial strength. These companies can usually proceed in the belief that if the strategy is otherwise sound it can—within broad limits—be financed. In this study we will not deal with any detailed methodological problems of financial analysis, such as alternative methods of calculating return on investment. They impinge upon our subject to some degree, of course, but they do not represent distinguishing characteristics of strategic long-range planning.

The other subject which is always intimately involved in development of a long-range strategy is the company's product line. "Product line" is construed here broadly to include an understanding of it from the standpoint of the customer as well as of the producer. This subject has a major effect upon the unifying set of assumptions which a long-range strategy seeks to provide, because a company's operating characteristics are always greatly affected by the kinds of products which it chooses to produce and/or market. Furthermore, this subject is highly acceptable to top management in the sense that, while it encourages the promotion of changes, these changes are usually transitional rather than jolting. That is to say, changes in product line are usually *manageable* changes; they can be executed without any catastrophic consequences for the company as a whole. In view of these features of basic importance and acceptability it is not surprising that product line is the area in which strategic long-range planning has made its greatest conceptual advances. Consequently it receives the most attention in the chapters which follow.

4. An activity. Strategic long-range planning is, at its core, an activity and not a form of organization. This fact needs stressing, because even now some top management executives believe that their responsibilities for any kind of long-range planning activities are discharged once they have established a special committee or task force to deal with them. They are mistaken on two counts. One is that, judging from empirical observation, strategic long-range planning is being carried on systematically and effectively in some companies without any formal organizational machinery having been established. There is, certainly, a growing tendency to formalize long-range planning activities, but this formalizing is a means, not an end in itself. In addition—and this is the other count—even when a special unit is assigned responsibilities in long-range planning, top management executives retain important responsibilities themselves. Their continuing support, advice, and, sometimes, direction are essential to successful results. Strategic long-range planning is an activity which demands top management's personal attention and continued participation.[4]

5. Relationship between strategic and implementational planning. While the two types of long-range planning are conceptually distinct, the same idea may fall into both categories. Thus a proposition which is properly strategic because it is an important elaboration of the grand strategy can also be implementational as a basic objective of the detailed planning in a particular area. For example, increased recruiting of scientific personnel may be an important elaboration of a company's grand strategy and at the same time a basic objective of the implementational planning in the executive personnel area. Moreover, a strategic decision to direct corporate activities in a certain direction will contain assumptions about the implementational planning necessary; for example, the company can negotiate the steps which will be needed to achieve that strategy.

The fact that it may be useful or even essential to have the same idea discussed in both the strategic and the implementational areas does not pose any major difficulties for the analysis of strategic long-range planning. However, it does mean that some things which will be said about strategic long-range planning will also apply to the subject of long-range planning generally.

REASONS FOR EMPHASIZING STRATEGIC LONG-RANGE PLANNING

There are several reasons why strategic long-range planning is receiving major attention in this study. One is its vast potential to any company which takes it seriously. By definition, strategic long-range planning is concerned with basic considerations which contain the seeds of success or failure for the company. Its importance was well summed up some years ago by General Robert E. Wood of Sears, Roebuck and Co., who is himself a strategic planner of the first order. "Business is like war in one respect," Wood observed, "if its grand strategy is correct, any number of tactical errors can be made and yet the enterprise proves successful." [5]

Its importance is not obvious to everyone and indeed there are some who view this kind of long-range planning as only a sophisticated extra, a topping on the administrative cake. Such people typically point out that a great many companies have been continuously successful over the years as a result of good implementational planning without any concern about long-range strategies. But this fact means that these companies have relied upon some intuitively reached strategies which have proved adequate for their needs. There are many other companies which have failed or have achieved very limited success, because their intuitively reached strategies have *not* proved adequate. Strategic long-range planning is valuable because it provides a means to deal explicitly and systematically with matters of fundamental importance which in the past have usually been dealt with implicitly and nonsystematically.

This brings us to the second reason for emphasizing strategic long-range planning. It deals with an aspect of top management responsibility which has only recently become systematized in a substantial number of companies. Consequently, a good opportunity exists now to explore and develop new concepts which will contribute to the understanding of this newly emerging responsibility. Today's fast-changing and increasingly complex world is making reliance upon intuitive strategies more and more hazardous.

Finally, conceptual clarity in strategic planning lags far behind that which has been achieved in implementational planning, and much work needs to be done in developing a good conceptual understanding of strategic long-range planning. Too many companies demonstrate greater proficiency in determining how they will accomplish a given strategy than in determining what such a strategy should be in the first place. The reasons for this situation are not hard to find. Implementational planning deals with concepts which are more tangible. Its importance is clear, and its purpose can usually be stated in some specific manner—for example, as a blueprint for additional production facilities or as a financial projection or schedule. By contrast, strategic planning is more abstract and is conceptually more difficult to deal with. Furthermore, its importance is not always obvious.

A CONCEPTUAL JUSTIFICATION OF THE SUBJECT

Some executives acknowledge that strategic long-range planning is important but doubt the feasibility of a systematized approach to it. They point out that the long-range future is shrouded in uncertainty and is affected by a great many variables which defy prediction. Under the circumstances, they say, strategic long-range planning can only wind up as an exercise in futility.

Of course, few executives allow themselves to be quoted publicly in this manner. The viewpoint is unpopular, and in some ways it suggests a defeatist attitude. Nevertheless, there are present-day counterparts of the following comment attributed to a major textile company some dozen years ago.

> How can we make long-range plans with synthetics coming in? The fiber we'll be using in ten years probably hasn't even been put into the test tube yet.[6]

The difficulty of grappling with this kind of problem is not to be denied, but it does not follow that long-range planning in these circumstances will prove fruitless. A systematic attempt at strategic long-range planning, in fact, is likely to provide a most useful way of understanding the situation that exists and of developing some basic strategy or strategies which will help clarify and unify the company's position in relation to (for example) the incoming synthetics.

In analyzing this matter there are two key concepts which, taken together, demonstrate the usefulness of a systematized approach to strategic long-range planning. Both stem from the pervasiveness of change in today's environment, and both help to explain the increasing difficulty of arriving intuitively at satisfactory long-range strategies. Let us examine each in some detail.

1. Discontinuities of change. It is axiomatic that there are a great many variables in the economy at large which change over time. Some changes are "continuous"; that is, they follow a pattern related to past performance or information. Thus the population of the United States increases each year by about three million people, and the gross national product for any given year will usually be within 5 or 6 per cent (higher or lower) of the previous year's figure. Similarly, forecasts in industry are commonly based upon the likelihood of this type of change occurring. A company produced 100,000 units of a product last year, for instance, and this year is producing 120,000. Forms of extrapolation are used to project past information in these situations and often result in accurate forecasts of changes.

Other changes are "discontinuous" in nature. Many of the most profound changes represent breaks in the linearity of projection. This can be illustrated by the example of a growing corporation. For a limited period of time, growth may proceed continuously: the production of the same product under the same conditions at a steadily increasing level of output. Somewhere along the way, however, there are going to be some discontinuous changes taking place in the type of products produced, in processes, in distribution methods, in corporate organization structure.

The contrast between continuous and discontinuous forms of change is perhaps more apparent in the following hypothetical case. The old maxim says that if you invent a better mousetrap, the world will beat a path to your door. The mousetrap manufacturer who accepts this maxim at face value presupposes that certain types of continuous change will take place over time. Estimates of likely sales volume in the future will be forecast on the basis of past performance, together with estimates of the impact of product improvements. The assumption is that the mousetrap market may be analyzed in terms of continuous change patterns. There is the possibility, however, that discontinuities in change may disrupt the otherwise sound analysis. The mousetrap market may suddenly collapse, not because someone invented a still better mousetrap, but because mousetraps are no longer needed. Suppose, for example, that one day someone markets a poison for mice which is completely effective, odorless, not harmful to humans or pets, and inexpensive. Such a product would sharply lower the demand for mousetraps. Or suppose that a market springs up for mice because of their fur, or for medical-serum purposes, which precludes their necks' being broken in the traditional mousetrap method. Again the market for mousetraps would be very hard hit indeed.

The important part of this example is not the specific possibilities suggested for massacring mice, but the illustration of the many opportunities for the intrusion of discontinuous changes, which have a major impact upon the affairs of a corporation.

Continuous types of change are likely to predominate in relatively short periods of time, but as the time span becomes longer, the greater are the chances for discontinuous changes to take place. Thus a short-term projection of the needs for copper wire will logically be based upon extrapolated information from the past. But by 1975 or 1980 it may well be that messages will be transmitted by radio signals which eliminate the need for copper wiring. In other words, a discontinuous change may take place at some point and upset all projections based upon continuity.[7]

Discontinuous change is a concept of great significance for strategic long-range planning. Major changes which represent a sharp, discontinuous break from past behavior can and do take place over time, and some of them have important effects upon a company's strategy formulation. Prediction of these changes—their timing and their form—is frequently very difficult. But a major function of strategic planning, in addition to forecasting continuous type change, is the anticipation of discontinuous type change. Peter Drucker writes that "long-range planning is necessary precisely because we cannot forecast," [8] and this comment underlines the importance of discontinuous changes—whether they be internal, competitive, or environmental in nature—in all long-range planning activities, and especially in the strategic form.

2. *The life cycle of a product.* The second concept which helps explain the need for strategic long-range planning is commonly termed the product life cycle concept. It has its roots in the (now discredited) idea of a corporate life cycle, which was popular for a time during the late 19th century. According to this idea, a successful firm would grow to maturity and for a while could remain af-

fluent, but inevitably it would sooner or later wither and die. The assumption fell into disrepute in the early part of this century when it became empirically obvious that some large companies had come to stay. They had become so firmly entrenched in the economy that only major legal or political changes could bring about their demise. Economic theory notwithstanding, their continued growth brought no signs of impending enfeeblement.

A major reason for this apparent immortality in a sizable number of companies in modern society has been their willingness to make changes in their product lines. For example, Du Pont today manufactures and markets very different products from those it did in 1902, even though it is still generically and legally the same firm. The company has been transformed by a succession of detailed implementational plans, each based upon emergent strategies which have provided basic direction and unifying purpose to these planning activities.

The corporate life cycle has all but disappeared from modern-day analysis of the business firm. It has been replaced by attention to the concept of a product life cycle, which, unlike its predecessor, does not claim universal application. The product life cycle concept holds that there are a great number of products which follow a general pattern of cyclic development that includes birth, increasing rate of growth, decreasing rate of growth, maturity, and (in some cases) level-off, decline, and (perhaps) total disappearance.[9] Although this concept is generalized and says nothing about the possible length of the cycle or any of its stages, it is nevertheless useful for understanding changes which take place over time in the business firm.

A difficulty in trying to apply this concept to specific examples is the ambiguous meaning of "product." The term can be applied to a series of different levels of abstraction with substantially different results. Take, for example, the case of a company operating in the so-called electrical industry and making just one line of products. That line of products may be described as "six-battery transistor radios." It may be described as "radios." Still more generally, it may be described as "commercial electrical transmitters." If the product is defined very specifically and as a low-level abstraction—for example, as a current model—then it can easily enough be translated into the life cycle concept. It will have a limited life in the market place, and it will be superseded by later and improved models. When the definition becomes more general (for example, "radios"), it is frequently more difficult to see the progress of the life cycle. Even when the broader definition of product comes closer to resembling an industry definition, there are few cases in which some kind of life cycle pattern does not become evident.

This widespread occurrence of a product life cycle has enormous impact upon the basic nature of a great many companies, which is the point of greatest importance in our analysis. The continued health and vitality of any given firm depend to a considerable degree upon its ability to make successful transitions from one generation of products to the next. The following example illustrates the transcending changes that have taken place in one company during one decade as the result of major changes in product life cycles.

Through the years of World War II and the Korean conflict, The Martin Company of Baltimore, Maryland, was one of America's major aircraft manufacturers. In 1952 Martin had annual sales amounting to $144 million, and it was busy producing B-57 jet bombers for use in Korea.

By 1959 Martin had made some radical changes in its product line. At the end of that year it had converted 80 per cent of its resources from airframe design and assembly to rockets and electronics. Its sales for 1959 reached $524 million, and its earnings of 16.8 per cent on net worth was the highest for any of the major aircraft manufacturers during that year. The conversion was completed in 1960 when Martin delivered its last airplane, marking the end of what was called "an historic era in our corporate history."

During the years between 1952 and 1959, Martin had become the prime contractor and integrator of the Titan Inter-Continental Ballistic Missile (ICBM) program. The company's top management had surmised that Martin would have to live in a "research and development climate." The president explained that "it was not so much a case of our converting from aircraft to missiles as it was of our converting from a production business to an R&D business." He continued: "Had we not sloughed off our emotional attachment to the airframe, we'd probably be struggling along, at best, with a third of the present volume."

Late in 1961 *The Wall Street Journal* reported that The Martin Company was actively planning to abandon missile making. This did not mean that the company had any intention of reneging on Government contracts: It had every intention of fulfilling these contracts and, indeed, of seeking contracts for later models of the Titan. It would, therefore, be continuing to produce missiles for a number of years to come. However, planning studies had led Martin executives to conclude that the missile business was eventually going to level off as a political stalemate was reached between the Western and Communist worlds. On the basis of this premise, Martin was already preparing to diversify into fields of manned space flight. The requirements for this sphere of activity included many elements radically different from those of missile weapons production.[10]

The Martin Company's experience offers a dramatic example of the way in which major internal changes in a firm are evoked through anticipation of product life cycle movements. It also demonstrates the kinds of problem, the sorts of analytical studies, and the radical nature of strategic decisions which are sometimes needed if a firm is to adapt successfully to the ever-changing environment in which it operates.[11]

The example also suggests several current-day trends regarding product life cycles. These deserve attention because of their significance in explaining both the importance and the rising interest in strategic long-range planning activities. One trend is that the life span of products and process is, in general, decreasing, while the time and cost of doing preliminary research and development work are, in general, increasing. Often today the time span of research prior to introducing a product commercially is materially longer than the time span between the point at which a product's rate of sales growth begins to decline and the point at which sales start declining. This suggests that such trends must be anticipated if the firm is to avoid product line gaps in the future.[12]

Melvin Salveson makes the impact of this trend graphically clear with some comparisons from history. Referring to a military systems example, he writes:

> . . . increasingly large amounts of time, cost, and knowledge are required to produce successive weapons. At the same time, their span of useful life is decreasing. For example, Lord Nelson's flagship was forty years old at Trafalgar and still was a first-class ship of the line. Its cost was minute in comparison to Admiral Halsey's U.S.S. Enter-

prise, which was obsolete within a few years of its construction. The B-17 took about as long to develop as was its useful life. The B-29 was tipped toward a shorter life. The B-36 was ten years to develop and was operational but three years. The Navajo cost one-half billion and never became operational before it was obsoleted. Some weapon types are not wholly obsoleted, e.g., rifles. However, within that weapon type, the trend is for successive models also to have shorter life span.[13]

Salveson also cites industrial examples—the automobile engine is a notable one— to illustrate lengthening research time and shorter commercial life cycle time. In effect he demonstrates the need for systematic and continuing attempts to anticipate these product life cycles. He also argues in favor of the diversion of resources, managerial as well as technical, from current problems of production and consumption to future problems. In the past a company could often exploit a market by entering it some years after its initial establishment; now this is frequently not possible. As a consequence, companies must determine their basic direction and purpose by means of well-thought-out strategies which anticipate, among other things, the likely changes in their own and related products' life cycles.

A second trend is the recognition that profits are generally substantially greater at early stages in the product's life cycle than when the product nears maturity. An innovation is followed by entry into the market by imitators, and the ensuing competition forces down the profit margin. This happens more quickly if entry to the market is easy and if the innovation is not restricted by patent or other unique skills or by some other decisive competitive advantage. Economists have long been aware of this phenomenon,[14] but only in recent years has it had a significant impact upon management decision making.

In view of the growing need for gaining early access to a product market, some companies see strategic long-range planning as a means for providing early signals about expected changes in product life cycles. IBM's long-range planning department frequently uses the military term "distant early warning," and it considers one of its most important responsibilities to be the reading of "distant early warning" signals.[15]

This discussion of product life cycles and the earlier analysis of discontinuous change demonstrate that the resolution of strategic long-range planning problems is often neither straightforward nor obvious. (The Martin Company provides a graphic illustration of this fact.) However, it is clear that a systematic, deliberate approach to the subject is of great value to a company, both in clarifying the basic problems and in determining the most appropriate strategies for the particular case at hand.

ANALYZING STRATEGIC LONG-RANGE PLANNING AS A PROCESS

The present chapter is intended to serve as a prologue to the main purpose of Part II, which is to develop a clear understanding of strategic long-range planning as a company activity. At this point, therefore, it is helpful to explain the analytic approach which will be adopted in the chapters to follow. The approach relies on the fact that strategic long-range planning, like all other forms of business planning, can be characterized as a process; that is, it is composed of a series of conceptual phases related to one another in a set order. Put another way, a strategic long-range plan in its final form is a composite of these various phases. In order to understand the subject clearly we must take a detailed look at each component phase, which is what is done in the succeeding chapters.

The phases of the planning process are *not* like steps in a procedure, the first of which is completed before the second is begun, and so on. They are interdependent and intertwined in practice; probably some work is done on all of the phases before the first is finalized. Although phases are artificial abstractions, they are useful for analytical purposes and they provide a convenient and orderly means for examining the subject. The five-phase classification presented earlier as a typical description of the planning process serves as a starting point for analysis of strategic long-range planning:

1. Establishment of objectives.
2. Establishment of planning assumptions.
3. Seeking the facts regarding possible courses of action.
4. Evaluation of alternative courses of action.
5. Selection of a course (or courses) of action.

The chapters which follow look at each of these phases, though they are grouped differently to facilitate analysis. Chapter 5 ("Corporate Self-Appraisal") includes elements of Phases 1, 2, and 3. Chapter 6 ("Establishing Objectives") is concerned with Phase 1. Chapters 7 ("Assumptions About the Future") and 8 ("Anticipation of Technological Change") are about Phases 2 and 3. And, finally, Chapter 9 ("Choice of a Strategy") encompasses both Phases 4 and 5 of the planning process.

Corporate Self-Appraisal

ONE OF THE MOST STRIKING FEATURES ABOUT STRATEGIC long-range planning is the important part played by an intensive corporate self-appraisal. The planning executives who were interviewed for this study repeatedly talked about the need for some kind of introspective analysis, echoing Hill and Granger's belief that "the nature of the present business must be understood and agreed upon before charting its future course." [1] These executives recognized that a company's inherited resources (both tangible and intangible) should play a very significant role in the determination of long-range strategies.

It might seem that a corporate self-appraisal is normally a simple matter, but this is not true. As Peter Drucker observes, the question, "What is our business?" is almost always difficult and can be answered only after hard thinking and study. The right answer, Drucker points out, is usually anything but obvious. [2] This fact helps explain why some planners have gone to great lengths in trying to determine useful ways for thinking about the corporate entity, and it is a measure of their success that we can today describe approaches to this subject in conceptual terms.

When planning executives undertake this type of analysis, they presuppose that their company has some predominant characteristics which can be isolated. These characteristics may relate to products, processes, equipment, distribution, finance, manpower, and/or research, to name some of the major possibilities. It is often assumed that the product line is not a conglomerate assortment of items, but that patterns of unification exist and that these suggest key strengths. One executive describes this type of analysis as a search for "hard-core skills." This search for predominant characteristics or "hard-core skills" is the subject of the present chapter.

POSSIBLE WAYS OF UNDERTAKING A SELF-APPRAISAL

There are two major approaches to corporate self-appraisal, and they may be undertaken separately or in combination.

One is to examine in turn each functional activity. This allows planning executives to draw some conclusions about the various strengths and weaknesses of their company, considering it as a composite of numerous parts. As a result, they can try to determine which strengths may best be exploited in planning for the long-range future. To the extent that top management policy formulation in the past has included any kind of corporate self-appraisal, the functional approach is the one which has been most relied upon. Of course this approach is generally undertaken today in a more thorough and more astute manner than previously, thanks to a greater understanding of the functions themselves as well as to refinements in the tools of managerial analysis. By the functional approach a company's planners can provide an inventory of strengths and weaknesses in a systematic way, thus lessening the chance of overlooking any obvious considerations.

The other approach to corporate self-appraisal is that of "total entity." Its primary aim is to achieve a better understanding of the company as a cohesive unit and to determine what characteristics in its nature may prove of special value in laying plans for the long-range future. The keystone of this "total entity" self-appraisal is an attempt to describe the essential nature of a company (or part of a company, such as a division) in a brief word or phrase. If this is to be done well, a sensitive and imaginative analysis is required, one which goes far beyond the obvious fact that a firm is manufacturing "automobiles" or "cigarettes." The analysis must assess not only the physical attributes but also the performance characteristics and must determine those assets which represent "hard-core skills."

The greater attention given to the "total entity" approach in the present chapter is not meant to depreciate the importance of the functional approach; actually, the most thorough corporate self-appraisals combine both. However, the "total entity" approach has been explored largely by companies doing pioneering work in strategic long-range planning. And, although this approach has received only sparse attention in management literature so far, it has now developed to a point where numerous valuable insights can be gained from it. In other words, the "total entity" approach is one which provides a good opportunity to see strategic long-range planning as practical and useful.

THE INFLUENCE OF EXECUTIVE ATTITUDES AND INTERESTS

One factor of the total-entity approach is of underlying importance to all the analysis which follows. It is the need of any corporate self-appraisal undertaken in connection with strategic long-range planning to include not only an examination of the products being produced and the markets being served but also a consideration of the attitudes and interests of the company's top management executives. That is to say, the self-appraisal needs to take account of the aspirations of these executives, their values, predispositions, prejudices, and preoccupations. These considerations are significant in making an appropriate final choice of strategy. In addition, they affect the perceptiveness and the accuracy of the appraisal itself.

To achieve this awareness challenges strategic planners. Their observations and interpretations need to be as astute and accurate as possible, because the conclusions reached become underlying assumptions in the analysis of more tangible, less personal data. But at the same time these conclusions will not normally be spelled out explicitly or formally. It is highly unlikely, for example, that a planner wants to reveal his interpretation of the top managers' prejudices *to* the top managers. Planning certainly needs to be logical, but it also needs to be intelligent and practical, and therefore planners often rely on their subjective judgments in observing and interpreting information.

Strategic plans are usually based upon corporate self-appraisals which are *acceptable* to management, but they are not necessarily impartial. The plans are developed with the idea of exploiting and building upon the company's strengths; they are designed to be positive and progressive. In developing them, planners do not usually believe that weaknesses outbalance strengths and that a plan should be developed which is actually a defensive, costly retreat. Strategic planning is usually adopted to facilitate "manageable" changes, and its great contribution comes in exploiting strengths rather than in mitigating weaknesses. Those companies which have been successful in strategic planning have usually been capable of overcoming weakness through strength.

Yet there are circumstances in which the best-managed company is placed in an extremely difficult position and in which strategic planning can help but little. Radical shifts in demand, or in supply, or in technology may suddenly render obsolete a heavy investment in fixed assets and skilled personnel. For example, if nuclear power were suddenly available tomorrow at competitive prices, most companies in the oil industry would have enormous problems in making adjustments. It must be remembered that strategic planning as presently practiced can be of great help in the exploitation of corporate strengths, but it is no magic wand for overcoming grave corporate weaknesses.

These factors are mainly silent influences, but they are significant nevertheless. They reflect the facts that companies are made up of people and that the attitudes and interests of those who are charged with direction of the company affect the way in which its basic nature and its "hard-core skills" are viewed. We need to keep this fact in mind in all the discussion which follows.

INDUSTRY CLASSIFICATIONS

When strategic planners attempt to appraise the corporation as a total entity, they frequently start with a general industry classification. This immediately leads to recognition that industries, like products, are not subject to any clear and unambiguous boundary lines.[3] Some industries are narrowly defined while others are very broad in their scope. The conditions governing the narrowness or breadth usually result from arbitrary circumstances well beyond the control of any one company.

Despite this arbitrary nature, observation shows that industrial classifications are continually used in business affairs for a variety of purposes. Industrial man needs to differentiate types of business companies and types of business executives, and industry classifications allow some broad distinctions to be made. If meaningful business statistics are to be compiled, clear boundary points must be established, and industrial classifications are useful. Further, they open up industry channels and enable communication with industry groups in spite of the vast variety of industrial activity. And, finally, industrial classifications give executives in similar types of activity the chance to associate with one another informally and through professional groups.[4]

Industry groupings are usually classified in one of three ways:

1. A single product, product line, or group of products. (For instance, the automobile industry, the shoe industry, or the furniture industry.)
2. A process or technology. (For instance, the chemical industry, the electronics industry, or the printing industry.)
3. An end use. (Such as the transportation industry, the communications industry, or the defense industry.)

CLASSIFICATIONS BY PRODUCT AND PROCESS

Historically, most industry classifications fall into either 1 or 2. In other words, a company has usually been classified in terms of the product(s) or process(es) which reflect its activities. It is described as an automobile company or a chemical company because in the past it has been engaged in the manufacture of automobiles or chemical processes. While classifications of these kinds have proved useful, it does not follow that they *necessarily* provide insights into the best course of action a company should project for the long-range future. Occasionally a company will continue to produce the same product or use the same process for a long period of time. The product life cycle is a widely observable feature of business operations today, and critical danger can come from assuming that a company will continue to produce the same products or use the same processes for a long period of time to come. In other words, if a company is guided solely or even predominantly by an industry classification according to product or process, it may become bound so closely to existing products or processes that its ability to make changes in planning for the future is impaired.

The history of business provides instances of companies, even whole industries, which fell upon hard times because their products became obsolete, or declined in demand, and which were unable or unwilling to adapt to the changing circumstances. Two examples serve to give point to this contention.

The cotton textile industry in general has had more than its share of problems during recent decades. There are a variety of reasons for this, some of them uncontrollable. But one which has had major impact has been the development of large synthetic-material markets. W. R. Maclaurin suggests that the firms in the cotton textile industry have largely themselves to blame for not participating in the synthetic-market upsurge. He claims that the firms defined their businesses too literally (that is, as manufacturers of cotton textiles) and were unable to see potential growth for themselves. Maclaurin points out that—

> Such technical contracts as they (the managers of cotton textile firms) developed were early divisions of textile technology or mechanical engineering departments rather than with chemistry and chemical engineering.[5]

They did not probe beyond a superficial level in any self-appraisal and were not aware of the relevance and importance of exploratory work in such prospective areas as nylon and orlon. These firms classified the industry to which they belonged according to a product line, but the limitations of this classification greatly restricted management's forward planning. The product life cycle was reaching (if it had not already reached) a mature state, and there was a growing prospect of discontinuous change (a switch to synthetics). Yet through lack of intensive self-appraisal these managers failed to realize the competitive problems which would follow.[6]

A more patent example is that of the motion picture or movie industry. Many companies in this industry have had financial difficulties in recent years, caused in great part by management's failure to make an introspective analysis of the nature of its business. There have been two outstanding examples of failure to adapt to changing circumstances, and both can be directly attributed to lack of understanding about the real nature of the motion picture industry. The first is the transition from silent movies to talkies. The talkie was commercially introduced in 1927, and less than one year after its introduction not a single silent picture was being produced in Hollywood. The talkie contained no single element that had not been known and made available to the movie industry for a generation or more. Companies in the industry had chosen, however, to stay with their traditional product line and not to hasten any technical advance.

The movie companies were not badly hit by this delay in bringing out talkies because there was no direct outside competition. This was not true, however, with the advent of commercial television after World War II. The history of technology in television parallels that of the talkie. By the middle 1930's television was technologically workable and available for development as a commercial proposition. But the movie companies were not interested in taking an active part in its introduction, even in the postwar years. One reason for this reluctance was that many member companies had vertically integrated their operations to include not only production facilities but also investment in many picture theaters throughout the country. With this kind of investment at stake the companies continued to think of their industry as the movies, and their management discouraged any change in the *status quo*.

T. Levitt comments on the consequences of this lack of probing self-appraisal in acid terms:

> Hollywood barely escaped being totally ravished by television. Actually, all the established film companies went through drastic reorganizations. Some simply disappeared. All of them got into trouble not because of TV's inroads but because of their own myopia. As with the railroads, Hollywood defined its business incorrectly. It thought it was in the movie business when it was actually in the entertainment business. "Movies" implied a specific, limited product. This produced a fatuous contentment which from the beginning led producers to view TV as a threat. Hollywood scorned and rejected TV when it should have welcomed it as an opportunity—an opportunity to expand the entertainment business.[7]

The motion picture companies were well equipped to enter the new television industry. They had skills and resources which companies starting from scratch did not have. For instance, they had production facilities far greater than any other type of corporation in existence. They had a great accumulation of copyrighted literary property. They had, in some instances, great stockpiles of documentary films. And by no means least, they had a great many skilled people gathered together under their roofs: directors, writers, film cutters, cameramen, animators, publicity men, and, of course, actors. Despite all this, the motion picture companies failed to see television as anything but a threat, inconsistent with the nature of their established business. Their self-appraisals had failed to go beyond the industry classification by product line.

It is easy to dismiss these examples as exceptional. Nevertheless, there are many less spectacular examples of companies which have suffered some setback because they failed to make self-appraisals which perceived changing factors related to their business. Furthermore, the question is not just one of protection against a threat. Many companies miss out on potentially attractive expansion moves because their failure in self-appraisal has caused them to overlook possibilities. For example, many companies have diversification possibilities for which their existing resources and skills make them peculiarly well suited. However, because they frequently require a company to venture across product or process industry borders, they are sometimes not recognized as opportunities.

It is not hard to see why companies have historically relied upon a product or process type of industrial classification. It has the advantage of being tangible. It is also distinctive and readily observable, and it has the appearance of permanence. After all, the automobile company of today will continue to manufacture automobiles tomorrow, next month, next year, and probably for many years after that.[8]

These types of classification do have a place in any attempt at self-appraisal—indeed, there are no better starting points for analysis. But problems resulting from overdependence upon them arise because there are many gradual changes occurring in the environment at large over time. The force of these changes resembles the movement of hands on a clock; over a period of time it is substantial, but at any given point in time the movement is difficult to perceive. The importance of such changes is underestimated when product or process classifications are relied on solely or predominantly in making a corporate self-appraisal. Where this is the case, the company's long-range strategy is built upon an unreliable foundation. Significantly, those companies which have recognized the importance of a self-appraisal have always carried their analysis well beyond these simplest and most obvious forms of industry classification.[9]

CLASSIFICATION BY END USE

The third way in which industries are sometimes classified is by a product's end use, or the grouping of products according to their performance characteristics rather than their physical characteristics or production methods. The product mission (as this approach is often called) allows a company to gain greater insight into the nature of its operations by taking the customer into consideration. Thus, it is sometimes said, if the railroads had seen themselves as part of the transportation industry, they would not be in their present dire difficulties. Or if the movie companies had seen themselves as being in the entertainment industry, they would have been able to view the advent of television as an opportunity for expansion, not as a threat to their very existence.

This way of thinking about the nature of a business can stimulate further analysis, but it is by no means a panacea. One difficulty arises from the fact that most end use methods of classification are vague and quite general. "Transportation," for instance, is a term which can be applied to a great variety of products—automobiles, aircraft, railroads, even bicycles—but it adds very little to a better understanding of the basic nature of a particular company. There are no common skills of either a mechanical or conceptual nature which clearly apply to "transportation." There are no common patterns in distribution methods for "transportation." The potential customers for "transportation" obviously vary widely in their needs and expectations. In short, this type of classification will not, by itself, provide all the information necessary for an effective in-depth corporate self-appraisal. [10]

No sound corporate self-appraisal can be limited to a one-dimensional analysis of this kind. An analysis solely by end use classification is not sufficient, any more than is an analysis solely in terms of a product or process classification. Even if it is helpful to recognize that a company is in, say, the transportation industry, a variety of other considerations need to be taken up if the self-appraisal is to be thorough. Nevertheless, attention to industrial classification by the end use of a product has underscored the significance of a customer orientation in analyzing the basic nature of a firm. Today one finds that planners who are engaged in introspective analysis are placing great emphasis upon customer orientation as a most useful approach in opening up new perspectives for reconceiving ("rethinking") the nature of their company's activities.

There has not always been this emphasis upon customer orientation in planning activities. While many American companies have built their success over the years upon skills in salesmanship and in customer relations, neither economic analysis nor management literature has given much attention to the customer in its theories of the firm. Indeed, Chester I. Barnard created quite a stir when he wrote in 1938 that an organization was not comprised just of a specified group of people with behavior coordinated in terms of a specific goal but that it also included the actions of others, notably consumers.[11] This view was challenged following publication of his book, and Barnard felt obliged to spell out his analysis in greater detail.[12] Richard Donham also recognized the importance of the customer in making a self-appraisal of a firm. Writing in 1933, Donham observes:

> . . . The sole reason for a company's existence is not to manufacture steel, or automobiles, or cotton cloth, or shoes, but through such products to aid in supplying some of the wants of the people. Once the executives of a corporation are aware what fundamental wants their product is helping to supply it becomes easier for them to recognize how many and diverse are the products with which, directly or indirectly, they must compete.[13]

Companies have generally displayed much greater attention to the customer during the postwar years, and executives report that there are constant attempts to incorporate more of the so-called marketing concept into their management activities. The writings of Peter Drucker, especially *The Practice of Management,* have had a notable influence in this regard.

OTHER APPROACHES TO SELF-APPRAISAL

The emphasis upon customer orientation has suggested a number of other ways of viewing the nature of a firm.

1. Basic wants. One way is to try to find out what is the basic want which a product is attempting to satisfy. There is a distinction between a permanent need (say, light for the home) and the product which customers currently buy to satisfy that need (the electric lamp). By trying to uncover the basic wants of the customer (even though he may be unaware of them at a conscious level) the company is attempting to remove its attachment to products which may have only transient appeal.

The postwar changes in The Martin Company, described in Chapter 4, provide a good case in point. In making the change from aircraft production to missiles and manned space vehicles, the management demonstrated its intention not to confuse a customer demand for aircraft with a basic want for aircraft. The more basic want, as The Martin Company's management apparently saw it, was high-speed air transportation. Aircraft, therefore, was a transient product line, and it could be superseded by such items as intercontinental ballistic missiles and manned space vehicles. This kind of alert thinking helps a company throw off any emotional attachment it may have to particular products now past their prime.

2. A product system. A second concept based upon customer orientation is the product-system type of analysis. A company frequently finds, upon inquiry, that there are whole families of products which have some relationship to its existing product line. Once it recognizes and becomes sensitive to this fact, the company may find itself in a favorable position to exploit and develop these relationships. It may forge expansion policies which enable it to develop in these related areas while still retaining its present corporate cohesiveness. This is illustrated by the so-called electrical industry. Passer has pointed out how electrical products have often been marketed as part of a product system from early times. They became part of a lighting system or a power system. Passer continues his analysis:

> To ensure that the component parts would operate together in a satisfactory manner, manufacturers found it advantageous to produce all, or nearly all, of the components of any system they chose to market. They also found it advantageous to sell and install the complete system. It was primarily the system characteristic of electrical products, therefore, that led an electrical firm to manufacture a full line of products and to assume the responsibility for placing them, in operating condition, in the hands of the users.[14]

There are many other instances. Companies in defense work have sometimes viewed their skills and resources in the light of product systems or families. The concept of systems management, which is sometimes an outgrowth of this type of self-appraisal, has become very important in defense work and is described in a later chapter. Other examples include companies which have product lines requiring component parts or continuous service needs. It becomes clear, in short, that this approach provides another insight into the real nature of the firm, and it is one which is most useful in developing strategies of "link diversification," a concept which is developed in Chapter 9.

3. Product territory. Still another customer-oriented concept is the product territory viewpoint. By this is meant that it is helpful to identify those market areas which surround the firm's existing product mission, as seen from the standpoint of the customer. This approach broadens the context of a company's product line; for instance, a firm which manufactures children's pencil sets may perceive that its product is closely related to other school stationery supplies. Or it may reveal close association between products with quite different physical characteristics. A manufacturer of home water sprinklers may find that his business is really closely associated with outdoor faucets. In each case, the concept of product territory use-fully examines the associations which a product-in-use has, whether the products associated have similar or dissimilar characteristics.

DETERMINING THE REAL NATURE OF A BUSINESS:
SOME CONCLUSIONS

These conceptual approaches whereby a company's management tries to view the nature of its business reveal the sort of thinking and analysis being undertaken by long-range planners in some of the most progressive companies. Some important conclusions are as follows.

1. Deceptive simplicity. There is a deceptive simplicity about the idea of a corporate self-appraisal winding up with some brief phrase which describes the nature of part or all of the firm's activity. The essence of simplicity is shown by the conclusion that American Tele-phone and Telegraph's business is "service," or that Polaroid's busi-ness is "the relations between light and matter," or that Standard Oil (New Jersey)'s business is "energy." But usually a great deal of corporate introspection has preceded such conclusions. Furthermore,

they are backed up by an intimate understanding of the nature of
the company. It is this self-awareness which is so valuable as a basis
in developing long-range planning strategies.

2. *Subsequent impact.* The results of a self-appraisal have important ramifications in the selection of a particular strategy and
therefore affect vast numbers of subsequent decisions made at different levels of the company. Take, for example, the case of a firm
which manufactures suitcases. One self-appraisal may result in its
viewing itself as a specialist in suitcases. Consequently, its policies
may emphasize a complete line of suitcases, a high-price line and an
economy-price line, special attention to the quality of materials
used, and perhaps consideration of vertical integration moves. An
alternative self-appraisal may result in prime emphasis being given
to the firm's place as a leather goods manufacturer. The policies in
this case relate to wider dispersion of company resources, as contrasted with the relatively intensive concentration in the first case.
Attention might be given to a search for new products and familiarity
with the most appropriate channels of distribution for various
products. A third possible self-appraisal might view the firm as being
in the travel accessories business. Here the dispersion of resources
is still wider, since the manufacturing activities presumably would
not be limited to leather or other closely associated materials. The
conclusion, to repeat, is that a single choice in this type of situation
will have great impact upon many subsequent decisions made within
the firm.[15]

3. *Multidimensional nature.* A single insight does not reveal the
real nature of a business. Company analysts need to utilize a number
of different insights, each having different conceptual focuses and
different standpoints. The problem is complex, and a one-dimensional view of things presents a distorted picture. We must view the
inherited resources of the company as its physical characteristics,
the processes it utilizes, and its performance qualities. We must
consider the attitudes and interests of top management executives
in relation to these other considerations. From this overall analysis
the self-appraisal is likely to reveal some strengths which are the
basic ingredients of future company success. Edith Penrose summarizes the situation:

> In the long run the profitability, survival, and growth of a firm do

not depend so much on the efficiency with which it is able to organize the production of even a widely diversified range of products as it does on the ability of the firm to establish one or more wide and relatively impregnable "bases" from which it can adapt and extend its operations in an uncertain, changing, and competitive world.[16]

4. General characteristics of analysis. While there are variations in the importance given to these different concepts by different companies, two general characteristics of analysis can be observed.

One is that it is *always* useful to carry industrial classifications according to product lines and processes to higher levels of abstraction. This facilitates giving attention to the broad sphere of activity within which a company is currently doing business. Thus some manufacturers of jeweled-movement watches have been able to broaden their concept of their product to "precision time pieces." Since their companies faced the postwar period with an apparently mature product, the broader concept suggested diversification of strategies such as the development of timing machines in defense contract work. Again, General Motors is said to have seen the great reservoir of transferable skills it had built up through its automobile manufacturing in terms of "engineering for quantity production." It was this recognition which played an important part in its decision to produce the Frigidaire refrigerator.

The other general characteristic is that *every* self-appraisal of this kind requires that attention be given explicitly to the customer orientation. We have already seen instances in which major errors in strategy have resulted from ignoring the customer, from which we can generalize that any company which ignores the customer in its self-appraisal runs the risk of basing its strategic plans upon a dangerously distorted self-concept. This holds true even when firms appear to have a heavy stake in the continuance of a given product. For example, if companies which have large investments in a given commodity (say, minerals or agricultural items) are to maintain demands for it, they must analyze its usefulness from the standpoint of customers and try to develop new uses. The changing energy sources utilized in the United States over the past century are pertinent in this connection. One hundred years ago wood was the principal fuel, providing over 80 per cent of the nation's energy requirements. Fifty years ago the dominant fuel was coal, and it provided about 75 per cent of the total requirement. Today the situation is again transformed. The use of wood as fuel is now negligible, while coal's share of the market amounts to only 23 per cent. To remain competitively successful, timber and coal merchants have had to adapt to changed circumstances, and the only way in which this has been possible has been, basically, through a new customer orientation. It is well known that demands for timber have developed and enlarged in many different areas. By contrast, the alternative uses uncovered for coal are limited and the fortunes of coal companies have generally declined as a result.

5. Basic characteristics of hard-core skills. The skills and resources which a company's management seeks to clarify in a self-appraisal can be summarized in terms of three qualities: (1) value, (2) uniqueness, and (3) permanence.

Value is a quality which depends ultimately upon the judgment of the customer, but it is not related only to economic considerations of price. There is a wide range of considerations which may be relevant: quality, service, reliability, promptness, and so on. The value of a company's productive activities will also depend upon how necessary they are in meeting the basic wants of the customer. These wants may not even be clear to the customer—wood was considered an "indispensable" fuel until the advent of large-scale coal mining, for example. Nonetheless, the quality of value as the customer determines it represents an essential criterion in any corporate self-appraisal.

Uniqueness is a quality found in a variety of different situations. It may apply to patents, to special equipment, to special manpower skills, to long relationships with customers, or to long experience in merchandising in a particular way. Since companies operate in a competitive environment, they want to be sensitive to those aspects of their operation in which they have unique skills or experiences or resources which can be exploited.

The third quality to clarify in a self-appraisal is permanence. In any company there are some characteristics which are relatively transient, others which are relatively permanent. The transient factors fade and alter with the passage of time. One generation of products gives way to a new generation of products; one generation of process technology gives way to a new generation of process technology; one generation of managers gives way to a new generation of managers. Yet there are other factors which appear to be relatively permanent. There are some skills, some resources, and some wants being met, which can be regarded as permanent, at least within the direct impact time of the intended strategic plans. Their immutability provides a basis upon which a company can better understand its own basic nature and thereby better plan the extension and adaptation of its operations to a world of continuing change.

While self-appraisal is only one part in the complex process of strategic long-range planning, its importance is becoming clear to increasing numbers of planning executives. It helps in providing a sound basis for determining future courses of action. It encourages companies to face impending changes which might otherwise be ignored (such as the fact that a company's major products have reached a stage of maturity in their life cycles). In addition, the better understanding it provides of the company helps not only in long-range planning but also in day-to-day administrative activities as well. Strategic planning is producing a new kind of company psychiatrist to serve top management, one whose object of study is the nature of the corporate entity itself rather than of the people who work within that entity.

Chapter 6

Establishing Objectives

The establishment of objectives is a subject of great importance whenever a company embarks upon any kind of long-range planning. It is also a subject which is very difficult to understand and explain. One corporate executive interviewed for this study asserted flatly that "objectives are the most difficult and the most obscure part of long-range planning," and this opinion, while outspoken, was by no means uniquely his. Widespread confusion about what objectives are, what they should do, and how they should be expressed has suggested the same conclusion to others.

Because the subject is at once so important and so difficult, this chapter is primarily a conceptual exposition in which there is an attempt to clarify the meaning of objectives, their relationship with the planning process as a whole, and the ways in which they can be expressed. Although the subject is treated in the context of strategic long-range planning activities, much of the analysis applies, with minor modifications, to long-range planning generally.

THE MEANING OF "OBJECTIVES"

The word "objectives"—like the word "planning"—suffers from an acute case of semantic fuzziness. Its meaning has become blurred partly because it is used in so many different organizational settings, partly because of careless use of language, and partly because of a lack of clear understanding about the concept itself.[1] In such circumstances it is important to explain the meaning of the word as it is used here. "Objectives" here are the statements of planning purpose developed within any kind of business plan. They are established *within* the framework of a planning process, and they normally evolve from tentative and vague ideas to more specific declarations of purpose. Objectives, furthermore, are always present in a planning process, even though they are sometimes unconsciously established.[2]

94

It is important to observe the difference between objectives, as just defined, and "company objectives," which are statements of those primary purposes toward which a company (or, sometimes, a given unit of that company) is directing its activities. Sometimes a statement or statements from the company objectives is incorporated as an objective or objectives within the strategic long-range planning process, and there is clearly a close relationship between the subjects treated in each instance. However, the two are conceptually distinct and must be treated as such.

THE PLACE OF OBJECTIVES WITHIN THE STRATEGIC PLANNING PROCESS

The place of objectives within the process of strategic long-range planning is not easy to describe, because the relationship between objectives and process is neither simple nor direct and because objectives do not assume a fixed, unchanging form throughout the process. The "establishing objectives" phase is interconnected and intertwined with all the other phases of the strategic planning process; it is not completed once and for all at the start of planning activities. Objectives in strategic planning are only "first" because it is convenient to present them at the beginning of a final report which details the planning decisions made. To understand the subject properly, therefore, it is useful to view the development of objectives in terms of a series of sequential stages.

The first is the *preliminary* stage. At the outset, a company's strategic planners are likely to have some vague and highly generalized notions of purpose, normally containing ideas about growth, profitability, survival, and stability.[3] These notions provide a useful starting point in that they give the planners something to work with—a preliminary basis for planning analysis. However, they are no more than a starting point and require subsequent refinement and a greater degree of particularity before assuming final form.

During the second stage *tentative* objectives are developed. As planning analysis proceeds, planners develop certain working objectives to guide and assist in testing and checking the feasibility of certain ideas. Tentative objectives normally reflect attempts to develop more specific statements of purpose than those which constitute the initial preliminary objectives. Instead of an objective about corporate growth expressed in nonquantitative terms, for example, a tentative objective may state that the company should aim for an average annual growth of 20 per cent in dollar sales volume.

The third stage in developing objectives supersedes the second as the analysis progresses further. It is the development of *revised* objectives, and this is the point where planners have the chance to correct, adjust, or confirm the earlier objectives in the light of subsequent investigation and study. The planners may have realized, for example, that the tentative objective of a 20 per cent growth rate is not realistic and that 15 per cent is the highest growth rate that could reasonably be attained and sustained over a period of years. This stage demonstrates once again the evolving nature of objectives, and the importance of flexibility in objectives while the planning analysis is proceeding.

The fourth stage is the development of *final* objectives. By final objectives is meant the objectives as stated in the formal written document which constitutes "the plan" in its final form. Progression to these final objectives represents two advances from the revised objectives stage. There is the need first to incorporate any subsequent revisions or refinements of the revised objectives. Second, there is the need to choose which objectives need to be incorporated formally in the written document. This second point deserves further attention.

In the course of analysis, planners are likely to develop a number of tentative and revised objectives which aid them in analysis but which need not be stated in the final written document. For example, the desirability of stable employment may prove a useful working objective in the course of analysis, but in most cases it need not be made explicit in the final objectives. Many times, in fact, planners seek some way of expressing the final objectives in one brief statement of central purpose. This is not always possible, but planners generally seek to keep the final statement of objectives as brief and succinct as possible. They have probably used many other working objectives in the course of analysis, but working objectives, like working papers, do not all have to be included in the final document which summarizes "the plan."

This four-stage analysis of the phase of "establishing objectives" illustrates how it is interwoven and interconnected with the rest of the planning process. Greater clarity in understanding objectives usually develops as the planning activity itself proceeds. The situation can be compared to a three-dimensional figure which can be readjusted to any rectangular shape so long as it remains the same in total area. In the case of objectives for strategic long-range planning, planners usually start out with wide breadth by superficial depth—the preliminary objectives stage. Subsequently, the planners strive for more particularity (greater depth) without, however, sacrificing anything significant in total breadth or height. This is done by determining, in the course of analysis, which factors are strategic. As a result, the breadth of the two-dimensional figure is narrowed to allow greater depth, but it is narrowed in such a manner that nothing of strategic importance is excluded. This is essentially what is happening when tentative and revised objectives are developed. In their final form the objectives are more precise and more perceptive statements of purpose than were possible at the start of the planning process.

ADMINISTRATIVE CONSIDERATIONS

Intermittent attention given to objectives serves as a most useful controlling mechanism for the activities of the planners themselves. By meeting together every so often to talk about objectives, they have a continuing check which discourages straying into unproductive areas. In other words, the need for reappraising objectives from time to time throughout the planning process has the beneficial effect of keeping planners on the track, thereby facilitating their efficient use of time and skills. When planners meet to discuss objectives, they also have the opportunity to become clearer about the relationship of their own activities with those of other planners. They develop a community of thinking about basic elements of planning activity and provide each planner with bench marks to prevent too great a departure from the thinking and the activities of the rest of the group.

Another administrative consideration is the very important point that some objectives are going to require approval from above. That is to say, the chief executive and perhaps others in top management are going to have the final say in endorsing, modifying, or rejecting objectives proposed by the planning staff. This in practice does not apply to all objectives: for example, those which are direct derivations from the company objectives normally require no express approval. However, some objectives *do* require express approval which should be sought before a great deal of analysis contingent upon them is carried out. At the same time, if an objective is tentative, the planners need to convey this fact clearly to the top management executives. It can be very harmful to have top management become greatly enthused about the proposed objective of a 20 per cent growth rate and then to have to report subsequently that anything above a 15 per cent growth rate is unrealistic.

These administrative considerations are highly significant as factors to be taken into account while developing objectives. Together they demonstrate the need for a combination of analytic skill and administrative awareness on the part of the planners.

BEDROCK OBJECTIVES

We have defined strategic long-range planning as an activity aimed toward "the continuing health and vitality of a company over the long term." Actually, this statement can be translated into four bedrock objectives, because all planning of this kind is intended to steer a company in the directions of (1) stimulating growth, (2) increasing profitability, (3) assuring survival, and (4) achieving greater operational stability. We need to be clear about the relative importance and the interrelationships of these four bedrock objectives, because they provide the foundation for the more specific objectives which evolve later in the planning process.

The objective of stimulating corporate growth has always received major emphasis in the literature on top management planning activities. Edward H. Hempel, whose *Top-Management Planning* (1945) is the first attempt to deal with this subject at book length, emphasizes the primary importance of growth:

> The decision, how big an enterprise should be conceived and made, when to enlarge and how much, or when to mark time, is definitely the most fundamental and vexing task of top management.[4]

Subsequent literature has, in general, continued to show a preoccupation with the central role of stimulating growth. A typical example comes from the management consultant Bruce Payne:

> Long-term planning, properly conceived, answers the question,

"How fast should we grow?" It points up the obstacles to growth and prepares management to overcome them. [5]

Interviews with planning executives also revealed this emphasis upon corporate growth. They frequently observed that long-range planning was essentially planning for long-term growth, and that their company's plans were being developed with this objective in mind.

Although widely held, this opinion is an oversimplified view of things. Each of the four objectives influences the shaping of plans, whether it is recognized as such or not. Thus one apparent reason why growth receives most attention is that it comes the closest to being all-encompassing. In other words, pursuit of plans which seek to stimulate growth are consistent for the most part with plans designed to increase profitability or to assure survival and sometimes also help in achieving greater operational stability. But the plans are not *necessarily* consistent.

The relationship between the growth objective and the profitability and survival objectives is fairly readily seen. Empirical evidence strongly suggests that a healthy company is usually a growing company, and vice versa. It also indicates that firms which fail to achieve some measure of growth over a period of years usually show substantial declines in profits and stock price quotations as well as a sharp diminution in their ability to attract top caliber managers. [6] And while some firms overextend themselves financially and expand their way into bankruptcy, this does not weaken the case, because the growth objective does not necessarily mean growth at high speed. As generally expressed, it means only "development in the direction of growth."

The relationship between the bedrock objectives of growth and of stability is not so close. A company seeks stability in order to become administratively more efficient and manageable. Plans which have the primary objective of increasing stability usually take one of two forms: either a company seeks to lessen seasonal fluctuations, thus hoping to gain greater utilization of production equipment, distribution facilities, and manpower resources, or it seeks to lessen its dependence upon products which are cyclically volatile. Stability objectives are usually formulated as supporting strategies. Rarely if ever are they part of a grand strategy, and so they are generally overshadowed in importance by the other bedrock objectives, most notably growth.

To repeat, then, there is no doubt that the growth objective is the major focal point in strategic long-range planning undertakings. It not only encompasses all of the objectives more completely than any of the remaining three, but also is closest to the challenge of providing "continuing health and vitality over the long term."

QUANTITATIVE TARGETS

Although strategic long-range planning is primarily an activity designed to provide guidelines for corporate action, these guidelines are sometimes set as quantitative targets. These targets approximate what is being sought and encourage incentive by establishing a point for the company to aim at.

Not all companies choose to express strategic long-range planning objectives as quantitative targets, but those which do establish them as bedrock objectives (for instance, aiming to sustain growth of such-and-such a rate) and/or as more specific bench marks (such as achieving at least 30 per cent of total sales volume each year from products which have been marketed by the company for less than three years). Whenever quantitative targets are adopted, there are two conceptual alternatives in their selection: One is the "carrot" type of target; the other is the "realistic" type.[7] The "carrot" target is based on the premise that people exert their maximum effort only if asked to do a little more than they can reasonably be expected to achieve. The "realistic" target represents the best estimate of what achievements can in fact be accomplished, having in mind both the skills and the limitations of the company as it now exists.

Between these two conceptual poles there is a whole range of intermediary positions, and some planning executives have established quantitative targets which were designed, in effect, to achieve a balance between the two extremes. Thus General Electric urges its managers to set "optimistic, difficult-to-attain goals," and planners in other companies similarly suggest targets which are "somewhat higher" than previous achievements. A planning executive at IBM also expressed this kind of approach when he commented:

> If you set objectives that are altogether out of reach, they discourage. If you set them too close, then they are "consumed" too quickly. Objectives must be attainable, but not too easily attainable.

In practice this striving toward an intermediary position frequently takes the form of oscillation first toward one extreme, then toward the other. This tendency is partly explained by the problems inherent in both carrot and realistic targets.

The difficulty with establishing carrot targets is that if they are rarely reached, or if it soon becomes apparent that they cannot be reached, they are recognized as artificial. Thereupon the pressure toward achievement slackens, sometimes with an accompanying drop in organizational motivation. In such circumstances there may be a replacement of the formal carrot target by an informal realistic target, which represents a judgment of what top management really expects. When (as in the case of strategic long-range planning) there are many interdependent plans being developed throughout an organization, this kind of informal adjustment can create serious problems of coordination.

Problems also exist when objectives are established as realistic targets. This type of target allows no margin for underestimating capabilities without losing some incentive value. Neither does it encourage more efficient accomplishments by units which are inefficient in the first place. Devons has reported, for instance, that in Great Britain's wartime aircraft program, grossly inefficient firms would sink to even more incompetent levels when realistic targets (targets which fully acknowledged their inefficiency) were set for their output.[8]

In many cases where quantitative targets are established in strategic long-range planning, the actual figures are determined in a fairly arbitrary manner. Indeed, sometimes some very detailed analysis is predicated upon an objective whose target figures have seemingly been plucked out of the air. There are those who argue that this is not a serious matter, because a self-correcting mechanism adjusts targets which miss their marks by wide margins. And it is true that reliance upon "crude objectives or measurements that are not completely accurate" is sometimes necessary in starting a planning program.[9] Often there is little information from past performance to guide long-range planners in determining targets, and they have to make do as best they can.

However, there are some serious difficulties about this approach. Frequently it is impossible to obtain definitive feedback information about the progress of a long-range plan, and therefore there is a long delay before past performance information can be incorporated into later plans. A second problem is psychological, and it relates to the incentive which targets imply. The then director of long-range planning at IBM, Michael Kami, stressed the importance of this factor when he said:

> Originally I did not think it mattered much how or where the original objectives and goals were set. I thought that the planning process would soon show which objectives were reasonable and which were not, and that succeeding cycles in the planning process would bring about readjustments in a fairly automatic fashion.
>
> Now, however, I have come to realize that early and tentative objectives can be either constructive or destructive. It is easy to create a negative attitude towards them in people's minds.

Planning and planners can quickly become scapegoats if targets are well out of range of reality at either the high or the low end. The relationship between planners and others in the organization is a fairly delicate one, and it thrives only when there are sincerity and candor at all times. If the planners attempt anything that implies underhand methods, or, indeed, anything that might be considered less than frank, the goodwill of the relationship is likely to crumble quickly and future planning activities may be impaired.

It is clear, in short, that arbitrary methods of establishing targets can create some serious problems in strategic long-range planning endeavors. Some of these problems can be alleviated by careful administrative handling in carrying out the plans, but the high risks of arbitrary targets and of targets that seem arbitrary point to the need for greater care in this phase of planning.

A CONCLUDING COMMENT

Objectives are an emergent, interrelated part of the planning process. There may be some who consider that this statement only makes an already confused subject still more confusing. But the fact is that, although the subject of establishing objectives has sometimes been presented in terms of a few clear-cut categorizations, this does not accurately describe their application in strategic long-range planning. Again, although objectives are sometimes said to be determined at the start of the planning process and from then on are "fixed," this is patently false in the context with which we have been concerned. In much of strategic long-range planning, "a problem well defined is a problem half-solved," and the importance of objectives in the planning process becomes apparent only in the light of interrelated characteristics.

Chapter 7

Assumptions About the Future

ONE ESSENTIAL CHARACTERISTIC OF ANY PLAN IS ITS DEVELOPment against a background of certain events and circumstances expected to apply in the future. By definition planning is always concerned with the future, and to be logically meaningful a plan requires some estimate of the future setting for which it is being designed. It is fair to say that the appropriateness of any plan always depends upon the validity of these assumptions about the future.

The complexity of strategic long-range planning would be greatly reduced if assumptions about the long-range future could be expressed clearly and precisely. But clarity and precision in this regard are usually difficult to attain for two major reasons: (1) The broad scope of strategic long-range planning requires assumptions about the future in all kinds of subject areas, some of which defy efforts at accurate prediction, and (2) the time period encompassed by this kind of planning makes it exceedingly difficult to determine even outstanding characteristics of the future with a high degree of confidence. Nevertheless, a systematic approach to the analysis of planning assumptions can be most useful.

THE PLACE OF ASSUMPTIONS IN THE STRATEGIC PLANNING PROCESS

The phase of "making assumptions" is closely interconnected with other phases in the overall strategic planning process. Assumptions, like objectives, usually emerge as the result of analysis; only a few are fixed and settled from the start. Therefore, making assumptions can be thought of as a complete subprocess in several stages within the main planning process.

The nature of the analysis used in developing these assumptions varies widely, ranging from emphasis on quantitative forecasts to emphasis on qualitative factors to reliance upon intuitive presuppositions. Furthermore, many different subjects are included, ranging from the possibility of unique events (such as war and natural catastrophe) to determination of expected levels of quantity (for example, national product, population). But at the heart of all these considerations, however dissimilar they may appear, lies the basic problem of trying to grapple with uncertainty about the future.

UNCERTAINTY ABOUT THE FUTURE

Planning is a process of groping forward. The future is enveloped in fog, which grows denser the further we try to peer. Prediction of future events and circumstances means grappling with the uncertainties looming in this fog and trying to make incomplete and indirect information as intelligible as possible. Uncertainty is never completely absent from planning activities. Business is a risk-taking activity, and uncertainty is a fundamental fact of business life. Nevertheless, an understanding of the problems rising from uncertainty helps the planner see which uncertainties or which effects of uncertainties might be reducible and which are irreducible. Such an understanding also helps the planner interpret assumptions so that uncertainties which remain in the final form of the plan are not there unnecessarily.

There are several possible ways in which a planner may seek to reduce uncertainties or their consequences. One possibility is to increase the accumulation and study of existing data. Another is to average out uncertainties by relying on large-scale organization. A third is to try to control some aspects of future developments. The appropriateness of any or all of these approaches depends upon the circumstances of a particular situation. The task is to determine how far to go in attempting to predict accurately. As Frank H. Knight observes, it is a question of economics in that refining alternatives is eventually subject to diminishing marginal importance, or diminishing return.[1]

In today's world every long-range planner has to make some assumptions, either implicitly or explicitly, about the possibility of nuclear war. On the basis of present knowledge, we know that there is a possibility (though it cannot be measured quantitatively) that a nuclear war will take place at some time in the future. However, no one knows whether such an event will or will not take place. In making assumptions about the future, therefore, the long-range planner must determine whether the possibility of nuclear war should be seriously considered or ignored. Of course, the uncertainty itself in this situation cannot be affected, but a company may well conclude that it can plan to provide a degree of protection for itself and its employees if a nuclear war should take place. Thus a long-range plan based upon this assumption might project building smaller plants in the future, with the idea of the company's becoming geographically less centralized. Or, the plan might call for the construction of civil defense shelters at each plant site. In each case the plan, based upon interpretation of the assumption, is designed to reduce the effects of uncertainty about nuclear war.

The alternative is to ignore altogether the possibility of nuclear war. This assumption (which appears to be the one most usually adopted by companies engaged in long-range planning activities) concludes that the uncertainty must be accepted as irreducible and that there is no point in trying to make plans which would have importance only in the event of a nuclear holocaust.

Even when there is great uncertainty in trying to predict the future, however, further study and the accumulation of additional data may help a company to draw firm conclusions.

In 1954 a major company in the United States with substantial holdings in Latin America established a survey task force to analyze conditions in various countries south of the border in order to help guide its long-term investment policies. The task force investigated .the situation in these countries and was able to contribute further information to company knowledge. In particular, it concluded that there were several prime economic indicators which would help to gauge likely changes in political and economic conditions. At that time no one could have predicted in detail the political and economic changes which would actually take place in Cuba during the next decade. Nevertheless, the task force, by careful analysis, was able to determine that these primary economic indicators suggested that major trouble might well come in Cuba sooner or later. They were particularly alarmed by the extremely small share of the country's national income received by the peasant population. As a result, the task force concluded that the uncertainties in making further plans for investment would be too great to justify, and so it recommended against further investment in Cuba. The company took this advice.

Another aspect of uncertainty which deserves attention here is the quantification of data. In developing assumptions about the future in so broad an undertaking as strategic long-range planning, arbitrary figures are frequently used to provide approximate bench marks. This is both useful and necessary in many circumstances, but problems may arise if the figures subsequently have greater certainty attributed to them than their original means of development justifies. Because a strategic long-range plan serves as a basis for many supporting planning activities, an error of this kind may have a multiplier effect upon the company as a whole and produce adverse consequences.

Devons has provided a vivid description of this problem in one of his essays on aircraft planning activities in Great Britain during World War II:

> If the statistical division estimated M.A.P. (Ministry of Aircraft Production) labour requirements as somewhere between 1,500,000 and 1,750,000, and surrounded this estimate with qualifications indicating the extremely flimsy basis on which it was drawn up, some official would sooner or later quote 1,625,000 as the best available figure, and this would become *the figure* of M.A.P. labour requirements. The degree of precision in the estimate might be further distorted by subtracting from this requirement figure that of the actual labour force employed by M.A.P. If, for example, actual employment stood at 1,534,000, this would give an additional requirement of 91,000. The use of this latter figure rather than, say, 90,000 or about 100,000 would give the whole picture an air of precision much greater than the basic information really warranted. And in the heat of interdepartmental battles on labour allocations, the wide margin of error in the figures was completely forgotten; and discussion and argument proceeded on the assumption that the various factors involved were known with accuracy. There was indeed something Freudian about the way in which the original basis on which the figures had been drawn up was hidden away and forgotten. For to have recognized the inadequacy of the figures would have meant admitting that policy decisions were not being taken on a rational basis.[2]

Devons' analysis is applicable to strategic long-range planning. Assumptions for strategic planning are always based on many subjective considerations, and the assignment of weightings or choice of approximate numerical estimates, even if roughhewn, can be most helpful at times. The danger is that these figures will subsequently be misinterpreted to imply an exactness which is not in fact justified, or a reduction in uncertainty when in fact no such reduction has been achieved. This sort of misinterpretation is most likely to occur when the strategic plan is communicated in abbreviated form. Actually the plan is founded upon a variety of assumptions about which there is some degree of uncertainty. For the plan to be properly understood, a reading of the fine print and the footnotes is necessary.

This brief discussion of uncertainty in its relationship to assumptions about the future reveals some of the difficulties which face the strategic long-range planner when he strives for accuracy. It is desirable to see the implications of uncertainty as the planner seeks to develop assumptions in practical planning.

POSSIBLE METHODS FOR DEVELOPING ASSUMPTIONS

The development of assumptions for strategic long-range plans always poses a problem in economics. There are countless numbers of possible assumptions which a planner might make and endless investigations which he might conduct.[3] There are, however, two considerations which must always be taken into account as well. One is that some uncertainty about the future is unavoidable in business life. The other is that investigations take time and are expensive in their use of planning resources. Thus the problem always arises: How much time and what resources should be devoted to the development of assumptions for strategic planning purposes?

In practice assumptions can be and are developed in a variety of ways, and so it is useful to make a classification of the major alternatives. There are five categories that need concern us here:

1. "Imposed" assumptions. Some assumptions are imposed by direction of the chief executive or others in top management. The planners do not need to take time to investigate these assumptions further: They are "givens" in their planning task and can be accepted without question.[4] Thus assumptions may take the form of instructions about the general environment or the industry environment, for example, "to disregard the possibility of a nuclear disarmament treaty" or "to ignore the possible impact of a specified technological advance." Or they may take the form of information about the company's own resources, for example, "to assume that the company can obtain any additional skilled manpower needed to carry out the plan decided upon."

2. *"High probability" assumptions.* In any plan there are a great many underlying assumptions which can be made with a high degree of confidence, based upon past experience. This is true in strategic planning, even though planners need to be wary about making assumptions concerning the long-range future on the basis of projective thinking. There are many factors which either remain constant or can be treated as constant because changes in them are slow-moving, persistent, and easily predictable. For example, it seems clear that a company may validly assume that there will be a continuing supply of many highly competent people in the economy. Their identity will change, and the knowledge they have will change, but the basic assumption can be viewed as unchanging and taken for granted as a "high probability" assumption.

There is, in fact, a myriad of assumptions which fit into this category. Other examples might include:

- The average life span of Americans will continue to rise gradually.
- Weather patterns in any given region can be expected to continue to resemble those of recent years.
- The U. S. political system of government is unlikely to change radically during the next decade.

Assumptions of this kind are normally accepted without detailed analysis unless there appears to be some *prima facie* reason for questioning their validity or unless a particular subject is of such central importance that it needs to be investigated more thoroughly.

3. *"Irreducible uncertainty" assumptions.* There are some subjects which have a substantial degree of uncertainty. Attempts to analyze these subjects quickly reach a point of diminishing returns beyond which further analysis is not fruitful. A case in point is the one cited earlier: the possibility of all-out nuclear war. It is certainly possible for planners to embark upon an extensive study of this subject: It has multiple facets, and an immense amount of literature is devoted to it. Yet, even after a year or more of study, the most able of planning task forces would probably be unable to provide any dramatic new insights which would be useful for incorporating into planning

assumptions. The basic analysis can be undertaken quickly, and there is usually no point in carrying it further. The distinguishing feature of this category, then, is not that the assumptions can be quickly determined with a high degree of certainty but that a point of diminishing returns is soon reached in analysis and at this point the remaining uncertainties must be accepted as unavoidable.

4. "Previous information" assumptions. Since any company which undertakes this kind of long-range planning activity is a going concern, it is bound to have accumulated studies of many subjects, and some of their findings prove most useful to planners in developing assumptions. For example, a detailed study of technological feasibility or resource capability often proves invaluable and saves a great deal of needless duplication of work. Of course, the planners have to judge the continuing validity of such studies' findings.

5. "Planning analysis" assumptions. Finally, there are those subjects which demand special investigation by the planners in order to develop assumptions, a category accounting for most of the planners' activity in this phase of forecasting. Not only does it require analytic skill and an ability to think insightfully about the subject, but also it demands skill to select those subjects which are sufficiently important and uncertain to deserve more detailed attention. The ability to distinguish between "high probability" assumptions and those which require further analysis before being confirmed, modified, or rejected is extremely important in strategic planning. The planner must always guard against accepting potentially important assumptions on superficial evidence.

This analysis makes it clear that the task of the strategic planner is not to conduct an exhaustive investigation of every significant subject area in which some assumptions are needed. In practice, there are some assumptions which are provided for the planners by others in the company or as a result of investigative work already done. Also, there are some subjects which are of such a nature as to discourage detailed study. Therefore, the planner's task is the selection and analysis of those subject areas which deserve special attention.

STAGES IN DEVELOPING ASSUMPTIONS

The evolving nature of assumptions makes it useful to think of them as developing in several stages. It is convenient to describe these stages as (1) initial assumptions, (2) working assumptions, and (3) final assumptions.

Initial assumptions are developed early in the planning process, and their main purpose is to provide some bases on which the planners may work. Some initial assumptions are imposed by top management; certain pre-established assumptions which form limits in the planning assignment.[5] Other initial assumptions can best be characterized as conditional or preliminary; they have been made without analysis or study and are "on trial." Some of them are high-probability assumptions, but others are quite uncertain, being tested with the knowledge that experience will demonstrate whether they are sound and reasonable.

Working assumptions are developed during the course of planning analysis. As with the establishment of objectives, various assumptions are seen as relevant only after some planning analysis has been carried out. There are other assumptions developed on a temporary basis, to show how some possibility would work out, given certain conditions. Still other assumptions represent deliberate abstractions from reality, often being used as simplifying assumptions to help clarify and understand the controlling factors which operate in a particular situation. Thus working assumptions cover a number of different considerations, and they reveal clearly the emergent character of assumptions in strategic long-range planning.

During this stage there are some administrative activities which are of considerable importance. At various times those people who are charged with the planning work meet to discuss assumptions, in much the same way as they discuss objectives. They not only review their collective judgments about assumptions on individual subjects, but they also make an overall review, which enables them to appraise their work as a whole. Are the assumptions too risky? Too ambitious? Too conservative? What are the major uncertainties among them, and has sufficient thought been given to the development of contingency plans in the event these assumptions prove inaccurate? Discussions of this sort provide way stations in the planning activity. They allow an appraisal of what has been done, and they provide a good time for making adjustments and alterations. Also, they provide a point of liaison at which each individual planner can check whether his own activities are proceeding in harmony with those of others of the planning staff.[6]

Final assumptions are those which are incorporated in the written presentation of "the plan" in its completed form. There are three important considerations in making the transition to final assumptions. First, there is a need to re-examine the validity of individual assumptions in the light of the tentatively selected strategy. Second, there is a need to re-examine the assumptions collectively, again in the light of the provisional strategy. And third, there is a need to decide which assumptions ought to be included in a final statement of "the plan."

The highly selective character of the final assumptions stage is one of its most important features. The selections are made so that they include only those major assumptions which should be understood (1) in assessing the plan as a whole and (2) in using the plan. They are not intended to provide a compact summary of the innumerable assumptions made during the course of the planning process, and in this respect they differ markedly from final objectives, which are intended to be a reasonably complete, compact summary of the emergent objectives of the plan.

The selection of final assumptions is usually made with particular attention to the needs of the *user* of the plan, who must have information which allows him to judge when and if the plan needs to be qualified, modified, or even abandoned at any time. For example, one important assumption in a given plan might be that no nuclear disarmament treaty will be signed during a specified period of time. This assumption would probably be stated in the final assumptions, because later it might provide valuable guidance to the user. Thus, if a treaty were subsequently concluded, the user would recognize that the plan needed immediate reappraisal.

The significance of these different kinds of analyses and the different stages in development of assumptions becomes clearer through consideration of the assumptions themselves.

SUBJECT AREAS OF ASSUMPTIONS

The subject areas of the many different assumptions which are needed in strategic long-range planning activities fall into three major categories:

1. "General environment" assumptions.

2. "Industry environment" assumptions.
3. "Factors of production" assumptions.

We shall examine each in turn.

1. "General environment" assumptions. The broad scope of any strategic long-range planning activity necessitates developing some assumptions about the general environment in which a company operates. Assumptions about political, social, economic, scientific, and technological factors are all likely to have an important impact in determining the eventual strategy.[7] An example of the way in which these general assumptions may be expressed is provided by The Pacific Telephone & Telegraph Company, which undertook a long-range study to appraise the needs of customers within its territory through the year 1970. In the course of the study the following judgmental assumptions were formulated concerning the expected political and economic characteristics of the intervening years:

1. There will be no major war.
2. Defense spending will be above current levels.
3. There will be increased welfare expenditures.
4. There will be no major depression.
5. The political and social structure will not change materially.
6. California's and Nevada's growth will be faster than that of other states in the nation.
7. Real income (in 1960 dollars) will continue to rise.[8]

In addition to these judgmental assumptions[9] more detailed quantitative forecasts were developed about general environmental factors, including population, economic growth, land settlement, and a variety of other subjects. In developing these assumptions, planners in Pacific Telephone stated that they were particularly anxious to overcome "a tendency to project current business conditions in future planning, even though these may represent short-term peaks or troughs of an economic cycle."

There is no need to discuss quantitative forecasting techniques in any detail, since the subject is highly technical and consideration of it would take us far beyond this books's scope.[10] However, the following brief illustration suggests the way in which a forecast may be developed to provide a general environment assumption for use in strategic long-range planning.

Another company requires some assumptions about the economic environment as it is likely to be in 1975. One important piece of information needed may well be a forecast of the total workforce in the United States at that time. This forecast may be developed by studying past and present information and trends about workforce levels and projecting this information in terms of its relationship to total population. Since all those who will be part of the 1975 working force have already been born, one might expect that this forecast could be developed with a fair degree of accuracy, provided a further assumption is made that no major catastrophes will occur during the intervening period. The resulting forecast might then become an assumption within the strategic long-range planning process, or it might be interpreted for further use in formulating another assumption. The significance of these general environment assumptions rests not only in the ability to make them on the basis of sound analysis but also in the ability to interpret them effectively in the light of a particular company's situation. For, in the final analysis, the value of these assumptions is measured by the contributions they make to emergent long-range strategies.

An outstanding example of perceptive interpretation of general environment assumptions in formulation of a strategy comes from the business history of Sears, Roebuck and Co.[11] The way in which Sears redefined its strategy to meet the environmental changes in the years following World War I is described by A. D. Chandler, Jr.:

> At Montgomery Ward, [General Robert E.] Wood began to advocate a new business strategy. More than any other mail-order executive of the time, he was aware of the impact of increasing urbanization and of the coming of the automobile on the national and, particularly, the mail-order market. This awareness apparently came from an odd passion for reading the *Statistical Abstract of the United States* developed during his off hours in Panama. Such statistics emphasized, Wood told his colleagues at Ward's, that the United States was rapidly becoming an urban nation. Since the mail-order buyers lived in the rural areas, Ward must adjust itself to these changes. Moreover, the mass-produced automobile was making it possible for the farmer to get to town more easily and to buy from a much broader assortment of goods than was available at the crossroads general store. Wood pointed out in October 1921 to

Theodore Merceles, Ward's President, that chain stores like J. C. Penney were already beginning to exploit this small-town market. With its existing branch houses as distributing points, its highly developed purchasing organization, and its long-established reputation, Montgomery Ward could easily compete with, Wood insisted, the chain stores in any market.

Merceles paid little attention to Wood's proposals. . . . So, in 1924, General Wood left Montgomery Ward.

Rosenwald [Sears, Roebuck chairman], interested by Wood's ideas on retail activities, asked him to join Sears. He would not take any other executive's place, but would come as Vice-President in charge of Factories and Retail Stores. . . . Now Sears had a retail office also, if no retail stores.

Wood began at once to plan Sears' move into the new type of marketing.[12]

This quotation suggests several important features of the analysis of general environment assumptions. In the first place, the information about the environment need for developing these assumptions was available and was duly noted. Second, the assumptions were made explicit and were carefully analyzed. And third, they were interpreted meaningfully. The combination of these three factors provided the ingredients of successful strategy for Sears, Roebuck, which suggests several other significant considerations.

Assumptions about the general environment are not simply projections of the past. Since changes are not noticeable from day to day, the present environment is liable to be viewed as permanent. However, important discontinuous changes are taking place; one planning executive observed that it is foolhardy to assume uncritically that environmental conditions remain the same indefinitely. Second, the challenges which general environment assumptions present to the planner are generally challenges of adaptation. Rarely can a company hope to influence significantly any of these assumptions. The assumptions are designed to set the boundaries within which the company operates; the company has to recognize their dimensions and organize its activities accordingly. Third, companies are aided in their quest for information about general environment subjects by the growing number of management service organizations. Some provide economic information, while others issue regular newsletters and commentaries. A few, such as the Stanford Research Institute's "Long-Range Planning Report Service," have been developed especially for corporate long-range planners.

As attention to strategic long-range planning grows, more of these services are being offered to planning executives. The gathering of information is a laborious and expensive task for any individual company and consumes the time of highly skilled people. More subscriber services devoted expressly to long-range considerations are likely to be an answer.

2. *"Industry environment" assumptions.* A second category of assumptions attempts to determine the future industry environment. In the term "industry environment" the word "industry" includes concepts of product line, process, and product mission.[13] A company, in drawing up strategic plans, needs to take special account of (*a*) expected changes in competitive relationships with an industry and (*b*) anticipated developments of a technical, distributive, and organizational nature within that industry.

Assumptions about competitive actions resemble assumptions about the general environment in that they frequently are not controllable by the planning company. However, this does not mean that actions based upon these assumptions are necessarily defensive. By anticipating likely competitive moves a company is often able to plan on staying a jump ahead of its competitors. For instance, in one company the staff planning unit found it valuable to assume the role of major competitors and try to determine what actions they would consider taking, given current circumstances. Members of the planning unit stated that they believed this role-playing device was most helpful in developing accurate assumptions about the industry environment.

Knowledge about possible competitive actions which may alter the *status quo* comes from a variety of sources. Some information obviously comes from company intelligence sources, though, not surprisingly, little is made public about their extent and importance. Industry publications and management service organizations reports provide a good deal of information, both about the technical research activities of competitors and about organizational changes that competitors are contemplating. The latter may be very important; for example, an automobile company must make assumptions about the extent and type of added vertical integration to be undertaken by competitors during the coming years. Similarly, it is important for an oil company to make assumptions regarding the likelihood and the potential impact of large-scale competitive expansion into areas like atomic energy or shale oil. Another source of knowledge about anticipated competitive actions comes from an understanding of the industry itself. The analyst may recognize that a certain market area is going to develop rapidly, and he is able to anticipate competitive developments with a high degree of confidence. For example, an aircraft industry planner draws some conclusions from the knowledge that the volume of goods to be carried by air freight during the next ten years is considered likely to rise at a near-exponential rate.

In addition to anticipating changes in competitive relationships, a company undertaking strategic long-range planning also must make assumptions regarding developments of a technical, distributive, and organizational nature within an industry. There are two features of these assumptions which have distinctive significance for strategic long-range planning. The first of these is the way in which progress in one area is frequently dependent upon commensurate progress in supporting or related areas. Developments in the aircraft industry are an example of the fact that progress and change take place on such a wide front today that one element of progress cannot usually be considered in isolation from other elements.

In the 1920's and 1930's the aircraft industry was emerging as a commercial giant. During those years it appeared self-evident that technology was the only major factor limiting increases in the speed of commercial aircraft. This was the underlying assumption in the activities of the major aircraft manufacturers and was valid at that time.

The assumption did not remain true after World War II, however. While technology remained important, there were other important limiting factors in considerations of aircraft industry advances. One was the need for expensive airport facilities with longer runways. Of even greater significance was the matter of traffic control. Traffic in the sky had become a problem of major concern with the advent of mass air transportation. Today it is apparent that large sums of money will have to be spent on the development of modern techniques for traffic systems. Thus advances in aircraft speeds today are no longer a simple function of aircraft technology. Assumptions must also take into account the need for support systems such as airports and adequate traffic control facilities in order for faster planes to be able to fly commercial routes safely.

The second significant feature, the need for sensitivity to the potential of peripheral items, is illustrated by the following example. Arthur D. Little, Inc. is an industrial consulting organization which has an even greater need than most companies to detect the peripheral item of today which may be the major item of tomorrow. The company's early attention to the study of cryogenics is an instance of successful anticipation in this regard, and is described by an Arthur D. Little executive:

> About 11 years ago, ADL concluded that cryogenics—the study of low-temperature phenomena—was a completely new area in which only a small amount of basic research was going on. We made the decision that this was an area that looked as if it would have real technical significance. We formed a group to start work in that field, to make ourselves proficient and skilled in fundamental research and in the application of research in cryogenics.
>
> The reason we have grown in the cryogenics field is because we were ready. . . . When government and industry started becoming interested in cryogenics as a practical field, we were in a position to offer services and to offer knowledge.[14]

We expect consulting firms to be sensitive to the potential significance of peripheral items and to develop plans based upon assumptions about them, but interviews for this book indicated that manufacturing companies also attach great importance to this kind of consideration. At one large defense industry company, for example, a senior planning executive talked about the potential value of detecting a small-scale or insignificant item today which might well become significant tomorrow. He observed that sometimes a new item, or a new concept, might receive casual mention in a military contract or an industry journal. A skillful planner might help the company greatly by encouraging it to spend, say, $30,000 or $40,000 in exploratory research work on this item.

In another company the head of a corporate planning unit told of one of his subordinate economists who was very skilled in "reading" figures from a myriad of different sources and seeing in them significant interrelationships between apparently different and widely separated figures. As a result, he made the company more aware of possible relationships between existing activities and newly emerging changes in the industry environment.

A technical aid in carrying on this kind of analysis is the Leontief input-output grid. It is used in some companies to aid in making assumptions about the industry environment and sometimes the general environment as well. The Leontief model compiles information about all facets of the industrial economy in a grid which shows the sources and amounts of materials embodied in specified products, as well as the volume produced and ultimate destination of these products. Thus it reveals the relationship of one segment of the economy to every other segment, and enables a company to learn which industries are dependent upon its products, and to what extent. Grids for succeeding periods of time reveal changes in trends and help in the early detection of those peripheral items which are likely to have later significance.

The establishment and interpretation of assumptions about the industry environment require astute understanding of a great many different factors. The task of the planning executive in developing these assumptions is analogous to that of providing information about the weather. In reporting information about the expected weather in different locations, the forecaster must be able to interpret and analyze technical information and communicate his findings in terms which are intelligible to nontechnical personnel. In short, it is a task demanding (in the words of one planning executive) "a combination of plain common sense and logical and deductive reason, spiced with a little 'salt and pepper' of intuitive imagination."

3. "Factors of production" assumptions. The third category of assumptions important to developing strategic long-range plans treats the availability and the quality of factors of production. This is to say, certain assumptions are needed about capital availability, material and equipment availability and quality, and manpower availability and quality.[15]

Most attempts at systematized long-range planning are initiated by companies with considerable financing strength. Therefore, while financial planning plays an essential part in implementational planning, capital availability is not usually a controlling factor in strategic planning. Within broad limits, a strategic plan is developed with the assumption that, if it is otherwise good, financing will be available. Only rarely is the final plan significantly limited by the unavailability of finance. Considerations of capital are important in the implementational planning which embodies the basic strategy.

All manufacturers rely upon the supply of materials and equipment from nature or from corporate suppliers. Sometimes the planning can proceed without concern about the availability of materials or equipment. In other cases, however, there are difficulties because of (a) limitations of supply in nature, (b) inability of supplier capacity to meet demand, (c) price increases to an uneconomic level, or (d) work stoppages in supplier companies. Since a permanent difficulty due to any of these considerations impairs the usefulness of a plan, the assumptions made in regard to them deserve careful attention and explicit investigation.

Another factor of production is manpower, which includes both workers and managers and applies to both supply and skill. The following report suggests the types of problems encountered and the types of assumptions that need to be made. During an interview a management consultant observed that some companies overlook the ramifications of problems regarding manpower availability. These companies, he said, make the mistake of concentrating their technological efforts upon the goal of reducing unskilled and semi-skilled labor requirements. They do this in the belief that they can gain big cost reductions because of the large number of workers presently employed who fit these categories. This reasoning (according to the consultant) results in less emphasis upon the search for labor-saving improvements in jobs which require highly skilled labor—often, for example, in technical maintenance and repair operations. And by about 1970 there is going to be an acute scarcity of this kind of worker in many industries: They are going to be "scarcer than gold." As a result, these companies will be faced with major operational bottlenecks which will not be easy to manage or to resolve and which will certainly prove very costly to them over the long run.

The problem is complicated further by the rapid changes taking place in the skills required within many industries. Sometimes a new skill has a period of ascendancy which lasts only a comparatively short time, thus increasing the need for major retraining programs. The general manager of planning at Standard Oil Company (Indiana) observes that—

> We appear to be reaching the point at which we can no longer ex-
> pect to train our young people in a trade with the expectation that
> they can follow it the rest of their lives.
>
> Long-established skilled crafts are suddenly disappearing, as tech-
> nology renders them unneeded. New skills are being called for, and
> even some of these are turning out to be short-lived. One dramatic
> example of this is the flight engineer on our airlines—a highly
> skilled profession, the need for which arose and disappeared in the
> short space of 15 years.[16]

The supply of manpower with requisite skills, like the other
factors of production, cannot be taken for granted in assumptions
for long-range planning. This is especially true in companies which
demand large numbers of highly trained personnel with newly
developed skills, and it also applies to top management skills in large
corporations.

In summary, strategic long-range planning always requires making assumptions, sometimes in explicit terms, about factors of production. The supply of materials and men may change significantly
and affect the appropriateness of a suggested course of action; thus
assumptions which can be taken for granted in day-to-day planning
do not always hold true for the long range.

CONCLUDING COMMENTS

There are a great many different assumptions about the future
that must be made in the course of developing strategic long-range
plans. They are established in a wide variety of ways, ranging from
imposed assumptions which are really directives from top management, to quantitative analysis, to qualitative judgments, to intuitive
presuppositions. They cover a large number of different subject areas
in the general environment, in the industry environment, and in
factors of production. Despite the complexity of assumptions, however, several general conclusions can be drawn.

Planning analysis in this phase is most often directed toward subject areas which are external rather than internal to the company.
More particularly, the major areas of investigation are usually economics and technology—attention to the latter being of recent origin. By and large, political and social considerations have been less

thoroughly examined, partly because they are frequently irreducible uncertainties.

Assumptions about subjects which are internal to the planning company are sometimes imposed by top management and are sometimes unstated. They are usually considered to be more important in relation to supporting strategies and in providing a link between strategic and implementational planning. Only rarely are they considered of central importance in the development of a grand strategy.

The strategic planner must be able to distinguish between those subject areas which deserve further study before assumptions are drawn and those which can be taken for granted as being "highly probable." The planner has to be wary of assuming that present-day occurrences will continue to take place indefinitely. Yet there are many areas in which he has to assume that the future will continue to follow the patterns of the present. He must, therefore, distinguish between the acceptable and the questionable.

Finally, it is important to note that even when planners engage in detailed investigation of a subject in connection with assumptions, the task is not simply one of utilizing techniques of analysis. The compilation of more information and more statistics is not always the best way to come up with sound, useful assumptions about the future. Reflective thought is frequently found to be a most useful aid in making judgments about the future, and one of the benefits of formalized long-range planning activities is the substitution of considered intuition for spur-of-the-moment intuition.

Chapter 8

Anticipation of Technological Change

AMONG THE MANY ASSUMPTIONS ABOUT THE FUTURE WHICH are necessary in developing strategic long-range plans, none are potentially more important than those attempting to anticipate technological change. The pace and the pervasiveness of technological change are perhaps the two most significant economic facts of our time. We see in today's society constant demands for new industrial and consumer goods and services, new markets, and new forms of transportation. These changes not only affect industry, education, medicine, and the military, but also bring about very profound changes in the social order. It follows that predictions of changes in technology and secondary waves of influence resulting from such changes have a great effect upon the long-range strategies finally adopted, and the present chapter is therefore devoted to a study of technological change and the possibilities of accurately predicting the path it will follow and the pace at which it will progress.

TECHNOLOGICAL CHANGE: AN ECONOMICS ANALYSIS

While managers have long recognized the importance of technological change and have tried to keep their companies in the forefront of technological advance, they have not usually thought about it as a subject reducible to systematic analysis. It has been regarded as "something that happens." Only since the late 1950's has there been any marked tendency within companies to inquire into its nature and to venture predictions of possible future changes. And even then, most such investigations have been undertaken exclusively from a technical standpoint, since they have usually resulted directly from problems raised in research and development.

However, some long-range planners have recently become interested in trying to analyze technological change, and their experiences reveal that it is a complex force which affects and is affected by

123

a great many different forces in the economy. Technical considerations are, of course, critically important, but there are other influential factors as well—for example, the competitive character of an industry, the availability of investment capital, and the economic feasibility of a proposed change. This being the case, it is useful to examine the subject of technological change in economics terms so as to determine more clearly its nature and to assess more astutely the possibilities and the limitations of predicting future changes in technology and their derivative effects.

Several economics terms need to be defined.

- *Production function* describes the various inputs (quantities and appellation) of factors of production which, when combined in a specified manner, produce a particular product or service.
- *Invention* refers to the discovery of a product or process which adds knowledge not previously understood or recognized. An invention *may* be developed commercially, but this is not a criterion of its meaning.
- *Innovation* is the establishment of a new product function by means of (1) a new process, (2) a new product, (3) a new organization form, or (4) a new market. The term includes, therefore, not only any invention which is developed commercially but also a variety of other types of change as well.
- *Best-practice techniques*[1] are those which embody the most recent technological advances in a given process and which reflect economically appropriate inputs of factors of production in terms of current factor prices at any given moment of time. That is, they correspond to the idea of the most up-to-date techniques currently in use.

From these definitions two facts become clear. First, technological change qualifies as one form of innovation, since it necessitates the formation of a new production function. Determination of the economic character of this innovation requires a comparison of two (or more) production functions established at different points in time. Second, the production function which incorporates best-practice techniques for a particular process changes only when additional technological knowledge is developed which can be justified commercially[2] or when there is a change in the price relationship of factors of production. That is to say, one or other of these conditions must apply in order for there to be technological innovations in best-practice techniques. To understand the significance of this, the two conditions need to be examined more closely.

1. Additional technological knowledge. The reasons for the development of additional technological knowledge vary widely from individual case to individual case. Nevertheless, there are three factors which affect the extent and the frequency of additional technological knowledge in a particular company or in a particular industry.

First, the amount of research undertaken in a particular company or industry is likely to affect the extent and frequency of additions to technological knowledge. Companies and industries which are highly research-oriented normally tend to achieve faster rates of change in best-practice techniques than those which are not. It does not necessarily follow, however, that the greater the amount of research undertaken, the faster the rate of progress will be.

Second, the rate of addition to technological knowledge is also likely to be affected by the competitive structure of an industry. Technological innovations are usually best encouraged when elements of monopoly and competition are both present in an industry structure. Some competition is necessary in order to provide the stimulus of trying to steal a march on competitors. On the other hand, a highly competitive situation tends to discourage those investments which are not likely to provide quick financial return, and this frequently results in postponement of major research undertakings.[3]

Third, and probably most interesting of all, the extent and frequency of additional technological knowledge is affected by the tendency of innovations to cluster together. Many times a major innovation will appear and then be followed by a succession of related innovations. This is a central concept in the theory of economic development propounded by J. A. Schumpeter.[4] Schumpeter attributed the clustering tendency to the imitative nature of many companies in an industrial economy. The concept has special significance in the prediction of derivative effects of major technological innovations.

While these three factors are usually the major ones, some additions to technological knowledge never become included in the best-practice techniques of a given company. One of two prerequisites has to be met if a technological improvement is to become a commercial reality: Either competitive pressures must impel the adoption of the improvement, or it must have sufficient long-term financial attractiveness to justify the investment.

Insistent competitive pressures are most commonly found when one company has incorporated a technological advance and other companies thereupon feel obliged to make a corresponding move to maintain their competitive position. Sometimes this occurs even when these other companies regard the technological advance they contemplate as being financially precarious. A case in point is provided by the policies of the major internal airlines in the United States in the 1950's. Most felt, and continue to feel, that they would have been financially better off if they could have concentrated upon building fleets of prop-jet aircraft. However, when one or two companies broke ranks and ordered pure-jet aircraft, all others felt compelled to follow suit.

Unless competitive pressures prevail, the major factor for determining whether or not a technological improvement shall be adopted is long-term financial attractiveness. Of course the decision in any particular case depends upon the determinations and the financial criteria used by management. However, the minimum attractiveness acceptable in any situation (ignoring competitive factors) is that the improvement be able to offset the cost of scrapping the existing plant and equipment which would be obsolete, disposing of obsoleted inventory, and tooling up for the proposed innovation.

2. Changes in factor prices. The second reason why changes may occur in best-practice techniques is that the relationship of the relative prices of factors of production may change.

Take the hypothetical case of a company which has been utilizing a particular production process in its manufacturing activities since 1924. The level of technological knowledge about this process has not changed, to all intents and purposes, during the 40 years from 1924 to 1964. During that time period, costs of machinery associated with the process have gone up 30 per cent, while labor costs affecting those who work at the process have gone up 300 per cent.

In such a circumstance it is entirely possible that the best-practice technique for the particular production process has changed substantially. For example, in 1924 the best-practice technique may have placed major emphasis upon manual methods, since labor at that time was so much cheaper (relative to the position in 1964). By 1964, however, the threefold increase in labor costs may well lead management to conclude that the best-practice technique to be adopted now requires greater emphasis upon machine operations.

This example, although hypothetical, has many approximate counterparts today, for the normal tendency in an industrial economy is the gradual substitution of machinery for labor in production functions.[5] The price relationships between factors of production usually change slowly, but the differential can grow into a very significant amount when measured over the long run. Thus it can be of great benefit in attempts to assess developments in best-practice techniques for a long period of time ahead.

Both of these conditions needed for technological change to occur —additional technological knowledge and changes in factor prices —are essentially continuous processes and, as such, are significant in long-range planning which treats heavy investments in fixed assets. There is usually a steady stream of new techniques developing in a given industry, and factor prices tend to change slowly. Additional technological knowledge sometimes takes the form of breakthroughs, but the cumulative effect of many small unpublicized innovations can be just as powerful when considered over a long period of time. This means that there is usually a steady stream of new techniques developing in a new industry. Factor prices, as we have already noted, tend to change slowly, but the changes are continual, which also encourages a continuing flow of changing techniques.

The special problem which this presents for the long-range planner is that of delayed reaction to improvements in best-practice techniques, because an investment in fixed assets for a given undertaking commits a company to a fairly rigid level of capability for that undertaking over a considerable period of time. Although some flexibility can be incorporated into many fixed-asset investments at a later date,[6] the fixed assets in existence at any given time represent, in effect, "a fossilised history of technology over the period spanned by their construction dates." [7] The year-to-year model changes in the automobile industry illustrate this point.

A 1955 model automobile represented an approximation to the

best-practice techniques of style and engineering in the commercial automobile industry during the year of its manufacture. However, the same model was reckoned by many standards to be obsolete in 1964, ten years later. By that time it had been subjected to ten years of wear and tear, and it had been superseded by ten years of later automotive models, which incorporated ten years of progress in developing improved best-practice techniques of style and engineering.

This example suggests, in simplified form, the changing technological environment in which companies must plan today. The fixed assets purchased in 1955 represented the best-practice techniques when purchased, but ten years later they need to be replaced by an investment which incorporates accumulated improvements.

It is easy enough to recognize the effect of these factors on past events. But the real difficulty lies in utilizing the findings of this analysis for the prediction and interpretation of future technological innovations. Unfortunately, formal economic analysis has had little to offer so far in this regard. The theory of economic development developed by Schumpeter does little toward developing a theory of foresight. It provides a useful framework for inquiry into the economic nature of technological innovations, but that is all. Yet prediction of technological change, even imperfect and sometimes vague prediction, occupies a vital place in strategic long-range planning.

IS PREDICTION POSSIBLE?

Technological change is one of the most difficult areas in which to make accurate predictions. Those who are skeptical about long-range planning frequently seize upon the "futility" of attempting to predict technological change as a prime argument to support their contention. These people claim there are too many random factors to allow accurate prediction, and to support this view they cite many examples from science, medicine, and industry in which major discoveries of great consequence were seemingly stumbled upon by chance.

Up to a point these skeptics are right: There are some instances in which technological change does indeed seem to defy prediction. Some reliance upon assumptions about the technological future is unavoidable because, although long-range planning is concerned with the future, it requires decision making in the *present*. Planners therefore have the choice of acting without giving any detailed thought to possible future developments in technology or acting in the light of some attempts at prediction. Faced with this situation, strategic planners have come to recognize that some degree of prediction is both possible and desirable.

A would-be predictor can readily gain some information about existing best-practice techniques, existing research and development activities, and existing frontiers of knowledge. Armed with this knowledge, and following careful analysis of it, he is in a position to come up with some predictions which, although they may be highly tentative, are better than total ignorance.

The chance element in discoveries and inventions is usually less significant than first appearances indicate. Even though a specific technological advance may appear to be "discontinuous" in relation to past developments, it is usually based on an accumulation of past knowledge and achievement in the particular subject area. Because environmental conditions were ripe for it, the advance often appears in retrospect to have been more inevitable than accidental.

The best evidence in support of this view is the phenomenon of simultaneous technological breakthroughs made by researchers working independently. Examples include the discovery of electricity, the transmission of speech by telephone, and the liquefaction of gases. This phenomenon may also be observed in the social sciences: For example, three economists working independently in three different countries unveiled what was in essence a theory of marginal utility within a few months of one another.

Although prediction of technological change necessarily relies upon intuitive thinking and judgment, there is a great deal of difference between spur of the moment intuition and intuition which is supplemented by careful analysis, discussion, and reflection. Planners who rely upon intuition of the latter kind can come up with insights which will prove most useful for the company.

Today more and more company planners are trying to make predictions about technological change, whereas ten years ago very few of them took the subject seriously.[8] They have begun to realize that it is more fruitful to grapple with problems of prediction than to reject it as being futile. Systematic analysis is useful even when the predictive assignment is extremely difficult and must necessarily be based upon highly tentative evidence. It is worth noting that a decision to delay a planning choice until the technological situation becomes clearer can represent a very effective piece of planning.

THE TASK OF PREDICTION

Predictions about technological change are made in many different ways. They normally encompass both the general and the industry environment within which the planning company operates, though the industry environment as a rule receives more detailed attention. At present the task of prediction is usually undertaken in a subjective manner, and the techniques of analysis are anything but routine. As in many other aspects of strategic long-range planning, a great deal of ingenuity and insight is needed if the prediction is to be meaningful. In particular, skill is needed in identifying those elements of the problem which are likely to be of strategic importance and in asking discerning and probing questions about them.

Predictions about changes within the industry environment may be causative in nature, that is, the predictions themselves may affect the nature of changes which subsequently transpire. This phenomenon can be observed in a number of predictive situations,[9] and wherever it occurs, the difficulties of accurate prediction are compounded because the predictors need to include some estimate of the consequences of their own predictions.

The current direction and pace of technological change are affected significantly by the expenditures of the U.S. Government. The Government appropriates vast sums of money for research in defense, space, medicine, agriculture, and many other areas. This research and resultant technological advances have both direct and indirect ramifications for large numbers of companies. Therefore, many planners include a considerable amount of political second-guessing in their efforts to anticipate future technological change.

The task of predicting technological change contains three component parts. First, there is prediction of the technical innovations themselves. Second, there is prediction of the time when these innovations are expected to take place. And third, there is prediction of the derivative social and technological changes expected to come about as a result of the initial innovations. While these component parts are obviously interrelated, it is useful to discuss them separately here.

1. Changes in technology. In Chapter 4 we saw that variables which are affected by time may change in a continuous or a discontinuous manner. That is, they may follow a pattern related to past performance or information, or they may break the linearity of projection from the past. Changes in technology may be either continuous or discontinuous, and attempts to predict such changes consider both types.

"The principle of opportunity and suitability," [10] which is primarily associated with prediction of discontinuous forms of change, states that discontinuous changes in technology are usually traceable to accumulated past knowledge and achievements in a particular subject. This type of thinking helps to identify existing gaps in technology and to locate likely thresholds of further advance. It is concerned with the efforts and forces by which technological changes are brought about, and it focuses particularly upon the potential significance of technological developments which currently appear to be only of peripheral importance. [11]

The other feature is associated with attempts to predict changes in technology which are of a continuous nature. The cumulative effect of many small innovations is often just as important over the long run as a few spectacular innovations, and so quantitative analyses of trends in productivity are of great significance in developing predictions.

The two features are, of course, complementary and apply to predictions about both the general environment and the industrial environment.

2. Time when predicted changes will occur. Sometimes it is clear that a particular technological change is going to take place; the difficulty is predicting when. The problem usually comes up in the context of industry environment developments, since approximate-time prediction is needed in appraising a company's competitive position and in incorporating lead-time requirements into long-range plans. Knowing when a predicted change will take place is also important when trying to determine its effect upon present fixed assets and production processes.

An example from the aircraft industry provides a good case in point. It is clear that supersonic commercial jet aircraft will one day be flying passengers on transcontinental and intercontinental routes. The main difficulty in prediction comes in trying to estimate the year in which these operations will begin. Yet this prediction is of great importance for aircraft companies and others closely associated with or dependent upon activities in the aircraft industry, for if a company concluded that no supersonic jets are likely to be on the commercial market prior to 1975, its long-range strategy would probably be quite different from that which it would adopt if predictions suggest that these aircraft will be ready for delivery any time after 1966.

This kind of prediction is often causative: It may affect the actual time when the technological change will occur. If, for example, competitive pressure becomes concentrated upon achievement of a particular technological advance, that advance may come about sooner than originally anticipated. This is what happened in the case of the commercial introduction of the first pure jet aircraft; it might possibly happen also in the case of the supersonic jet aircraft.

Recognizing this cause and effect relationship, some company planners have developed time predictions as spectrums of different alternatives.[12] This enables greater flexibility to be incorporated into alternative strategies, and in particular insures that sudden intensified efforts by competitors in a particular technological direction do not take the planning company too much by surprise.

3. Derivative social and technological changes. A major advance in technology may bring about succeeding waves of change, both social and technological. Social changes may take place in areas far removed from the technological environment of the original innovation, and sometimes they are not readily seen as a result of that innovation. Technological changes often take the form of clusters of innovations in the same technological area, though sometimes they also occur in seemingly remote areas. The impact of these derivative changes can be very strong,[13] and the task of predicting them, while extremely difficult, is significant in strategic long-range planning.

The far-reaching impact of major innovations can be better understood by considering again one of the most influential technological advances by the 20th century—the airplane. One result is that nations have come into closer contact with one another. No longer can the British Navy—or any navy—rule the world. No longer can the United States rely upon the Atlantic and Pacific Oceans as impenetrable fortresses. Today planes can fly from country to country at high speeds, carrying statesmen, businessmen, tourists, or bombs. A second result is that additional knowledge has been stimulated in a variety of diverse academic subjects, including physics, aeronautics, engineering, and meteorology. The airplane has also opened up enormous new business opportunities. It has not only been directly responsible for two large-scale industries (aircraft manufacture and airline transportation) but has also led to the development of hundreds of smaller industries and has spawned a new giant offspring, the aerospace industry. Finally, the airplane has contributed to the need for Federal regulation of business activity, as seen in the formation of the Civil Aeronautics Administration and the Civil Aviation Board.

Making predictions of this kind when the innovation is still in the future is, it bears repeating, an extremely difficult undertaking. The analysis is necessarily highly subjective, and the predictor needs to be very sensitive to the potential impact of all kinds of developments in many different areas of the economy. However, progress can be made.

INTERFUNCTIONAL LIAISON

The most noteworthy administrative development emerging from the growing attention to the prediction of technological change is the encouragement of closer liaison between a company's technical and commercial people. Some planners, recognizing the need to look at technology from both technical and commercial standpoints, have arranged meetings to which people from each of these general areas were invited.

According to these planners, the meetings have proved most useful and have had interesting consequences. They have allowed the marketing person to become more familiar with the problems of making choices about technology while at the same time providing the benefit of his counsel at a much earlier stage of planning activities than is usually the case. They have also encouraged the technical man to see more clearly the commercial and competitive consequences of technological developments. In particular, he has been encouraged to see that progress in technology is a continuing thing: Sometimes in the past the technical man's enthusiasm about a particular advance has tended to blind him to the fact that other developments are coming along which sooner or later will supersede that advance.

A planning executive presented a representative viewpoint when he observed:

> We are convinced that most of today's markets can be considered as a combination of needs and of technologies and that there is a particular role to be played in linking the skills of the technical man and the marketer.

MODELS OF FUTURE CONDITIONS

There is one recent development which is of special interest in our analysis of strategic long-range planning. It is the attempts which have recently been made in several companies by long-range planners to try to construct models of future conditions in the belief that products and their supporting technologies should be considered in time frameworks. They therefore usually take the form of expressing expected levels of technology and environmental conditions at certain points of time in the future. In other words, their aim is—

> To help management foresee what succession of decisions will best assure the company's success at any given time in the future, taking into account that each of the firm's products is in a continually varying stage of its life cycle, that the expected capability of competitors is always changing, that consumer demand is fluctuating, and so on. [14]

A large company in the defense industry has tried to develop this kind of model of future conditions as part of its planning activities. This company does most of its work under contract to the Federal Government, and its long-range planners believe that in the past there have been certain decisions made at the national level which have had major derivative influence upon the company. They also believe it is possible to develop a national "decision network" which will tell a great deal about when and what will be the important decisions to be made at the national level in the future. While they acknowledge that such a decision network will not allow complete prediction of the future, they believe it will allow their company to be better prepared when it comes to taking calculated risks.

Among the benefits which a company might look for in using a decision network of this kind are:

1. The disclosure of capability gaps.
2. Greater ability in selecting subjects which deserve study by the company.
3. Greater ability in determining what the nature of Government contract requirements will be.
4. Better awareness of technological gaps and technological state of the art in the company's industry environment.

This model of future conditions, while still very much in the exploratory stage, is indicative of the active interest now being shown in the possibilities of better predicting of technological change. We can expect that as planners improve their skill in this predictive task, their skill in developing sound and imaginative long-range strategies will be correspondingly broadened.

Chapter 9

The Choice of a Strategy

SOMEONE HAS OBSERVED THAT "PLANNING IS FUNDAMEN-
tally choosing," and the remark has particular relevance here because
problems of choice are prominent throughout the strategic planning
process. Some are choices of technical method; some are choices of
exclusion. Some are implicit choices which everyone accepts and
which never come up for discussion; some are explicit choices which
are made only after detailed analysis. But they are all significant in
the sense that they all have bearing upon the ultimate choice of
strategy.

For the purpose of analysis we will concentrate attention upon
those choices which may be termed "climactic"—those which appear
to be of critical or decisive importance in determining the major attributes of the eventual strategy. Usually these include choices made
in developing alternatives and in selecting the eventual strategy itself, but they may also include some key choices regarding the objectives and assumptions to be adopted. We will first discuss the nature
of these climactic choices and then illustrate their possible types by
means of examples.

THE PLACE OF CLIMACTIC CHOICES IN THE
STRATEGIC PLANNING PROCESS

Choice is an extremely difficult subject to deal with conceptually.
There is, for instance, the basis question of who makes the choices.
Ultimate responsibility for the outcome of strategic plans clearly lies
with the chief executive, but in practice some choices are made by
the chief executive himself, some are formulated and recommended
by others in top management and ultimately approved by the chief
executive, while still others are formulated and recommended by
staff or line personnel who are not members of top management at

136

all, the ultimate approval again coming from the chief executive. [1]

A second difficulty, and one of more immediate concern here, is the wide variety of analytical approaches which can be adopted in making choices. For example, one choice relating to strategy may require judging among a number of alternatives which appear to be equally plausible. Another choice may depend upon nothing more than drawing an obvious conclusion which has emerged as the result of a series of findings and judgments made earlier in the planning process. Thus it is not easy to generalize about the form which choices in strategic planning take, nor is it easy to generalize about the analytical processes whereby these choices are made.

However, as a starting point we may think about climactic choices as being of four major types. They are defined below.

1. Early choice concerning a strategic factor. Sometimes a choice is made early in the planning process which, in effect, limits the area of activity of the staff planners. Usually a choice of this kind is made by the chief executive, perhaps in association with others in top management. In practice it means that some limiting or strategic factor becomes a "given." The staff planners may be told that the company will not consider any major changes in its present product line nor any moves which necessitate further outside financing. Choices of this kind have a great effect upon the eventual strategy. They may be incorporated in the objectives or the assumptions of the plan; they may be informal instructions which nevertheless represent climactic choices in the planning process.

2. Part-way choice concerning a strategic factor. The second type of climactic choice is one made during the course of analysis, usually in the light of some preliminary findings. For example, staff planners make intermittent contact with members of top management, discussing their investigations and reporting on progress. The chief executive may tell the planners that they have shown him enough to conclude definitely that (for instance), "the Latin American market clearly offers the best prospects for our proposed international expansion." By making this part-way choice about a factor which limits the strategy for the planning as a whole, the chief executive has made a climactic choice which will have a very significant effect upon the shape of the eventual strategy.

3. Choice of strategy alternatives. A third type of climactic choice is the selection of major alternatives for consideration as possible long-range strategy. The selection of alternatives is normally arrived at by paring down a wide number of possibilities. The choices become more clearly climactic in nature as they move into a semifinal stage: the selection of a few alternatives from which a final choice is later made. The choices at this stage are sometimes made by staff planners, sometimes by members of top management. Some evolve as analysis progresses; others are deliberately chosen fairly late in the planning process. Whatever the precise method adopted, however, the important point is that some climactic choices have to be made in developing these alternatives.

4. Final choice of strategy from among alternatives. Lastly, there is the choice of the eventual strategy itself. The manner in which this choice is made can vary widely, and the choice itself may be obvious or exceedingly difficult. Thus the choice may require consideration of a substantial number of feasible alternatives, or there may be only one practical possibility. Again, the choice may have to be made by members of top management, or it may be formulated and recommended by the staff planners, the chief executive and top management reviewing the recommendation and giving approval.

While the differences among the types of climactic choices are evident, a discussion of the following concepts has relevance for each type.

1. The role of top management.
2. The qualitative nature of choices in strategic planning.
3. The place of flexibility in choice.

ROLE OF TOP MANAGEMENT IN CLIMACTIC CHOICES

Climactic choices in strategic planning are more likely to be effective if two extremes are avoided. One is the temptation of top managers to make climactic choices in an arbitrary and perhaps even idiosyncratic manner. If this is their attitude, they probably do not properly understand the implications of the questions being raised. Choices which concern matters of crucial importance to the whole company deserve seasoned and reasoned judgment. Thus attention should be given to the background material, anal-

ysis, and ideas which have been developed by staff planners or others
who have been intimately acquainted with the subject at hand.

The other extreme is the tendency of top managers to allow staff
planners to make all the climactic decisions. Responsibility for long-
range planning is not only being delegated; it is being abdicated.
Far-reaching decisions are being made for the company as a whole
by staff people who have not the responsibility, the experience, nor
the perspective of top management.

Strategic long-range planning will have a better chance of being
successful if top management takes a middle road. It should be prepared to rely upon the staff planners' analysis; but not too much. It
should not halter the staff planners; but it should not give them unlimited free rein either. As with many other considerations in long-
range planning, a balance between extremes is needed.

QUALITATIVE NATURE

Perhaps the most distinctive feature of climactic choices in strategic long-range planning is their qualitative nature. They are qualitative because they necessarily are affected by a variety of judgmental
and subjective considerations which impinge upon the strategic
planning process at a number of different stages. For example, establishing objectives, making assumptions, designing analysis, developing alternatives, and making a final choice all rely upon some
important judgmental and subjective considerations. The following
hypothetical case serves as a simple illustration.

Assume that two companies of similar size, resources, and financial
strength are producing the same product. Each has the opportunity
of committing itself to an identical course of action requiring a substantial financial outlay. The investment in each case promises very
good financial returns over the long term and appears to have a
strong probability of success.

However, the investment must be regarded as speculative to the
extent that there is a small possibility of an adverse circumstance
which, if it should occur, would threaten the survival of the invest-
ing company.

Company *A* sees the small risk of potential failure as being quite
intolerable, believing that corporate survival is something that can-

not be gambled with or compromised in any way. Company B's managers, on the other hand, see the small chance of bankruptcy as being the kind of business risk which it must accept, given the type of economy in which it operates. Consequently it may well be prepared to make the investment.

Both of these management attitudes can be found everywhere today. Each reflects a different disposition toward risk taking and entrepreneurial aggressiveness, and there are no absolute standards by which these considerations can be appraised. Some companies are deliberately conservative, while others are deliberately venturesome; there is a place for both attitudes in business. However, each is likely to result in radically different choices in the process of developing long-range strategies.

One consequence of this qualitative nature of climactic choices is that quantitative techniques for solving problems (such as operations research) are normally not applicable.[2] The issues cannot usually be stated numerically or in a clearly defined scalar manner. They are, rather, unprogramed problems which can be resolved only by a type of problem solving often called heuristic.

In talking about this kind of decision making, Herbert A. Simon points out that in the past, human thinking, problem solving, and learning have all been mysterious processes which have been labeled but not explained. Men have therefore resorted to gross techniques for improving decision making. For example, they have selected men who appear to have skills in this area to do the work. And they have organized special full-time groups to undertake the necessary assignments. "We cannot say that these traditional techniques have failed," Simon writes; "decisions do get made daily in organizations." But he continues: "Neither can we say that we might not do very much better in the future as our knowledge of the decision making process grows." [3]

Some embryo developments in this area suggest that substantial advances in the ability of man to solve qualitative problems by means of more rigorous analytic skills are likely to be made in the coming years. Concepts from the theory of games (such as minimax, bluffing, and building coalitions) are being incorporated into qualitative problem-solving methods to an increasing degree. Again, some planners are presently experimenting with weighting techniques and methodological models which they believe will prove helpful in qualitative problem solving. They hesitate to rely upon these kinds of analyses in strategic planning, but as time goes by they are certain to become more confident about the usefulness and applicability of such techniques.

Top management's attitude is likely to be one of initial caution and wariness—and rightly so. The choices to be made are of very great importance, and top management is reluctant to take the claims of staff planners at face value until it becomes satisfied that the specific approaches actually do have merit.

Human judgment is obviously going to remain a very important part of climactic choice in strategic planning activities, but it does seem likely that significant analytic advances in the processes of qualitative decision making will take place in the future.[4]

THE PLACE OF FLEXIBILITY

Flexibility is the ability to adjust or adapt to change. Businessmen have adopted this concept, too, from the military, where it has long been recognized as a vital factor in contingency planning. Flexibility in the context of business planning has received relatively less emphasis[5] although today it is widely considered a highly desirable planning characteristic.

Three aspects of the future show the need for flexibility in long-range planning. First, the future itself is always clouded in uncertainty. Second, a large part of the environment of the future is not controllable by any individual company.[6] And third, it is certain that the future—whatever its form—will differ in a great many ways from the present.

Given these three facts, it seems logical to conclude that long-range planning decisions are usually best formulated on a sequential basis, if that is possible, rather than as a once-and-for-all commitment. This suggests that two different aspects of flexibility are of importance in long-range planning.

Built-in flexibility. First, there is the notion of flexibility as a quality to be built into the planning strategy. For example, one company with major product commitments in the present U.S. armament program recently conducted an inquiry into likely Cold War relationships between East and West in the years immediately ahead. It concluded that the present relationships are likely to continue for an indefinite period. Nevertheless, the company felt that it should develop some plans for alternative courses of action in the event that some radical changes in this Cold War relationship should take place—changes which the company did not believe *would* happen but which possibly *could* happen. In particular, it was interested in developing contingency plans to apply (1) in the event that a general mobilization should be ordered and (2) in the event that substantial progress should be achieved on a nuclear disarmament treaty.

Deliberate-postponement flexibility. A second aspect of flexibility is the deliberate postponement of some choices while taking action on others. The reasoning is that, while certain information is now available which allows a company to take certain actions, it is probably best to delay some other decisions until further information becomes available.[7] The company retains the advantage of postponing certain choices while at the same time being able to go ahead with a part of the plan.

Examples of this second aspect of flexibility are frequently observed when top management is anxious to learn of some important governmental decision or to learn the results of an important election. Thus a Defense Department decision regarding the choice of one particular weapons system over another is often anxiously awaited because it is likely to have widespread ramifications for the given company's future strategy. Again, an election for President has far-reaching implications because of the effects it may have upon such matters as economic policy, labor, social welfare, and defense. In both cases, companies frequently seek to delay some of their long-range planning commitments until the awaited information becomes known and its impact can be appraised.

While the advantages of making choices which incorporate flexibility are clear, flexibility must be tempered by decisiveness. There is such a thing as *too much* flexibility, as the following considerations suggest.

First, lip service to the need for flexibility can sometimes cover up a lack of courage or an indecisiveness on the part of top management. There are circumstances in which a decisive commitment must be made, and building flexibility into the plan is not appropriate.

Second, incorporating flexibility into a decision is sometimes uneconomic. Flexibility can often be considered as a cost worth incurring in the sense that an optimal strategy for one particular set of assumptions may be modified to offer better prospects for a range of possible occurrences. In such cases the costs of building in flexibility resemble an insurance premium, and therefore they need to be examined in terms of risks entailed and possible benefits accruing. When viewed in this manner, it is evident that the costs of flexibility sometimes represent an unjustifiably high premium.

Finally, there can be excessive preoccupation with flexibility which results in continual revision of strategy. It has been said that "if you keep pulling up the plant to see how the roots are getting on, it does not grow very well," and the analogy is true for strategic planning. If a "revise" rather than "strive" attitude develops, the strategy does not get a fair trial, and top management spends a disproportionate amount of time being concerned about revisions.

These examples illustrate abuses of flexibility but are not criticisms of the notion of flexibility itself. Flexibility is a most valuable attribute in a plan when it is carefully considered and constitutes more than a vague slogan. The skillful planner seeks to make choices so that the advantages of flexibility are considered along with the alternative advantages of commitment or delay in a particular circumstance.

EXAMPLES OF CLIMACTIC CHOICES

The considerations at issue in making climactic choices can be demonstrated in a more pragmatic way by referring to some typical situations which arise when a company is trying to develop a strategy for long-term growth.[8] Two frequently encountered situations are: (1) the choice between internal growth and growth by acquisition and (2) the choice of strategy as it relates to product line.

1. Internal growth and growth by acquisition. Every company which seeks to grow can plan to do so in either one, or both, of two possible ways. It can choose to expand by means of internal development of its own resource capabilities and/or by means of financial acquisitions of other companies or products. The choice which has to be made between the two or the determination of a balance be-

tween the two is climactic. There are several important factors which
have bearing upon the choice to be made.

First, there are considerations relating to the desired pace of company growth. Growth by acquisition clearly offers more scope for
rapid growth in small- and medium-size companies than does self-
generated growth,[9] because it immediately incorporates the momentum of a going concern. Growth by internal means is limited by
many time-consuming requirements: time to expand a sales organization, time to develop new products, time to gain market acceptance,
and so on. It is significant that in the past the business tycoon or empire builder has usually relied upon acquisition rather than internal development as his primary means of promoting corporate
growth.[10]

Growth by acquisition can be embarked upon with much less preparatory effort than internal growth. It requires at the outset only
financial resources and bargaining skill; only later do the problems
of welding together the enlarged corporation manifest themselves in
acute form. By contrast, the achievement of a strategy of growth
based on self-generation of resources and skills requires much more
managerial acumen from the start. It requires production and marketing know-how plus the development of functional resources so
that they will be able to cope with the planned-for growth.

The ensuing problems of integration for the company which grows
by acquisition, however, can prove to be very complex and difficult.
In practice there is normally a low ceiling to the number of corporate acquisitions which can reasonably be made over a given
limited period of time (say, one year)—that is, if the acquiring company is to remain an operating company and not become a holding
company. This conclusion is applicable even to very large companies,
because inevitably when acquisition takes place there are many human relations problems of adjustment and integration which require a great deal of top management's time and attention.[11]

One consequence of these problems is that it becomes progressively
more difficult for companies to select acquisition as their primary
mainspring of growth as they grow larger and larger. Very large
companies are likely to make some acquisitions but it is not feasible
for them to acquire large numbers of small companies over comparatively short periods of time, and there are few other large companies
which will consider acquisition offers. Society does not like the idea

of "big fish" continually swallowing "little fish," and the Justice Department continually looks for antitrust law violations in very large companies. The Justice Department has increased its activities during recent years in consequence of the amendments to the Clayton Act. These provide power to prevent those corporate mergers that could be said to lessen competition, and today many large companies feel that almost any merger is open to challenge. It is no surprise to find, therefore, that as a company grows larger it is more and more likely to rely upon a strategy which encourages growth primarily through the development of internal resources and skills.

This conclusion is supported by empirical observation. In particular, it is clear that some aggressively managed medium-size companies are able to sustain a much more rapid rate of growth over a period of years than can any of the modern-day giants of American business—say, as a rough measure, companies which have sales of more than $1 billion annually.[12] Indeed, simple extrapolation of trends reveals that some giant corporations would fast approach projections of the gross national product if they continued to grow at the rate achieved over a period of years in the past. For example, a 25 per cent increase in sales volume each year results in a trebling of sales every five years. On this basis a company doing $5 billion in sales in 1965 would grow to a colossus doing over $400 billion in sales by the year 1985!

Long-term growth rate is especially significant in strategic planning when a company's top management places heavy stress upon a "desired" rate of growth in formulating company objectives. Objectives need to be tailored to meet the realistic limitations which gross size imposes as the company becomes a giant. The spectacular leaps forward of 30 per cent, 40 per cent, and even 50 per cent in a single year, which may have been possible when the company was a comparative fledgling with annual sales of, say, less than $.5 billion, have become a thing of the past.

One other interesting ramification of this tendency toward declining growth rate deserves further scrutiny. Perhaps by accident,[13] some companies have made organizational arrangements to formalize their long-range planning activities at about the same time that a slackening in their corporate growth rate became noticeable. The problems which can arise in such a situation are suggested in the following experience. In one large company (its annual sales volume was nearly $750 million) there had been a notable decline in the rate of growth during recent years as measured by annual sales volume. During the previous three years the rate had fallen to about half that attained during the three years before them.

The staff planners were puzzled and concerned by the apparent inability to sustain the higher rate of growth of previous years. They sought ways to counteract the decline. They did not believe that the quality of planning within the corporation had degenerated, yet the evidence of comparative annual reports indicated to them that something must be wrong.

The staff planning unit itself had been formed at about the time when this decline in growth rate became evident, and members of the unit were worried lest their own positions as long-range planners should be undermined. They were aware that there was a close trend correlation between rise in money spent on formalized planning on the one hand and decline in rate of sales growth on the other.

The staff planners in this company (and perhaps top management as well) had not developed any clear awareness of the problems of declining growth rates which giant corporations have to face sooner or later. Insecurity and confusion were almost certainly impeding the usefulness of an otherwise very capable group of planners. Unrealistic ideas of rapid growth are sometimes dreamed up by top management or staff planners, and they must be overcome through better understanding if the planning is to prove effective.

Some aspects of choice emerge logically as the result of analysis, while others have to be deliberately selected in an appraisal of alternatives. There must be careful attention in weighing the various factors; although the subject matter is in many ways subjective, the choices are too important to be made arbitrarily. Again, the importance of qualitative considerations in this kind of choice is clearly seen: particularly, for example, in determination of the rate of growth which is deemed "desirable" by a company's top management. Finally, there is implicit attention to flexibility in making this kind of choice. A strategy of acquisition normally incorporates a good deal of flexibility, because it is dependent in substantial measure upon happenstance. In other words, many companies call for acquisitions if the "right company" or the "right product" happen to be available at the "right time" and at a "reasonable price."

2. *Choice of strategy in relation to product line.* As is pointed out

in Chapter 4, considerations of product line are of central importance in strategic planning. Decisions in this area have a major effect upon the character of the unifying set of assumptions which a long-range strategy seeks to provide.

Again, the choices that are open to companies provide for the selection of one, or both, of two broad alternatives. The first is *intensive* strategy, or the continued use of resources in developing products with the same physical characteristics and/or the same performance characteristics as those of existing products. The second alternative is *extensive* strategy, or the use of resources in developing products which incorporate simultaneous changes in both physical and performance characteristics when compared with the company's existing products.

In general terms there are three different types of intensive strategy.[14] The first and simplest is market penetration, which tries to acquire increased sales for existing products. The company does not change the existing products but concentrates its efforts upon selling them to more people or selling them in greater quantities to existing customers. This kind of strategy is predicated on the belief that the products are at stages in their life cycles which indicate strong continuing market demand over the future time period envisioned in the planning. There is also the presumption that these products are not likely to be rendered obsolete by some sudden technological advances in competitive products.

The second type of intensive strategy is market development. In this case the physical characteristics of the products remain essentially the same as those of the company's existing product line, but new uses and consequently new markets are sought. One example of market development is the entrance of the Checker automobile into the general automotive market: Previously the automobile had been produced and sold for use as a taxi. There is always the implicit assumption when such a strategy is adopted that the products have, and will continue to have, the strength to compete for the additional markets that are sought.

The third intensive strategy is product development. In this instance the end uses of the current products remain unchanged, but new characteristics improve the end use effectiveness. Most research and development work is geared to this type of strategy. For example, mass-produced automobiles do not change their end use significantly from one year to another, but each year the automobile manufacturers do provide new models which introduce new designing and styling features.

Extensive strategy is involved with what is usually termed product diversification, and it has become a vital aspect of expansion activities in a great number of companies today.[15] Again, several possible choices can be broadly stated.

The first type of extensive strategy is vertical integration. This occurs when a company expands its operations to include production of component parts or ownership of raw materials needed for end products already manufactured; it also occurs when a company packages and sells products which it produces, instead of having other companies act as middlemen in assembly and merchandising. Vertical integration often has the effect of associating a company still more deeply with the fortunes of its present product line. This is not necessarily wrong but the long-term assumptions which it presupposes need to be very carefully analyzed.[16]

The second type of extensive strategy, which is termed link diversification, is in many ways the most significant, because it answers most fully the challenge of retaining those strengths among a company's inherited resources and skills which are valuable, unique and permanent, while adapting to the ever-changing environmental conditions of the world. Its key feature is the planning of diversification to place some reliance on the operating resources and skills which the company has already acquired and is utilizing in existing operations. Link diversification strategy is normally adopted as a result of management's perception of one of the following three possibilities:

1. Expansion opportunities which are the direct outgrowth of some existing company undertaking.
2. Expansion opportunities which arise from the existence of surplus capacity in some part of existing operations.
3. Expansion opportunities which are likely to dovetail with existing operations in providing economies of scale.

Almost every major company today has relied in some substantial part upon a strategy of this kind (even though it may have been implicit and not well thought out). Two illustrations demonstrate how this is encompassed into climactic choices.

A statement made by the president of the giant Lever Brothers organization in Great Britain represents a brief yet meaningful summary of the type of climactic choice relating to product line which this company makes:

> We have a highly diversified business ourselves, and we believe strongly that we are unlikely to survive, let alone grow, in a rapidly changing world, unless we take a flexible view of the kind of activity we are prepared, from time to time, to engage in. But that is very far from saying that we take an unlimited view of our capabilities. We are not an investment trust, concerned to find capital and leave management to others. We normally go into businesses we can run ourselves, and there are many things we should never think of going into, just as there are others that we take to very readily. Our aim is to employ our existing resources more fully, or extend them along their natural lines of development.
>
> Many of our existing resources are designed to promote the activity we are most skilled in, which is making and marketing consumer goods in everyday use in the households of the world, and especially goods sold retail through grocers' shops or their equivalent. That gives us a wide field of choice, but it is narrow enough to be manageable. It is not a principle which can be applied to every side of our business—our trade in chemicals is an obvious exception to it—but it is one that is likely to govern a good deal of our future expansion.[17]

The second example is drawn from the experiences of a watch-manufacturing company, and it illustrates the way in which this company was able to envisage expansion opportunities through link diversification as the result of being aware of the wide applicability of its distinctive and unique skills.

Hamilton Watch Company was founded in 1892 and produced a wide range of quality watches. Until World War II its business had been almost totally concentrated upon watches; it had embarked upon only two small diversification projects previously, and both of these were discontinued by 1931. Then during the war the company produced a variety of defense products, including military and railroad watches, fuses, chronometers, and miscellaneous instruments.

It became apparent in the years after the war that the jeweled watch market had reached a stage of maturity. A 1957 *Long-Range Planning Report,* written by top management personnel in Hamilton, noted that no more jeweled watches were being sold in 1957 than had been sold in 1947. One result of this level-off was that the company's prime strategy from about 1950 on had become growth through diversification.

In the years which followed, the company's diversification projects included:

1. Defense contract work in time fuses and small precision parts.
2. Industrial applications for its spring alloys, notably minia-ture precision parts.
3. An automobile clock.
4. Miniature electronic and electromechanical instruments and systems.
5. A precision hole gauge.

The *Long-Range Planning Report* explained the company's ap-proach to diversification in these words:

> A concentrated effort is to be made to develop new products that can be manufactured with the skills and facilities that now exist in our factory, adding new skills and new equipment when necessary, or which can be procured from outside sources, and be distributed as a profit by either our consumer or our industrial marketing divi-sions.[18]

The third type of extensive strategy is termed conglomerate diver-sification and calls for expansion in areas which appear to be quite unrelated to the existing operating resources and skills. Normally it is embarked upon through acquisition of other companies or prod-ucts, and the attractiveness of expansion is gauged in terms of finan-cial measures without reference to operating resources and skills. This strategy is often found in holding companies and sometimes also in companies that uncover an investment opportunity which is considered to be "too good to turn down," even though such com-panies may have no apparent experience or skills (beyond general management skills) to assist in the exploitation of the new invest-ment.[19]

It is obvious that any one, or any combination, of the various in-tensive and extensive alternative strategies may be appropriate for a given company in a specific situation. The choice facing each individual company is affected by a vast number of individual considerations and a good deal of qualitative judgment by top management. Most frequently the strategy adopted is one which implies "continuation with certain modifications," and the climactic choices to be made focus upon what these modifications should be.

Climactic choices and the variety of ways in which they can be made are the heart of the planning process, and even though the choices to be made in strategic planning have a high degree of qualitativeness, they require a great deal of time and careful attention.

This completes the discussion of the conceptual analysis of strategic planning, and a consideration of the organizational problems and challenges which surround this subject follows.

PART III

Organization for Long-Range Planning

Chapter 10

The Role of Top Management
In Long-Range Planning Activities

Most efforts at making formal organizational arrangements for long-range planning are of very recent origin: Few companies have experiences in this respect which date back more than a dozen years. And so it is not surprising to find that most people associated with formalized long-range planning still think of their organizational arrangements as experimental, both in regard to work undertaken and acceptance by others in the company. Despite this newness, some useful statements about the subject can be formulated on the basis of practical experience.

Although strategic planning is the major focus of conceptual analysis in this book, in practice formal organizational arrangements for long-range planning activities generally encompass some elements of both strategic and implementational planning. This is highly desirable, because a full separation of the two would probably prove frustrating to the planners. The good strategic planner has an interest in seeing his plans take on more tangible form at the implementational stage, while the good implementational planner continually brings up questions of vital interest and importance in strategic planning. Thus this discussion, while focusing primarily upon strategic planning activities, also includes implementational planning.

TOP MANAGEMENT'S DILEMMA: FINDING TIME TO PLAN

Formal organizational arrangements for long-range planning have evolved primarily as the result of an assortment of pressures upon top management. Before World War II long-range planning activities were undertaken informally, if at all, by a company's chief executive, perhaps acting in association with some other members of top

155

management. In the years following World War II many top management executives began to recognize that long-range planning deserved their systematic analysis and continuing attention. Perception of this fact created a dilemma for them. They saw the importance, yet they also felt the need to keep the subject in perspective. After all, they had many other pressing duties, and they had to be concerned with the present as well as the future. As one manager succinctly expressed it: "If there's going to be a future, there's got to be a present."

A consequence of this dilemma is that top executives have been hard pressed to find enough time to devote to long-range planning activities. Not only is this conclusion suggested by observations, but many executives themselves have acknowledged it to be the case. One interesting expression of executive opinion in this matter comes from a study undertaken by Professor Sune Carlson in Sweden, in which he recorded and interpreted the day-to-day activities of a group of chief executives. Each of the subjects was asked to make a critical appraisal of his own performance as a chief executive. When he asked these executives what particular part of their duties they regarded as neglected, they answered, almost without exception: "long-range planning." [1]

There are several factors which help explain why these pressures exist when top management attempts to do all the long-range planning for a company without delegating any part of it.

1. Physical overload. Top management executives are very busy people. There is ample evidence supporting the claim that executives work longer than any other industrial group in society;[2] in fact, many work longer hours than did the pitworkers of early industrial England (albeit in a more congenial environment).[3]

Despite discussion in recent years about decentralization, top management executives still feel obliged to take on a great variety of time-consuming tasks. Peter Drucker tells of listening to a group of chief executives at a dinner party while they discussed the essentials of their respective jobs. He jotted down each "essential" mentioned, and by the end of the evening his list contained 41 separate functions. "The bottleneck," concludes Drucker, "is at the head of the bottle." [4]

Along with this schedule of long hours, top management executives often operate in an apparently disorganized manner. Some outside observers have viewed their work patterns as being crazy quilts of turmoil, concentrated mainly upon fighting fires as hot-spot areas develop. Sune Carlson expresses his personal disillusionment about the way in which he found chief executives managing their own jobs. "Before we made the study, I always thought of a chief executive as the conductor of an orchestra, standing aloof on his platform. Now I am in some respects inclined to see him as the puppet in a puppet show with hundreds of people pulling the strings and forcing him to act in one way or another." [5] The assignments frequently organize the man instead of the man organizing the assignments. [6]

2. Different requirements of temperament. The characteristics of temperament required in detailed long-range planning include not only the ability to make climactic choices about objectives, assumptions, alternatives, or the eventual strategy but also the ability to analyze, inquire, and speculate about factors likely to affect the long-range future and the company's opportunities for that future. These characteristics differ widely from those needed in many other facets of top executives' work. Most have climbed the ladder of promotion by demonstrating their ability as men of action, men who have the talent to see that plans are executed effectively. They are essentially driving, active, and outgoing, so their temperaments are somewhat alien to the requirements of the long-range planning process.

Some observers dispute this view. They say that long-range planning is known to be an important part of the top management job at the time promotions are made, and they reject as oversimplified and unrealistic the view that people cannot wear the hats of "planning" and "doing" simultaneously. [7]

However, while this view cannot be definitely "proved" or "disproved," it does have a substantial degree of validity. For the top management job, as Peter Drucker has pointed out, provides assignments for a "thought man," a "man of action," and a "front man." All three, he says, are most unlikely to be found in one man; yet "in all three major areas there are important activities that have to be discharged well if the enterprise is to prosper." [8] This suggests the kind of temperament conflicts which are apt to face top executives when they have *sole* responsibility for their company's long-range planning activities. If most are by nature "men of action," for example, they may find the role of "thought man" uncomfortable.

3. Preference for routine. The third factor limiting the time which can be devoted to planning is not so widely applicable as are the first two, but it does deserve mention. In some companies top managers may be hampered (consciously or unconsciously) by a Gresham's Law of planning, which claims that "daily routine drives out planning." This hypothesis has been advanced by James G. March and Herbert A. Simon.

> When an individual is faced both with highly programmed and highly unprogrammed tasks, the former tend to take precedence over the latter even in the absence of strong over-all time pressure.[9]

This hypothesis does not have a great deal of relevance for companies with a progressive, future-oriented top management.[10] In these companies, top management continually seeks to concentrate as much of its time as possible upon the creative and novel aspects of administration and policy.

However, in companies which are not characterized by this kind of managerial progressiveness, the hypothesis does have some validity. It has greatest relevance when top management's own self-interest seems best served by not encouraging long-range planning activities.

Often today there is a long time lag between the determination of a basic strategy or other long-range plan and the time when definite results of that strategy or plan can be discerned and assessed.[11] Ten years may elapse in some cases before a major research project can be judged a financial success or failure. If a company is just starting out in long-range planning, the investment may be reflected in financial statements as a severe drain on present operating results.

The top management executives in such companies frequently do not expect to remain in their present positions for as long as ten years. Some are getting close to retirement, while others look to further advancement. Thus it sometimes appears to be consistent with the executive's own self-interest not to become concerned in making major long-range plans. This is particularly true in the event that competitive weaknesses resulting from inaction will not become apparent for a considerable time to come.

To repeat: This kind of situation is more apt to arise in companies with mediocre management. It is less apt to arise in progressively managed companies, which have led the way in formalizing long-range planning activities.

The conclusion is clear: In many companies top management executives have found it increasingly difficult, if not impossible, to retain sole responsibility for all aspects of long-range planning while at the same time meeting all of their administrative responsibilities. They have therefore been under increasing pressure to make some organizational adjustments to alleviate this situation.

Side by side with these difficulties, there has been a growing awareness on top management's part of the importance and usefulness of *systematized* long-range planning undertakings. This development (see Chapter 3) is not merely a response to external changes in the economy; it results directly from advances in concepts of managing. Many top executives now recognize the importance of giving more detailed attention to both strategic and implementational long-range planning, which has led them to think more seriously about formal organizational arrangements.

It is not surprising, therefore, to find that organizational adjustments, designed to provide more attention to long-range planning, have been made with increasing frequency during recent years. The adjustments made have usually incorporated one, two, or all three of the following elements:

1. Some realignment of top managers' workload to allow them to spend more time working on long-range planning projects.
2. Increased reliance upon advice from, and analysis by, non-operating personnel, in particular the board of directors and management consultants.
3. Delegation of some responsibilities in long-range planning to people who are not members of top management.

Whenever formal organizational arrangements of this kind are introduced into a company, top management's role in long-range planning usually changes significantly. However, in every case it remains a pivotal one.

ADJUSTMENTS IN TOP MANAGEMENT WORKLOAD

One of the most significant recent trends in formal organizational arrangements is toward making adjustments in the workload of top management. These adjustments, which seek to provide top management with more time to devote to long-range planning activities, take two major forms.

1. Decentralization of authority. Prior to World War II, most managers believed that a centralized organization structure was the only one which could assure effective administration of a large industrial corporation. This view was questioned by some, but for the most part it was accepted. The typical organizational situation in large corporations at that time has been described by A. D. Chandler, Jr.:

> The executives in the central office were usually the president with one or two assistants, sometimes the chairman of the board, and the vice presidents who headed the several departments. The latter were often too busy with the administration of the particular function to devote much time to the affairs of the enterprise as a whole. [12]

The basic weakness was that "a very few men were still entrusted with a great number of complex decisions." [13] This weakness became magnified as companies grew larger and the decisions required became more numerous and more complex.

The trend toward greater managerial decentralization is attributable, in some measure, to a desire to lessen the administrative workload of top management, thus allowing more time for attention to these "complex decisions." Top management has been able to spend more time working on questions of long-range planning.

The far-ranging decentralization program of General Electric Company, developed and implemented in the years following World War II, provides an interesting illustration. General Electric recognized the need for "continuing, competent attention to the long-range future," and the company's president publicly stated that the whole decentralized structure hinged on the concept that—

> The "Manager," and especially the Chief Executive (or the General Manager of a business), must deliberately free up and devote more man-hours of his personal, normal working time to planning and organizing, as distinct from operating. [14]

The new organization structure provided for three basic kinds of responsibilities: Executive work, Services work, and Operating work.

Executive work included advice and assistance in the overall leadership of the company, and these were part of the responsibilities given to General Electric's group executives, who report directly to the president.

The *Position Guide* outlining the work required of group executives made suggestions regarding the need for predominant attention to be given to long-range considerations. An excerpt follows:

> Preponderant attention must be given to long-range rather than short-range factors, plans, problems, and analysis. Normally, therefore, approximately three-quarters of the Group Executive's work will deal with long-range affairs of both the Group components and of similar responsibilities as a member of the Executive Office, in order to attain the goals of the Company as a whole.

This example illustrates the widespread and growing concern within large corporations to insure that top management's time and attention are being devoted to matters of central importance to the corporation as a whole. The result is that today we have many instances of companies with top management "general executives," men who have been freed of many previously held administrative responsibilities in order that they may concentrate upon matters of broad, long-range interest.[15] The top management executive now has a silent reminder that a substantial amount of his total working hours should be spent engaged in matters of "long-range importance."

This concept of "freeing up" time is a most interesting one, because top management will always have a crucial role in long-range planning, particularly in its responsibility for making climactic choices. Thus it is of great significance that managerial decentralization allows top management to give more systematic and more detailed attention to long-range planning problems, even though there is also some delegation of authority to a planning staff.

2. Formation of a top-management line committee. Another adjustment in top management workload is the formation of a special line committee to deal with problems of long-range planning. The organizational arrangement can be charted as shown in Exhibit 1.

A committee of this kind may be set up in addition to a full-time staff planning unit, or it may be the only formalized organizational arrangement for long-range planning within the company. The circumstances in which either of these alternatives is appropriate will

EXHIBIT 1

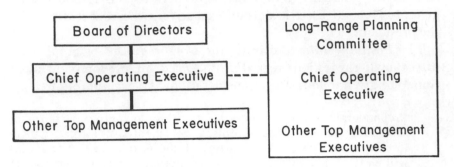

become clear as we discuss the various possible reasons for establishing such a committee.

One reason is to make judgments and decisions in the light of detailed analysis by members of a staff planning unit. In Eastman Kodak Company a staff planning unit does most of the detailed planning analysis, and top managers are members of an executive committee, an appropriations committee, and a finished products committee, whereby they participate in making key decisions which help to determine the final form of the long-range plans. The decisions may relate to aspects of strategic or implementational long-range planning. The great merit of this organizational arrangement is that it *insures* top management's active participation in the climactic choices of long-range planning.

Another reason for forming such a committee is to devote special attention to problems of strategic long-range planning. Sometimes this kind of analysis is undertaken in collaboration with a staff planning unit, but in other companies the committee is an organizational mechanism for keeping strategic planning analysis as the exclusive bailiwick of top management. The argument is that, while some aspects of implementational long-range planning can be delegated, the fundamental, broadly gauged issues associated with the determination of corporate long-range strategy cannot be delegated.

This "exclusive bailiwick" idea is of doubtful validity. Strategic long-range planning must of course be a centralized activity, but it does not follow that certain detailed work associated with strategic planning analysis cannot usefully be delegated to staff planners or others in divisions or departments of the company. Indeed, the technical requirements of analysis frequently demand the attention of technical specialists.

However, there are two types of situations in which a company can appropriately use only a top management line committee for strategic planning. It may decide that it cannot sustain the manpower or financial investments necessary for a planning staff, but that a line committee represents a sensible compromise. This situation is further discussed below. The other situation is likely to be found in a company which operates in a stable industry. It may have done some strategic planning and feels that its strategy is now determined and will remain appropriate (perhaps with some minor modifications) for a long time. In this case a top management line committee operates as a watchdog committee, keeping an eye open for any significant changes within the company, within the industry, or in the economy, changes which might have an effect upon the appropriateness of its long-range strategy.

A top management line committee, with a staff planning unit, is sometimes established by a small company which does not believe it can afford the manpower and financial investments needed to establish a full-time planning staff. The difficulties of establishing a small staff planning unit are not so great as commonly imagined, however. In view of the potential benefits, the investment in two or three highly skilled men is not very great if the company's management wants to engage in systematic long-range planning activities. While there are some instances in which the establishment of a committee only is sound, there are many others in which it would be strengthened by the addition of a staff planning unit.

A top management line committee is sometimes established on an interim or temporary basis, and this frequently proves to be a sound move. The reasoning is that long-range planning, and strategic planning in particular, is an extremely broad subject which should not suddenly be delegated to a staff planning group. Top management itself should first take a good look at the types of problems likely to be encountered and gather some ideas of its own about them and how the company might best organize to deal with them.

One hazard which impairs the effectiveness of a staff planning unit is premature establishment, without a clear awareness of its relationship to the rest of the organization. Thus an interim arrangement, which acquaints top management executives with the general problems and the types of planning activities that are needed, can be a most useful steppingstone to subsequent organizational arrangements for long-range planning.

GREATER PARTICIPATION OF NONOPERATING PERSONNEL
IN LONG-RANGE PLANNING

Another way in which organizational arrangements relating to long-range planning can be made is by drawing upon the services of nonoperating personnel. These are either (1) members of the board of directors or (2) management consultants or other outside advisers.

1. Board of directors. The distinguishing feature of this arrangement is that it stresses action at the board level in the formulation and development of long-range plans. Schematically, it can be presented as shown in Exhibit 2.

EXHIBIT 2

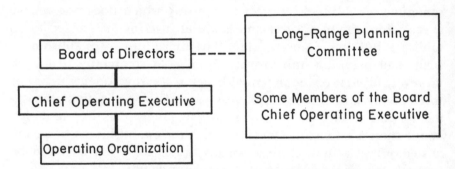

There is nothing new about this arrangement, since the board is always legally responsible for "managing the corporation." Theoretician and practitioner alike have long believed that the board is "in a position to take a long look ahead and to contribute a perspective and balance in policy-making." [16] Yet in practice the majority of boards do not play an active role in the formulation and development of long-range plans.

Under the type of arrangement advocated here, board members are brought into more active collaboration on long-range planning activities. Usually the chief executive is the prime mover in the arrangement: He is likely to determine what aspects of long-range planning are to be considered in the collaborations, and his views and attitudes probably carry much weight. The personal relationships and the power relationships of the chief executive with the members of the board are therefore very important.

The arrangement can encompass either strategic or implementational long-range planning (or both), but it is particularly useful in the former. Here there is the opportunity to introduce a dispassionate, objective viewpoint into analysis, a viewpoint of people who are concerned and, presumably, experienced, yet who are not intimately engaged in the company's operating activities. It is, in effect, an acknowledgment that one can be so close to the trees that the forest cannot be seen and that therefore the viewpoint of someone who is standing a little way off will be welcome and helpful.[17] In other words, the outlooks of operating and nonoperating executives can be blended to provide a better overall appraisal of the fundamental issues which require consideration in strategic planning.

This kind of active participation by the board in strategic planning represents a significant change in responsibilities. In a research study conducted in 1945 John G. Baker found that boards were mainly active in making decisions about financial considerations: capital expenditures and appropriations. In only a few companies did the board determine the content of postwar plans or help formulate the major policies in the various functional areas.[18]

The best-known example of a board which is intimately and continuously concerned with strategic planning is that of Standard Oil Company (New Jersey). Jersey's Board is composed of 15 full-time members who have no direct operating responsibilities (although each man has been promoted from within the company). The board's principal responsibilities include, among others, the duty to see that proper balance is maintained between the interest of shareholders, public, employees, government, and customers; to decide on long-range objectives of the company and the time table or methods for achieving them; and to review major policies and long-range objectives of affiliates as appropriate.

A board of directors is sometimes asked to work on problems of long-range planning which generally fall into the category of implementational. In particular, its assistance is requested with long-range financial plans, often through an appropriations committee, and with long-range manpower planning.[19] Attention to the latter usually stems from a recognition that although selection of a new chief executive occurs infrequently, succession to the position is not in most cases automatic. "Preparation for the selection of a successor to the chief executive should be a continuous process." [20]

The idea of drawing upon the talent of the board of directors in working on problems of strategic planning is sound in most cases. As a rule, the board members have wide and varied experience, and their positions enable them to be "stand off" observers who can contribute perspective and an outside point of view which often proves helpful in this kind of planning. At the same time, the arrangement is best seen as a useful adjunct to other formalizing designs. By itself this sort of arrangement is unlikely to satisfy all the pressures for formalizing long-range planning. In practice the services of board members have usually been employed in association with other formalizing arrangements, for example, the establishment of a staff planning unit.

2. *Management consultants.* Outside management consultants are frequently called upon by top management and by staff planning units to assist in some phase or another of planning. Sometimes consultants are called upon individually, and sometimes as a team; sometimes on a short-term assignment, and sometimes on a continuing basis. A National Industrial Conference Board study some years ago found that 50 per cent of responding companies used consultants at some stage in their long-range planning work. [21]

Interviews for this book indicated that consultants are generally called upon with the thought of gaining their assistance in one or more of the following three ways: to provide an independent appraisal of planning activities being undertaken; to offer new ideas which could prove of great value, especially in strategic planning; and to give advice regarding formal organizational arrangements. In each case, we again see companies making attempts to exploit the value of an experienced outsider's viewpoint. The combination of "independence" and "varied background" is said to make the skilled management consultant a most valuable person with whom to "talk things over."

One interesting development has been the increasing use of consultants on a continuous rather than a one-shot basis. The advantage is that the consultant can become familiar with a company's characteristics and problems and get to know some of the key personnel without losing the essential nature of his role as an outsider.

After 60 years of owner management, a medium-size manufacturing company located in New England chose an outsider as its president for the first time in 1957. (The company continued to be owned by the family of the original founder.) The new president, whose previous business experience had included more than 25 years with a large electrical company, soon felt that "I needed a mechanism to supply me with competent advice and constructive criticism, yet of such a kind that it would not restrict in any legal way my powers over the affairs of the company."

Working with a management consulting firm, the president devised the plan of an Advisor-Board to provide the kind of assistance he desired. He did not want "bankers, lawyers, and prominent citizens" on the Advisor-Board. These were, he admitted, "the type of men typically chosen for service on boards of directors." Instead, he was interested in "skilled practitioners of business," and he selected four men to meet with him for one full-day meeting every two months. The men he chose had the following backgrounds:

- Former vice president of finance in a large electrical company.
- President of a management consulting firm and specialist in manufacturing problems.
- President of a small tubular products manufacturing company.
- Former president of a large manufacturing company.

The arrangement he devised is schematically presented in Exhibit 3.

EXHIBIT 3

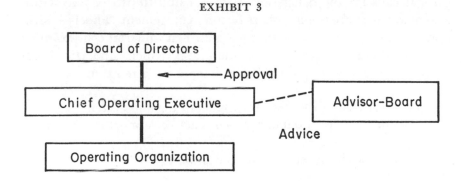

The Advisor-Board meetings covered subjects ranging from operating problems to long-range planning. The president suggested an agenda of subjects, but members of the board could ask questions or make suggestions about any subjects they wished. It was a ground rule of the meetings that board members assumed no formal responsibility for any actions subsequently taken.[22]

In addition to the advantage of using consultants on a continuing basis, this example contains two other features which deserve attention. First, there is an attempt to gain the benefits of outside counsel and assistance from a source other than the board of directors. The value of an outside viewpoint is still recognized, but the "skilled practitioner" is thought to offer something more pragmatically useful than the varied experience of the board members.[23] Second, the consultants in this case serve in an advisory capacity, and this contrasts with the participation of the board members described above. Only one person makes the crucial decisions: the chief executive.

For a small company which is led by a strong president, the Advisor-Board is likely to prove very useful. It needs modification, no doubt, if it is to be used in large companies with many capable executives. Nevertheless, the idea of an informal sounding board of consultants to meet with the chief executive, with a team of top management executives, or with members of a staff planning unit is a valuable one.

DELEGATION OF LONG-RANGE PLANNING RESPONSIBILITIES

The third principal kind of organizational adjustment in formalizing long-range planning activities is in many ways the most significant. It calls for the delegation of responsibilities to people within a company who are not members of top management. This is a development of such importance that we must first undertake an examination of several conceptual considerations which underlie it. In particular, the following three issues deserve our attention:

1. The desirability of separating planning and doing.
2. The need for top management's active support and participation.
3. The extent of centralization desirable.

1. Desirability of separating planning and doing. The question of whether "planning" and "doing" should be separated is one which is a source of lively controversy among executives today. Some argue that the two are separate tasks which should be undertaken by different people; others claim that the two must be done by the same person if effective performance is to be insured. These two conflicting schools of thought may be termed the "separationists" and the "nonseparationists," and their views can be summarized in the following manner.

Separationists. The case for separating the jobs of "planning" and "doing" within a company can be traced back at least as far as the writings of Frederick W. Taylor, who laid the guidelines for modern-day separationists when he expressed his position as follows:

> All of the planning which under the old system was done by the workman, as a result of his personal experience, must of necessity under the new system be done by the management in accordance with the laws of the science. Because even if the workman were well suited to the development and use of scientific data, it would be physically impossible for him to work at his machine and at a desk at the same time. It is also clear that in most cases one type of man is needed to plan ahead and an entirely different type to execute the work.[24]

Taylor was, of course, primarily concerned with the separation of "planning" and "doing" at the worker level. Nevertheless, his views regarding limitations of time and different personal qualities have been adapted by later writers to long-range planning. One representative opinion is that expressed by William E. Hill:

> Some managers are inherently planners, others are not. Since most operating men have such heavy responsibility for current operations that it is difficult for them to find the time to plan, they need planning assistance. This is true at top management as well as divisional and departmental levels.[25]

The case for separating long-range planning from operations has been put even more strongly by others, among them Walter B. Schaffir, who has written that long-range planning—

> . . . requires background study which is possible only through full-

time, continuous effort, painstaking research and often application
of special skills and techniques for which the operating manager
generally does not have the time—and perhaps the inclination.[26]

Thus, in summary, the separationists claim as supporting evidence
for their theories the time pressures on operating management, different personality requirements, and the need for skills of full-time
specialists in planning.

Nonseparationists. The nonseparationists are just as outspoken in
their views. Peter F. Drucker, for example, interprets the meaning
of Taylor's observations in a very different manner:

> To have discovered that planning is different from doing was one
> of Taylor's most valuable insights. . . . That we are able today to
> speak seriously and with meaning of management by objectives is
> a direct result of Taylor's discovery of planning as a separate part
> of the job, and of his emphasis on its importance.
>
> But it does not follow from the separation of planning and doing
> in the analysis of work that the planner and the doer should be two
> different people. . . .
>
> Planning and doing are separate parts of the same job; they are not
> separate jobs. There is no work that can be performed effectively
> unless it contains elements of both. . . . Advocating the divorce of
> the two is like demanding that swallowing food and digesting it be
> carried on in separate bodies.[27]

These arguments against separation of "planning" and "doing"
are summarized by Alvin Brown in three brief statements. First, it
is impossible to separate all planning from the job of doing something. Second, planning is done most effectively by the man who is
to carry out the plans. And third, withdrawing the planning assignment from the man who is to do a job decreases his motivation to
work.[28]

On the surface there seems to be a sharp conflict of viewpoints
here. However, an examination of the points at issue reveals that the
disagreements are in many ways less sharp than they appear.

Some of the confusion is removed by recalling that planning is a
process which includes aspects of *both* fact finding *and* decision making. This is significant, because the separationists generally have
concentrated their attention upon the fact-finding aspects of planning, while the nonseparationists have tended to equate planning

with decision making. Each has neglected to consider the other part of the process. In short, one contentious aspect of the problem is primarily a matter of semantics.

But the problem is more complex than this, as concentration on strategic long-range planning shows. Within the strategic planning process the interrelatedness between the fact-finding and decision-making phases makes it impossible to allocate one to staff personnel and the other to line executives without overlap. Actually implicit choices are made in every phase of the planning process, choices of exclusion, choices of direction, choices of interpretation, as well as many unconscious or unrecognized choices. Obviously, then, staff planning personnel have some influence upon the eventual strategy decided upon: Indeed, they may even gravitate to positions where they possess (as Ely Devons has phrased it) "enormous power" [29] in determining final choices. This is especially true in situations where strategic planning requires a good deal of technical analysis.

The fact is that the seemingly doctrinaire question posed ("Should 'planning' and 'doing' be separated?") has no doctrinaire answer. Certainly top management must continue to accept responsibility for long-range planning results, but it does not follow that staff personnel should not be employed in the development of these plans. Indeed, the need for full-time, highly skilled staff planners grows greater each year as the demand for more systematized and more thorough long-range planning increases. Were Malthus alive today, he might appropriately have pointed out that—

> The capacity of top management to keep informed appears to increase over time in an arithmetic progression. But the generation of information relevant for effective strategic planning increases over time in a geometric progression.

In practice, top management in large companies has little choice except to call upon the service of highly skilled staff planners.

The challenge to top management thus becomes one of keeping in close contact with these staff planners and of providing guidance and making choices where necessary in establishing objectives, making assumptions, developing alternatives, and, of course, determining the eventual strategy. This kind of continuing association with the staff planners allows top management to retain its overall responsibility for decision making, while at the same time it provides the company with the advantages of the full-time, specialist attention of a staff planning unit.

2. *Need for top management's active support and participation.* There was complete accord among the people interviewed for this book that top management, and in particular the chief executive, must demonstrate an active interest in long-range planning. They stressed that lukewarm support is insufficient; enthusiasm must be communicated throughout the organization.[30]

In almost every company visited there were specific instances given of active encouragement and support on the part of the chief executive and others in top management. The president of one company, for example, makes a point of opening regularly scheduled planning conferences, and he usually stays to listen to the conference discussions. The president of another attaches a personal cover letter to important materials prepared by his corporate planning unit for release throughout the organization.

The head of the central planning department of one large company said:

> In my opinion, the most fundamental requirement for building successful and realistic corporate plans is that top management must really believe in a systematic forward looking program. . . . If top management sees the value in economic forecasting and in forward planning in general, I do not hesitate to say that these activities are "worth the try."

Long-range planning (especially strategic) is concerned, by its very nature, with far-reaching decisions which will affect the basic nature of the company. This means that the subject matter is of direct and vital importance to top management, and the best way of insuring that the planning will be of high quality is to maintain a continuing relationship with the planning staff, providing guidance and direction as needed. The chief executive always has to remember that the final responsibility for the far-reaching decisions that are made is his.[31]

If subordinate managers are going to cooperate in the development or execution of any long-range plans, they first want to be assured that top management will measure their performance on the basis of long-range contributions and not simply on the basis of current-year operating results.[32] This is very important because most long-range planning, both strategic and implementational, requires an initial sacrifice of current profits as an investment in future well-being. Thus, for example, a 5 per cent return on sales might be more healthy in the long run than an 8 per cent return on sales if in the first case additional funds have been invested in major research projects. A further consideration is that subordinate management partly patterns its attitude toward planning in general on the basis of the attitude it sees reflected at the top level of the organization. This illustrates once again that top management's active support and participation in long-range planning activities can have far-reaching repercussions throughout a company.

3. *Extent of centralization desirable.*[33] In any planning activity there are two opposing organizational "pulls"—one toward increased centralization and the other toward increased decentralization.[34] This situation, which exists in all but the smallest of companies, is well summed up by Ely Devons:

> Every attempt at planning reveals these two problems: first, the need to split up the field to be covered so that each administrative unit can deal efficiently with its own sector; and second, the need to secure that the actions of these separate units all fit into the general plan.[35]

When we come to relate these organizational "pulls" to the subject of long-range planning, we must remember that in practice strategic and implementational planning activities are usually grouped together under one general supervision, partly because each is strongly affected by developments in, and insights gained from, the other. The effect of this grouping is to increase the degree of centralization.

In strategic long-range planning, the balance is tilted strongly in the direction of centralization, for several reasons. First, strategic planning requires a view of the company as an integrated whole, not merely as the sum of many parts. Persons at the executive level are in the best position to develop such plans, since they alone have the necessary perspective, the necessary experience, and the necessary liaison with others in the company. In addition, the issues are of such fundamental importance that top management must be closely associated with the planning that is taking place.

Second, strategic planning demands the attention of high caliber people in dealing with the types of fundamental issues which it raises. Top management usually believes that the best way of insuring this quality is to bring together the best staff planners it can find and maintain a close and continuing contact with them at headquarters.

Third, strategic planning often entails working with information and developing a strategy which is highly confidential. Top management therefore usually seeks to restrict the number of people having access to such information, and the best way of doing this is to limit participation in the planning to high echelons of management at headquarters.

The strongest "pull" toward decentralization in strategic planning is the need for realism. In some companies top management and staff planners purposely try to keep in touch with industry operations and to spend time with people at divisional and departmental levels. A number of planners interviewed for this book stressed the necessity for avoiding the label of "ivory tower planning," and they said they recognized the dangers of coming up with plans which are academically impressive but not realistic.

Implementational long-range planning is also essentially a centralized activity in most companies. One reason for this is its close interrelationship with strategic planning, but there is a variety of other contributing factors. Many implementational long-range plans are of great importance to the company as a whole and therefore require the attention and decision making of top management executives. It is the kind of planning which also demands top-level direction from people who are in a position to see the company as an integrated whole. Further, it requires the attention of highly skilled people, and top management usually believes that these people are best grouped together at company headquarters.

Of course, much of the detailed analysis associated with implementational planning is done on a decentralized basis. This is particularly true when some well-established plans have to be updated or when a problem requiring technical analysis is given to experts within a particular department or functional area.

However, much of implementational long-range planning has to do with new developments, developments which top management usually considers to be of considerable importance. In these circumstances it is hardly surprising that the heart of implementational planning is centralized, even though much of the detailed work associated with it is farmed out to subordinate levels.

MAJOR ORGANIZATIONAL PATTERNS OF DELEGATION

Having discussed these several conceptual topics, we are now ready to look at the major organizational patterns adopted when long-range planning activities are delegated.

1. Formation of a task force. A popular organizational arrangement in formalizing long-range planning activities is the establishment of a task force and the assignment of one or more special projects to it. The task force approach is sometimes used during a time of major change within a company, as the following example illustrates.

In 1945 a new management team assumed control at the top level of W. R. Grace & Company. Soon afterward an extensive study was started which was designed to assess the company's present position and to draw some guidelines to help in the establishment of policies for the postwar future. In other words, the study was to help in strategic long-range planning. A number of senior executives in the company were relieved of operating responsibilities so that they could become full-time members of a task force working on this project. After a detailed investigation lasting many months, the task force came up with some recommendations which subsequently were to bring about major changes in the character of the Grace Company.

On other occasions, a task force is used to initiate a continuing, formalized approach to long-range planning. Thus its purpose may resemble that of a top management line committee in that it is a temporary forerunner of a more permanent organizational approach. This is the case in Douglas Aircraft Company, as the following discussion shows.

In the early spring of 1961 Douglas Aircraft Company inaugurated an intensive corporate study on which many people throughout the organization worked. Its title was *Project: Forge,* and its chore was to develop ten-year corporate plans. The company hoped to discover in the process what lay ahead in markets and technology and what changes it needed to make for the future.

The project was organized into various *ad hoc* groups, each of which was given certain responsibilities. Senior corporate officers participated in the study, some being relieved of operating responsibilities so they could devote full-time energies to the project.

Following completion of the study, the chief executive decided to institute a reorganization of the company's organization structure, in August 1961, making it much more decentralized than previously. At the same time, an office of corporate planning and control was established as a permanent staff unit.

Finally, a third variation on the task force approach has been suggested by Ronald J. Ross of Sperry Gyroscope Company.[36] His method is a rotating organization structure: Managers are assigned to certain projects, and they move back and forth between operations and planning, first taking responsibility for one and then for the other.

Ross is concerned about the limited opportunities for participation in most attempts to organize long-range planning. He believes that the rotating organization structure approach using task forces helps to tap "the large reservoir of experience of men at the lower management level to effect better working arrangements in the conduct of the firm's business." [37]

There are three assumptions in a rotating organization structure which should be made explicit: first, that projects can be divided into managerial assignments suited to this kind of arrangement; second, that deemphasis upon specialization of function provides a net gain to the company; and third, that it pays the corporation in the long run to have two managers assigned to each task. Ross claims that this third assumption is true because of greater flexibility and effectiveness, better communication ties, and more extensive utilization of managers on the job.

Probably not one of these assumptions is generally applicable, although examples can be cited supporting each. The second assumption in particular is dubious. While strategic long-range planning emphasizes a general rather than a specific approach, implementational long-range planning (which, it would seem, is the prime concern here) requires technical skills in various functional areas, and, in fact, the quality of the technical analysis required is becoming progressively more stringent.

Despite these shortcomings, Ross's approach is an interesting and refreshing one. Much of the writing on organization structure travels well-worn ruts, and Ross seeks to avoid them. His suggestions remind us that there is a good deal which still can be done in introducing organizational innovations to deal with the changing managerial demands of the present day.

In general, the task force approach to organizing for long-range planning has some important advantages, even though it is essentially of a temporary nature. It offers great flexibility for short-term intensive studies. It allows the assignment of priorities and the direction of concentrated effort to problems which seem of critical importance. It also appears to be a most useful approach in getting long-range planning activities started, giving them an initial momentum and providing background acquaintance with relevant subject areas while demonstrating top management's active support. In particular, the task force often proves to be a more rewarding interim arrangement than a top management line committee, for it enables the chief executive to be more scrupulous in his choice of men and projects. This, together with the fact that the particular project assumes greater urgency in the eyes of the participants, often allows a more effective plan to be developed.

At the same time, the usefulness of the task force varies from case to case. Sometimes it is not possible or helpful to divide managerial planning assignments into task segments. Also, the task force approach usually gives less attention to long-range planning as a whole; it is best suited to those situations where top management has designated one or two facets as being the most crucial. Consistent with this, the task force is more appropriate for making an intensive effort in a particular area than it is for carrying out a continuing study of long-range planning problems. Its usefulness for a company is greater as a sprinter than as a distance runner.

2. Establishment of a corporate staff planning unit. The organizational arrangement for long-range planning which is most widely adopted among large companies calls for the establishment of a corporate staff planning unit. This unit reports directly either to the chief executive or to another senior top management executive, and it most commonly takes the form of a committee or department. In some instances, however, it consists of only one person, and for this reason the all-encompassing term "unit" is used. The position of a staff planning unit within an organization can be depicted as shown in Exhibit 4.

The unit best exemplifies the formalizing changes which have

EXHIBIT 4

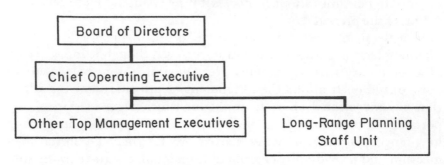

taken place during recent years in relation to long-range planning activities, and it is obviously of great significance. However, the unit is not a cure-all for long-range planning problems, as some managers have mistakenly believed. Neither is it a shortcut to long-range planning effectiveness. Therefore, we must hear a few cautions.

One is that it will be established too early. If established before anyone in the company has developed some clear ideas about what approach the organization should take in its long-range planning activities, the staff unit may thrash around uselessly, uncertain of its own role and of its relationship to the rest of the organization. As one executive has concluded: "I would wait until the company's concept of long-range planning had crystallized enough that the department could find its rightful place in the organization structure." [38]

A second and even greater danger arises when the top management of a company establishes a staff planning unit and thereafter pays it only lip-service. Sometimes top management will assume that "long-range planning is being taken care of" and nothing further needs to be done. The problems which this attitude can create are well illustrated in the following case. [39]

In 1953 a large manufacturer of industrial equipment established a product line planning and control department. The department, according to top management, would have responsibility for initiating, planning, and integrating among the several functional departments the work on all projects related to any change in the company's product lines. The top management was following a precedent set by some other large concerns in their own and other industries. The management had also recognized that the product line required simplification. Further, it had observed that operations were shifting from producing custom-engineered products to making standard items.

The man chosen to head this new department had previously been responsible for market research activities within the sales department. He had been with the company for 15 years, and his work experience included engineering and production assignments. He had, in other words, an extensive and varied background preparation for the new job. Furthermore, the job specifications appeared to offer ample scope for him to perform his assigned functions and make a most beneficial contribution.

Yet four years later, in 1957, an appraisal revealed that the product line planning and control department had not been able to operate effectively. The need for planning had been intellectualy recognized by top management, and a qualified man had been chosen to head the new department, but the department had not proved useful, mainly because it failed to receive support, encouragement, and backing from the chief executive and others in top management, in deeds as well as in words. As a consequence, functional vice presidents and others in the functional departments took little notice of the new department. They continued to bicker, as they had before, about delivery dates and product reliability and customer demands and engineering possibilities, while the product planning department remained hamstrung in most of its efforts.

While some contributions had been made, the company was perhaps worse off in 1957 than it had been in 1953. At least the management was not practicing self-deception in 1953; it recognized that it was not paying special attention to product planning then. In 1957, however, top management thought it could say that "product planning is taken care of." [40]

In this example formalizing planning activities was unsuccessful primarily because top management displayed a lack of responsibility. Top management failed to realize that formalizing a staff planning unit does not, of itself, solve planning problems. Formation of such a unit can only facilitate the confrontation and analysis of risks and problems. The basic responsibilities for success remain still with top management; they cannot be delegated.

While these dangers and limitations emphasize the fact that the establishment of a staff planning unit by no means automatically guarantees successful long-range planning, the staff nevertheless can provide a sound basis for high-quality long-range planning. This becomes clearer in the next chapter, where there is a detailed study of the nature of staff planning units and the various roles which they assume.

Chapter 11

The Staff Planning Unit

FOR THE PURPOSE OF THE ANALYSIS WHICH IS TO FOLLOW, IT is useful to discuss the activities of staff planning units in terms of a number of assumed roles. This provides a convenient conceptual base from which to analyze their responsibilities, and it allows us to observe similarities and distinctions among the units which have been established in different companies.[1]

ROLES ASSUMED BY STAFF PLANNING UNITS

The roles most usually assumed by staff planning units are of four major types. Two of these—the *integrator* and the *forecaster*—appear to be adopted universally. The other two—the *consultant* and the *instigator*—are sometimes adopted, sometimes not. The manner in which each of these roles is assumed becomes evident as we look at each one in turn.

1. Integrator. All staff planning units assume the role of integrator, directly or indirectly, because their organizational position inevitably places them in some sort of liaison with departmental or functional management. The planning units must strive to facilitate the development of long-range plans which harmonize with one another and which make sense for the corporation as a total entity, or they will wind up with an assortment of contributions which have neither coordination nor any kind of centripetal force.

The need for long-range plans to be developed and modified in the context of the corporation as a total entity applies not only in the obvious case of strategic long-range planning but also in the less obvious case of implementational long-range planning. In the latter instance, long-range plans developed in one functional area frequently make sense for the company as a whole only in the light of corresponding plans developed for other related functional areas. This suggests again that the staff planning unit can scarcely avoid becoming immersed in problems of bridging gaps between departmental or functional plans and corporate plans.

The role of integrator also requires awareness of the dynamic forces in the modern business world, and two concepts which aid in fostering awareness of the momentum of change should be particularly noted. The first is the "planning gap," which refers to differences or discrepancies between the company's consolidated plans and its initial objectives. The long-range planner, in his integrative role, discovers gaps, determines the reasons for their existence, and brings his findings to the attention of top managers.

The second concept derives from the first. If corporate objectives are not being met, the planning gap information provides a "distant early warning." This signal is important because time is imperative to accomplish whatever remedial action is necessary. In the past it was possible to exploit a market by entering it some years after initial establishment. Now, however, this is usually not possible. A business needs to be operating in a new product area near the start of that product's commercial life.

All staff planning units do not, of course, interpret or practice the role of integrator in exactly the same way. Sometimes the role is seen primarily as a personal responsibility for planning details; sometimes primarily as an organizational channel of communication or other organizational mechanism; sometimes primarily as an interpretation of key issues for top management. But in every case the maintenance of corporate cohesiveness in long-range planning activities is of basic importance. Staff planning units, in assuming this role of integrator, are always seeking to complement departmental drive and ingenuity with a spirit of corporate identification.

2. Forecaster. The role of forecaster is very different from that of integrator, and it is much more specific. By forecasting, members of a staff planning unit develop and synthesize information pertaining to the future: information which will become part of the data upon which long-range planning decisions will be based.

There is always a great deal of forecasting associated with long-range planning activities. While the type varies with the kind of long-range planning being undertaken, it remains true that forecasting of some sort constitutes an intrinsic part of any systematic approach to long-range planning. Furthermore, this need is one of the major reasons for the existence of planning specialists. Unlike the integrator role, the forecaster role does require some detailed knowledge of special skills and techniques of analysis—and as a rule top managers do not have this knowledge. Here, more than anywhere else, the long-range planning task demands specialist assistance.

The requirements of the forecaster role can be met by two different organizational arrangements. In some companies the staff planning unit becomes a full-fledged forecasting analysis group, which may be quite large. In one oil company, for example, there are over 100 people working in the staff planning unit, most of them engaged in detailed forecasting analysis. In other companies most detailed forecasting is done outside the staff planning unit—in other corporate staff offices and/or at divisional and departmental levels. In such companies the forecaster role within the staff planning unit is concentrated upon interpretation and appraisal of the different forecasts developed by others. An understanding of forecasting methodology is still required, but the planners are not concerned with the techniques of preparation. A number of distinctive features about the forecaster role deserve further comment.

In the first place, an intelligent blending together of staff and line activities is required in order to insure that the full-time planners keep in close touch with line personnel who have their fingers on the pulse of business activity.

Second, the technical expertise of staff planning members is usually enhanced by the fact that they have no vested interest in any particular figures and also because their relationships with top management are likely to be closer and more informal than would normally be the case with divisional planners. These factors can make the corporate staff planners less inclined to worry about losing face if they modify or abandon initial positions.

Third, the staff planning unit, in assuming the forecaster role, develops forecasts in the context of the company's overall capabilities and therefore can embrace a corporate point of view which departmental forecasters cannot. It can take into account such things as overlapping activities; the extent to which corporate resources can realistically be taxed; the detection of future gaps in projected output; and so on.

However, the basic questions which still have to be dealt with are: When should a staff planning unit become concerned with detailed forecasting analysis, and when should its task be confined to the interpretation and appraisal of forecasts? Two major factors influence the answers.

One is the extent of conjunctive relationships within the given company's product line. That is to say, if the various major products have substantial uniformity in their cyclical and/or seasonal patterns of activity, they lend themselves readily to analysis by a centralized forecasting unit. This kind of conjunctive relationship is most commonly found in companies where there is a major product line base of one commodity or perhaps a group of commodities. It is not surprising to find, for instance, that staff planning units commonly assume detailed forecasting assignments in oil, sugar, and steel companies.

The second factor is the extent of geographic and managerial centralization. In general, the more centralized the company's operations, the more likely it is that the staff planning unit assumes responsibility for preparing detailed forecasts. Since commodity-based companies have tended to retain centralized organization structures,[2] they are again seen as likely to employ staff units in developing detailed forecasts.

Thus the appropriateness of assigning detailed forecasting analysis to the staff planning unit depends on the extent of conjunctive relationships between major products of the company's product line and on the degree of geographic and managerial centralization in the company's organization.

3. Consultant. A third role which a corporate staff planning unit may fulfill is that of consultant. While the term "consultant" is most frequently used to describe an outsider who is called upon to provide assistance or guidance, the role of "internal consultants" is of special concern here.

Staff planning units which assume the consultant role undertake one, or both, of two major types of consulting activity. One is providing written materials to assist and guide those people within the organization who are charged with developing corporate or divisional long-range plans. The other is assisting and guiding these people through personal contact with them.

The staff planning unit's effectiveness as a consultant depends significantly upon the attitude of those for whom the consultative assistance and advice are intended. As some management consultants have pointed out in discussing their experiences, the receiver must exhibit a willingness to learn before an effective helping relationship can be established. The receiver also must have respect not only for the consultant's technical competence but for him personally as well.

Interviews for this book suggest that the character of the consultant role is likely to change over time. As formalized planning becomes better established, there is generally a tendency toward (*a*) "integrative approach" consulting, (*b*) "independent viewpoint" consulting, and (*c*) "new ideas" consulting. Integrative approach consulting is concerned with coordinating the interests of different divisions or parts of the company which have the same needs. Independent viewpoint consulting requires staff planners to appraise planning methods or the content of plans developed by others in the organization. Finally, in new-ideas consulting, staff planners are frequently able to provide suggestions gained from their varied experiences in planning activities.

4. Instigator. In the role of instigator the staff planning unit attempts to increase the scope, ambitiousness, and reliability of the company's long-range planning activities. In this case the staff unit's influence is catalytic. It also checks to insure that, when responsibility has been assumed for specified long-range planning assignments, these assignments are actually carried out.

Although the roles of both the instigator and the consultant are concerned with improving the quality of planning being done by others within the company, the consultant role is one in which the staff planner acts as an adviser who provides counsel, assistance, an independent viewpoint, and perhaps some new ideas. The instigator role is more external in nature, and it is characterized by prodding and spurring toward better performance. The two do not necessarily conflict: The same staff planning unit may assume both roles in the course of its activities. It is also possible that the consultant role will be assumed without the instigator role, or vice versa.

The instigator role has three distinctive features. First, it comes closer to being a control function than any of the other roles. It specifies guidelines for acquiring and presenting planning information and stimulates those who are charged with long-range planning to make sure that they actually carry out their responsibilities. In theory, at least, the result of this kind of activity by a staff planning unit is designed to help provide information more readily, to make for greater ease in comparison of past and present performances, and to offer better opportunities for improved planning as a result of more extensive and dependable information about the past.

A second feature of this role is that, like the consultant's, it provides the opportunity to introduce new ideas regarding both planning techniques and planning opportunities. The staff planner does not have direct responsibility for the content or caliber of the planning done by others, but he can make constructive and useful suggestions for planning improvements. The role demands much more than an ability to impose sanctions; and here, as in the case of the consultant role, the staff planners are likely to conduct extensive discussions with those responsible for detailed planning activities.

Third, the role of instigator has special importance during the initial stages in the establishment of a formalized long-range planning program. It also has special value when new techniques in planning activities are being introduced or when major reappraisals or reorientations of existing planning programs are being undertaken. Once the formalized program has gained momentum and is continuing in the same general pattern, there is normally less need for staff planners to spend much time in this instigator role. Inertia has been overcome, and the planners are able to spend more of their time assuming the other roles.

GENERAL COMMENTS

Finally, a few general comments relating to staff planning units should be made.

Seriousness of purpose. It seems trite to observe that when a planning unit is established, the job designated should be taken seriously both by planning unit personnel and by top managers. However, planning efforts sometimes fail because this obvious prerequisite is ignored. For example, in 1959 one large company reportedly had no fewer than three vice presidents for planning in its central organization chart. In addition, there were other "planners" scattered through the divisions of the company. The researchers who discovered this situation reported, further, that they found little evidence of sound forward planning in the company. Upon further investigation they found that the three men were all in their early sixties and had been "shunted" into these planning slots. Subsequently, arrangements were made within the company to retire these vice presidents of planning—and an estimated annual saving of over \$110,000 resulted. But the deeper implications stemming from their presence as the organization's leaders in planning still remained.[3]

The problems created by this kind of situation have to be seen in two time dimensions. In the present, the company is not likely to be gaining much in the way of effective planning activities. For the future the picture is, if anything, more dismal. When long-range planning becomes a more important requirement, problems of acceptance throughout the organization are likely to be exceptionally difficult. If planning has been allowed to become a laughingstock in the organization's ranks, it later becomes difficult to convince anyone of its merits.

Size of units. Staff planning units established at the corporate level are usually very small, except when responsibility is assumed for detailed forecasting analysis. Typically the number of men associated with such units ranges from four to eight; the largest one observed during the course of this research was ultimately intended to expand to sixteen.[4] The unit must remain small so that it can retain its informality and flexibility. This fact was recognized by the heads of most planning units, who emphasized the need for keeping the number of members very low. Some units had not expanded at all since their initial establishment.[5] In a few companies the staff planning unit consists of only one man. There are, however, some great disadvantages to this practice, especially in large companies. The most notable is that "few individuals have the breadth of experience and vision to do the whole task." [6]

Location of staff planning unit. In the majority of companies, the staff planning unit is located in the corporate headquarters building. This is scarcely surprising, for the advantages are obvious. There is easy access to top management when needed, and there is access to other headquarters officers and to company records. Further, there is the opportunity to keep in informal touch with company activities and problems.

One disadvantage is that sometimes the planners are called in as "firemen" to act in this or that emergency and get caught up in the mainstream of operating activities. This does not normally appear to be a great hazard, but it makes some staff units anxious to obtain a more isolated location.

In several companies the staff planning unit is geographically isolated from any pressures of day-to-day operations: In other words, it's in a "hideaway." This means sacrificing the constant formal and informal contacts with others in the headquarters building, but the advantage of providing an atmosphere which had no overt time pressures was felt to be an overriding factor. Whether a "hideaway" is a good idea depends importantly upon the ability of the staff planning unit to maintain frequent and close contact with top management executives. Every hideaway observed was within easy and rapid access to corporate headquarters. In one company, for example, the planners talked about headquarters as being "about an hour by plane."

Personal qualifications. The qualifications demanded in staff planners differ from those customarily sought when filling line management positions. The staff planning unit, taken as a whole, usually requires the following:

- An ability to engage in broad-gauged thinking about the company as a whole and its place in the operational environment.
- An ability to analyze complex data not only in quantitative but also in qualitative terms.
- An ability to communicate effectively with other members of the planning unit and with top management. Communication in this sense means many things. It includes, for instance, knowing what to say and how to say it, but it also includes knowing what *not* to say. Planning must be acceptable—and staff planners should be able to judge, say, how far it can carry self-criticism without injuring pride or otherwise antagonizing top management.

The individual members of the unit must be chosen with these overall requirements in mind. The requirements are imposing, and they suggest why industry spokesmen say that top caliber planners are extremely hard to find.

This emphasis upon competence and ability raises the question of what role, if any, status and seniority should have in the selection of long-range planners. There are some who say that they should be ignored altogether: for example, Theodore Levitt, who comments:

> If a corporation wants successful blue-skies planning . . . the best
> way is to appoint a group of carefully selected people who are
> known for their imaginativeness, audacity, and their broad-gauge
> interests and competence, regardless of their positions in the
> hierarchy.[7]

While this viewpoint should not be carried to the extreme where
no attention is given to considerations of status and seniority, its
primary emphasis upon ability is most appropriate. The success of
any staff planning unit depends upon the wise selection of men and
women who have this "imaginativeness, audacity, and broad-gauge
interests and competence." The chief executive can do a great deal
by means of direction and guidance to insure that the right kinds
of people are chosen.

There is some variation in opinion among planners themselves on
the question of whether line experience is a necessary background
for a good staff planner.[8] Some agree with one spokesman that
"anyone who takes an important planning job and who has no experience as a line executive cannot understand what it takes to get
things done." Others, however, say that it is competence rather
than line experience which is the all-important need; they admit
that line experience can be useful, but it is not absolutely necessary.
Most planners have had some prior line experience, which is perhaps explainable by the fact that formalized attention to long-range
planning is very recent in origin. As time goes by and these units
become more widely established, it seems likely that the more relevant qualifications will prove a more important consideration than
the question of line management experience.

The ages of members of staff planning units are generally within
the bracket of 30 to 45 years. Very few interviewed were under
30,[9] which is perhaps explained by the fact that most staff planners are chosen in the light of some work experience as well as academic accomplishments. The reason for the apparent age ceiling of
45 (there were occasional exceptions) is not so obvious, and the
question requires special investigation.[10]

Most of the planners had advanced degrees from universities;
either in a technical subject associated with a product of their company or in economics or business administration. Once again, this
suggests the concentration upon competence rather than status and
seniority in selecting these men.

Informal relationships. Although a detailed examination of the informal relationships of staff planners among themselves and with others was well beyond the scope of this study, there are two general comments which can be made. Each reveals that staff planners are not in any sense "backroom boys"—individualists working independently.

Staff planners typically meet together for several discussion sessions each week. The meetings are characterized for the most part by flexibility and informality. Frequently there is no formal agenda, and a major purpose of such meetings is "to keep ideas rolling." In some companies these planners are prepared to allow an informal "bull session" to continue for a full afternoon if they believe it to be worthwhile; at other times they cut short a meeting if they feel it is not proving useful.

Some staff planners are also in frequent contact with others in the organization, both at top management and at operating levels. One point of particular note here is that the planners sometimes have access to confidential information, and they have to be discreet and careful not to betray confidences. An unwise move might easily result in a staff planner's being considered as an "informant" by men at the operating level. At the same time, however, this liaison relationship provides great opportunities to facilitate better planning at both the corporate and divisional levels. The nature of the relationships suggests the professional nature of a staff planner's job. It is a job which requires not only technical competence and behavioral skill but integrity as well.

———

PART IV

Conclusion

Chapter 12

Implications for Top Management

LONG-RANGE PLANNING IS ASSUMING INCREASING INTEREST
and importance for top management in today's world. As this book
has indicated, the subject has a vast number of implications for
management, and, in summary, we shall draw attention to a few
which are of special significance and speculate about some of the
possible consequences of future corporate long-range planning activities.

THE VALUE OF LONG-RANGE PLANNING

Long-range planning, in both its strategic and implementational
forms, deserves the most careful thought, study, and attention in all
large companies today, and in many medium-size and small companies as well. It is much more than an elegant phrase with which to
adorn a description of top management responsibilities. On the con-
trary, long-range planning can be of great practical value, and top
management should be fully aware of this fact.

Its value usually increases when a company introduces formal
organizational arrangements for systematizing planning. Systematizing enables the company to group together technical specialists
for the special purpose of working on long-range planning problems. It also insures that continuing attention is given to advanced
planning, which usually receives a higher priority than previously.

Like other activities, long-range planning has its pitfalls. There
are two in particular which top management should strive to avoid.
One is disassociation from long-range activities once arrangements
have been formalized. If the planning is to prove successful, top
management must give continuing and active attention to the work
being done. For example, it should give direction in the clarification of objectives and assumptions, as well as in the establishment
of task priorities. While some aspects of long-range planning may

193

appropriately be delegated, the responsibilities cannot be relinquished.

A second possible pitfall is placing too much reliance on statistically demonstrable conclusions. R. H. Roy refers to this danger as "the deification of numbers," [1] and it is particularly misleading in long-range planning because much of the statistical analysis is highly tentative. Qualitative factors are often much more important in strategic planning than quantitative factors, and the temptation to allow numbers to dominate planning decisions must constantly be resisted.

DIFFICULTIES OF MEASURING EFFECTIVENESS

Long-range planning is an activity which is immensely important and worthwhile, yet at the same time its value is very hard to "prove." Measurement of effectiveness is very difficult, and in fact companies have given very little attention so far to this matter.

The reason is not hard to find. Measurements of efficiency in most kinds of planning require comparisons of actual with planned performances, but with long-range planning companies are not very practical. This kind of plan by its very nature encompasses a long period of time, and therefore any final comparison of "actual" with "planned" will not be available for years. Furthermore, most such comparisons would be meaningless anyway, because of the updating and revision of the long-range plans which take place as time goes by. Thus a comparison of a company's current results with its planned five-year estimates is not likely to have much meaning, since the initial estimates have probably been altered a number of times to incorporate new information and new judgments.

Sometimes it is possible to make comparisons of "actual" and "planned" results on the basis of preliminary information available at the end of, say, one year. But this, too, has its difficulties, especially in strategic planning. In a short-period comparison, performance reflects the influence of cyclical movements, whereas the long-range plan is likely to have been developed on the assumption that short-term cyclic influences would balance out. Then, too, the fruits of a strategy may not become evident for several years, and the preliminary comparison may actually prove misleading. Thus, if a company is seeking to develop greater research competence in certain specified areas, the results may not become apparent for five or six years.

The subject of appraising long-range plans is still in its infancy. Most top management judgments about their value today are based upon subjective opinions which indicate either "approval" or "disapproval." [2] For the present, at least, top management and staff planners alike are prepared to assume that this kind of planning activity is worthwhile and that questions of measuring effectiveness can safely be left until later. They are more concerned with the development of better conceptual and technical methods for developing the long-range plans. And, in view of the tendency to "deify members," this is probably a good thing.

ADMINISTRATIVE EFFECTS OF LONG-RANGE PLANNING

The influences of long-range planning activities are manifold, and sometimes they spread to phases of a company's operations which appear to be far removed from long-range planning itself. Top management executives should be aware of and take account of these influences, and we will draw particular attention to three examples.

1. Effect on management performance. One consideration is the effect which long-range planning activities may have upon managerial performance in operating work. Special benefits may emerge as the result of association (direct or indirect) with long-range planning activities; however, there may be some adverse effects upon management performance as the result of some people's *not* being associated with the planning.

Sometimes the skills, experience, and understanding derived from long-range planning are transferable to other aspects of management which are not directly related to long-range planning. For instance, exposure to problems of long-range planning can give an executive a broader perspective on company problems and can thereby help him in overcoming some functional or departmental bias which has previously been a shortcoming in his managerial ability.

In earlier chapters of this book we observed that strategic long-range planning focuses upon those matters which are considered to be of central or strategic importance. This characteristic of analysis is sometimes carried over into other aspects of an executive's work. For example, in one company where a task force of line managers had participated in a long-range planning project, a top management executive subsequently made the following observation:

> I can see in our weekly manager meetings that there are some changing features in our discussions. The managers are, by and large, talking about more important things, while bringing up less frivolous matters.

Long-range planning is a thought-provoking activity, and one side-product of it is often the sparking of new ideas and the development of previously inchoate ideas. These ideas often have applicability in areas which have no apparent relationship with long-range planning.

2. Effect on caliber of executives. There are two important considerations bearing upon the caliber of executives which should be noted here. When an executive is co-opted to work on some aspects of a long-range planning project, top management frequently regards this as an intensive test of his capabilities and potential. It furnishes good firsthand evidence of abilities (or lack of them) in some areas which cannot be assessed directly on the basis of day-to-day operating performance, and thus it allows top management to add to its information about the executive.

The second important consideration is that a company which provides opportunities for participation in long-range planning activities is likely to attract men who are challenged by this kind of work and who are able to handle it. In other words, the situation becomes a beneficial circle for the company: The challenges which the company offers encourage the hiring and retaining of able men.

It is worth noting, too, that the converse appears to hold. Those companies which have not grown in recent years and which have no long-term growth objectives are apt to be bypassed by the very people best equipped to help them grow.[3] In this case it is a malevolent coterie which forms and impedes progress.

3. Effect on financial reputation. A third administrative effect of long-range planning deserves mention, even though it has perhaps less significance than the first two. It arises from the fact that banks, insurance companies, and other sources of capital are "invariably favorably impressed by organized and formalized long-range planning that is operated in a practical way." [4] If a company has documented its plans for the future in a thoughtful and thorough manner, potential sources of capital take cognizance of this fact. But of course this is helpful only as it supports an overall impression of sound and progressive management. Furthermore, a company should develop its plans with an eye to internal use, rather than external review. In this connection, it is again important to avoid the danger of overemphasis upon numbers.

LONG-RANGE PLANNING AND ITS EFFECTS UPON THE ECONOMY

Another factor which top management should be aware of is the influence which long-range planning activities may have upon elements of the economy. Top management's task in planning ahead is not simply an efficiency requirement; it also entails taking account of the company's public responsibilities. The influences can be observed if we look first at the effects which corporate long-range planning activities can have upon economic stability and then look at their impact upon economic growth.

1. Economic stability. Spokesmen for business sometimes like to say that management's increased attention to long-range planning is going to make a great contribution toward making the business cycle more stable. *The Wall Street Journal,* for example, has said: "It cannot be stressed too often that modern long-range industrial planning is a tremendous factor in making the economic situation in the United States more stable than it ever has been before." [5]

Many other examples of this kind could be cited. The belief is that the cumulative effect of long-range planning activities will lessen the fluctuation of business investment levels over time by making the investments more regular.

Actually, however, this is an oversimplified and overoptimistic view of things. A determination of the kind and extent of impact which long-range planning activities have upon cyclical stability is very difficult indeed. Even among economists there appears to be no clear consensus.

It is not feasible or desirable to dwell on the subject at great length here, but there are one or two observations which should be made. In the first place, attention to long-range planning causes some companies which operate in industries requiring long lead times for investments to give greater attention to leveling out their own investment programs. They are more likely to plan their investments on a noncyclical basis, and this means that their programs are not normally postponed in the face of a cyclical recession. Furthermore, they usually become more aware of opportunities for leveling investments in repair and maintenance, as well as in replacement schedules.

These factors indicate that attention to long-range planning is probably likely to insure that certain business investments continue. even at depressed stages in the business cycle, and, to this extent, it makes some contribution toward greater cyclical stability. When a very large company embarks upon or continues an investment program through the depths of a recession, this can have important reverberations in building business confidence throughout the economy. One example of this is a $1 billion expansion program announced by General Motors Corporation during the 1954 recession.[6]

However, there are also some aspects of undertaking long-range planning, and some effects from it, which apparently work against the regularizing of investment and therefore against cyclical stability.

Today's accelerated pace of technological change means that current best-practice techniques are more transient than ever. Because of this, one effect of long-range planning activities is to reveal that plant and equipment which are acquired or built ahead of time in anticipation of a business boom are more prone than ever to become obsolete before fulfilling their expected productive capabilities. Even the dictates of long-range planning, therefore, frequently recommend the continued concentration of investment in boom phases of the business cycle. (Obviously, this has the greatest pertinence to industries where investments require relatively short lead time.)

A second characteristic of today's economy has consequences for long-range planning which may discourage greater stability in the business cycle. It is that the complexity of industrial activity often requires investments of a "lumpy" nature. That is to say, major expansion may require a large unit investment spread over perhaps two or three years, but thereafter no comparable expansion program may be required for the next several years. The effect of long-range planning here, therefore, may not increase in the degree of regularization of investment.[7]

Third, and probably most important of all, there is overcapacity, which appears frequently to be aggravated rather than alleviated by formal attention to long-range planning. Where companies operate in industries which require heavy plant and equipment investments and long lead times, there are strong competitive pressures toward overexpansion. Examples of industries which have been plagued by overexpansion of this kind during recent years include the steel, the aircraft, the oil, and some parts of the electrical. In each case competitive expansion programs, drawn up as long-range plans, have subsequently led to industrial overcapacity, with the result that a great deal of expensive plant and equipment has lain idle or else has been operated at levels far below capacity.[8]

Thus in some circumstances the effect of long-range planning can be one which makes for disequilibrium, and this remains as a critical problem for top management to contend with in many large concerns. There is a necessity for finding ways to overcome the unbalancing effects without sacrificing any essential attributes of competitive enterprise.[9]

The effects which long-range planning activities have upon cyclical stability in the economy are complex and not well understood, as we have seen, and these comments are intended merely to suggest some of the considerations. The one thing that is clear is that the impact of long-range planning should *not* be assumed uncritically to promote economic stability.

2. Economic growth. The impact of long-range planning activities upon economic growth is much less controversial: The effect is generally one of facilitating it. There are several reasons why this is so.

One reason is the great advances made during recent years in developing business statistics. Information reported about the past and projections about the future have become more widely available and more reliable, which has encouraged management to raise its sights and to make firm commitments for long-term growth on the basis of such information.

The creative and innovative nature of many long-range plans suggests a second reason. These plans are concerned with the active promotion of change, and they make possible many of the complex projects that have become a feature of industry today. Without long-range planning many advances simply would not take place; seen in this light, it is an important mainspring in economic growth.

THE CHALLENGE TO "THINK GREATLY"

Long-range planning (especially the strategic variety) can encourage and assist top management to become more statesmanlike in its policy making. For top management has responsibilities not only to stockholders and employees, but also to business and society in general. Long-range planning provides a perspective to see this total concept of the company not only from within but also as a part of the whole economic, social, technological, and political environment.

This is not meant to sound like a call for business altruism. Rather, it is a recognition of the fact that long-range planning presents a special challenge to top management to "think greatly" about its activities. The challenge was well expressed by Alfred North Whitehead some three and a half decades ago when he noted that "the behavior of the community is largely dominated by the business mind" and then went on to say that "a great society is a society in which its men of business think greatly of their functions." [10] As companies more and more take a long-range view of things, they gain the opportunity to recognize the ways in which corporate interests and the interests of society harmonize.

Top management will find, during the years ahead, that long-range planning facilitates meeting the kind of challenges just described. In particular, we will see advances in the three areas to be discussed below, since these are significant examples of the broad-scale challenges which are already presenting themselves to top management.

1. Attention of companies to social wants. Many social critics have drawn attention to the fact that society today gives much higher priority to the satisfaction of private wants than it does to the fulfillment of social needs. Perhaps unfortunately, however, the subject is frequently raised in the context of politics, and consequently it becomes enmeshed in disputes about the extent of government intervention and political centralization that is desirable.

But this is not the only way of looking at the problem. It is entirely possible that, at least in some circumstances, a company's own long-term interests would be well served by more active efforts to satisfy social wants. There is no *a priori* reason why private companies must be limited to satisfying private wants, making no substantive contribution to alleviating social needs while maintaining their profit-seeking status. Neil W. Chamberlain hints at the type of developments which could take place when he says:

> If G.M. and G.E. were involved in the planning process to do something about our transportation mess, I am sure we would get a better solution than if they were left out. If U.S. Steel and Goodrich sought actively to collaborate with government in meeting the housing mess, I suspect we would get further faster.[11]

Some argue—and rightly—that relations between business and government in the United States are always somewhat strained and that collaboration of this kind is difficult to visualize. But top management should constantly be on the lookout for ways to improve the situation, rather than rejecting such a possibility in discouragement. Some excellent collaboration between business and government, and between companies, has been attained in technological areas, particularly those associated with defense, and there are other opportunities for achieving cooperation, which could prove beneficial both to individual companies and to society.

When Mary Parker Follett developed her ideas of coordination some 30 or more years ago, she pointed out that there is sometimes the opportunity for resolving conflicts in a manner which yields positive gains to both parties. She observed that this sort of resolution requires cooperation from both sides: One may lead, but the other must respond in kind or there will be no integration.[12] This concept is relevant to the subject at hand, because it suggests the importance of management's attitude in considering possibilities of the type described above. In the past top management has usually been suspicious of changes in social patterns brought about by the government. Perhaps the perspective gained from strategic long-range planning will help clarify possible areas of cooperation and as a result encourage top management to take the lead in exploring new possibilities of corporate and social advancement.

2. Attention of companies to supporting functions of products. In Chapter 3 we cited the example of some able long-range planning work that was carried on about 1910. At that time American Telephone and Telegraph Company had to decide whether it should rely upon a use-of-operator telephone system or proceed with the development of an automatic-dialing system. The telephone company's plans were determined by information about a supporting function (operators), and there are many companies today whose principal product lines depend heavily upon the availability or skill of supporting functions. Thus, the commercial aircraft industry is affected not only by technological advances in aircraft but also by the availability of adequate airport facilities and reliable traffic control systems. Or, to take another example, automobile sales in 25 or 30 years' time will be affected by such factors as the severity of traffic problems, the availability of city and community parking facilities, and the expense of providing home garage facilities for two- and three-car families.

A long-range planning viewpoint sometimes suggests that supporting functions may have an important effect upon sales of a company's product in the long run. In such circumstances it may be wise for the company to become active in the development of these supporting functions. It may pay the automobile companies, for example, to study the subject of quick-service parking facilities in cities and large towns. Or, again, it may pay them to review problems of traffic control and perhaps become engaged in promoting the development of equipment which will help speed the flow of traffic.

Developments of this kind again reflect a perspective of the company within a total environment, and they often reflect a harmony of interests for the individual company on the one hand and the community as a whole on the other. The supporting functions are on occasion social needs, and so in part this development is related to the discussion above.

3. Greater candor in company relations with society. A third development which seems likely to emerge from long-range planning is an increase in candor displayed by management in its relation with society. There will be a closer identification of company interests with the interests of society, and so there will be less tendency to act in an opportunistic or exploitative manner.

This type of change can be illustrated by the example of the cigarette industry, in which short-term corporate interests appear to override long-range overall interests. The cigarette industry today faces some extremely difficult problems in relation to the potential health hazards of cigarettes. Exactly how serious these health hazards are in fact is uncertain at this time, but certainly the cigarette companies have been hurt very badly since evidence (most notably in the Surgeon-General's report on smoking) has proved positively that such hazards do exist. The companies have heavy investments in the cigarette industry, and absolutely definitive and incontrovertible proof that cigarettes cause lung cancer has been an enormously costly blow. It does not follow, however, that the difficulties can be combated and overcome by heavy doses of public relations. Yet this is the policy which a number of companies in the industry have adopted and continue to adopt. A longer-range perspective suggests that this is indeed a mistaken policy. Not only is it inconsistent with the interests of society, but it is not really consistent with the interests of these companies themselves. The threat of lung cancer will not be overcome by a great many declarations that "all is well." [13] Since the health hazards have been proved to be very real, the companies would be in a better position if they, say, concentrated upon developing blends which do not have these health hazards.

*   *   *

The remarkable growth in attention to long-range planning during recent years has had a profound effect upon the nature of top management's job. The primary role of top management has evolved through a number of different stages: from owner, to innovator, to entrepreneur, to organizer, and, most recently, to administrator. The emphasis upon long-range planning today suggests that the primary role is changing from administrator to anticipator, and we may expect this change to continue during the years ahead. The significance of this change is illustrated by the fact that many large companies have sought to lighten the administrative responsibilities of their top management executives over the last few years so that they can devote more time to projects associated with long-range planning.

"The manager of tomorrow," Peter Drucker wrote in 1954, "will have to be able to relate his product and industry to the total environment, to find what is significant in it and to take it into account in his decisions and actions. And increasingly the field of vision of tomorrow's manager will have to take in developments outside his own market and his own country." [14]

The requirements of "the manager of tomorrow," of whom Drucker wrote ten years ago, are the requirements of the top management executives of today if the task of strategic long-range planning is to be done effectively. Broad-gauged thinking is a prerequisite for "the manager of today" as he assumes his newly emerging role of anticipator. It is certain that top management's effectiveness in the coming decades depends greatly upon its ability to develop long-range strategies which are creative and imaginative and at the same time logical and sound.

Appendix

NOTE: The case descriptions contained in this appendix report on some aspects of long-range planning activities in two large divisions of the General Electric Company. The cases do not purport to present a full account of all the long-range planning undertakings in these divisions. Long-range planning is a complex subject which is affected by many factors rooted in the history and character of each company; consequently it is quite impossible to cover the subject exhaustively in case studies of this kind.

The case materials have been reviewed and approved for inclusion in this book by persons associated with each of the departments. I, however, bear sole responsibility for their treatment and interpretation.

B. W. S.

General Electric Company

(A)

YOU MUST APPRECIATE AT ONCE THAT GENERAL ELECTRIC IS AN atypical organization in almost every way." A representative of General Electric's Management Consultation Services component made this observation when describing some features of his company's approach to long-range planning. He continued:

> Ours is a company which affects the livelihood, directly or indirectly, of one out of every 30 people in the United States. We feel, therefore, that the job of planning ahead is not simply a requirement for efficiency but is also a moral responsibility. When a company like this one is going to try and shape the future, it has a moral responsibility to take careful cognizance of the factors involved. Consequently, our entire approach to professional management has been developed to incorporate a long-range point of view.

The General Electric Company is by far the largest electrical manufacturing company in the world. It ranks fifth on the list of largest corporations in the United States, and its 1964 sales volume was approaching the $5 billion level. The company was composed of approximately 100 separate product businesses, with individual sales volumes ranging anywhere from $5 million to $500 million annually.

Every company product had its base in "the fundamental business of creating and serving the market for equipment to make, transmit, distribute, and use electric power." [1] The electrical industry had expanded in so many directions, however, that in 1963 General Electric was considered to be an extremely diversified company. Specifically, it produced—

> diverse electrical end products and components for defense, industry, commerce, and the home, and also covers a wide range of business operations from raw material processing, through fabrication and manufacture, to widespread distribution, installation, and product-servicing units on both a national and an international scale.[2]

General Electric had never failed to earn a profit and had paid a dividend every year since 1899. The company's sales, profit, and dividend records for selected years during its history are shown in Exhibit 1.

NOTE: Unless otherwise indicated by footnote, quotations in this case study have been drawn from General Electric Company sources.

EXHIBIT 1

GENERAL ELECTRIC COMPANY

Sales, Earnings, and Dividend Records

(For selected years)

(Millions of dollars)

Year	Sales	Net Income	Net Income As Percentage Of Sales	Cash Dividend On Common Stock
1892	11.7	3.0	25.5	2.0
1900	28.8	6.0	20.9	1.7
1910	71.5	10.9	15.2	5.2
1915	85.5	11.7	13.7	8.1
1920	275.8	22.1	8.0	16.1
1925	290.3	38.6	13.3	25.1
1930	376.2	57.5	15.3	46.2
1933	136.6	13.4	9.8	11.5
1935	208.7	27.8	13.3	20.2
1940	411.9	56.2	13.6	53.3
1943	1,459.9	48.6	3.3	40.3
1945	1,467.2	58.4	4.0	46.1
1948	1,865.6	136.3	7.3	51.4
1950	2,233.8	179.7	8.0	97.1
1952	2,993.4	164.9	5.5	85.9
1955	3,463.7	208.9	6.0	145.9
1956	4,090.0	213.8	5.2	172.4
1957	4,335.7	247.9	5.7	173.2
1958	4,120.8	242.9	5.9	173.7
1959	4,349.5	280.2	6.4	174.3
1960	4,197.5	200.1	4.8	175.5
1961	4,456.8	242.1	5.4	176.4
1962	4,792.7	265.8	5.5	177.5

SOURCE: General Electric Company Annual Reports.

COMPANY HISTORY

General Electric was formed in 1892 as the result of a merger of two leading electrical companies. In 1900 the new General Electric Company had a sales volume of $28 million, and in the following 20 years the company increased this dollar volume tenfold, to $285 million.

It can easily be seen that during these early years General Electric rode a wave of rapid expansion in a spectacular growth industry. Consequently, as one historian puts it, "the forging of policies was hard put to catch up with the brilliancy of invention." [3] The company developed a centralized organization structure for all products and all functions. In common with many other growth companies of the period, General Electric's progress was guided by a few key personalities.

Most of the planning done during this period which we might today designate long range was informal and intuitive. One example from General Electric's early history provides an illustration of this. In the early 1900's General Electric was concluding an agreement valued at $1 million for patent rights on a new turbine engine. However, before the agreement was signed, its president, Edwin W. Rice, insisted on a clause which permitted the company to use these turbines on ships, if ships were electrically run.

There was no formal blueprint drawn up which showed General Electric's intention to build turbines for ships. As a matter of fact, most electrical engineers at this time were dismissing as impossible the idea of driving an ocean liner by electricity. The generating plant needed would be so large as to sink the ship, they said.

Fifteen years later, however, the value of the clause became apparent, and in fact it played a leading part in the destiny of General Electric. [4]

Between 1920 and 1930 the company's dollar sales volume grew a further 30 per cent, reaching $376 million. During this period General Electric remained predominantly a centralized organization, although certain divisions were given increased independent authority.

Then in 1929 a special meeting was held, attended by approximately 200 of General Electric's top managers, whose purpose was to consider a long-term organization plan to accommodate the prospective size and character of General Electric as foreseen at that time. The dominant theme of the meeting was decentralization, and looking back in retrospect, General Electric regards this conference as the forerunner of many of the ideas later incorporated in its postwar reorganization. Excerpts from the presentation to this meeting by Charles E. Wilson (later to become president of General Electric) are reproduced in Exhibit 2.

Shortly after this meeting took place, however, the Great Depression of the 1930's took charge of the economy. It halted General Electric's growth pattern for a decade: In 1939 the sales volume ($342 million) remained lower than the peak achieved in 1930. During this period of continued depression, action was delayed on the planned decentralization.

THE PRECIPITATION OF CHANGE

Then came World War II and with it a huge increase in demand for electrical products of all descriptions. By 1943 the General Electric Com-

EXHIBIT 2

GENERAL ELECTRIC COMPANY

Excerpts from Statement by C. E. Wilson
on Desirability of Decentralization, 1929

The outstanding advantages of the vertical or decentralized form of organization are simplicity, clear definition of duties and responsibilities, and the ease of securing action and results. We recommend:

First, a more complete decentralization of those departments which are now partly decentralized; and
Second, the adoption of vertical or decentralized type to the extent that it is practicable by other departments now operating under the functional or centralized type of organization. . . .

The multiplicity of problems attendant upon the rapid and widely diversified expansion of the company's business makes it impossible for those heading the functional form of organization to know, as they should know, the distinctive and special problems which are inevitably involved in the many different lines of our endeavor. . . .

We believe that the ideal form of organization for departments which serve, in the main, one or perhaps two or three classes of customers, and whose products are of the same general nature, is that headed by a vice president or general manager who would have full responsibility for the "business." This officer should have full responsibility and final authority in engineering, manufacturing, and sales. The highly specialized general departments . . . are still necessary, but their function should be to study, to guide, and to educate. . . .

We believe there are departments which would be greatly benefited by the adoption of a vertical plan. These departments are in competition with many small concerns who prosper and who, in the aggregate, obtain a large proportion of the available business because they are able to move quickly—are faster in new development—more agile in meeting sales problems and more flexible in their sales policies.

SOURCE: General Electric Company records.

---

pany's sales volume had skyrocketed to $1.37 billion, which represented a fourfold increase in four years.

It seemed clear that its volume of business in the postwar era would continue at a level much greater than it had been before the war. With this in mind, the company inaugurated an intensive study of "the new problems of organizing and managing such a large and rapidly growing enterprise." Direction of this study, which began in 1943, was assigned to Ralph J. Cordiner, at that time vice president and assistant to the president.

The operational aim of this study soon became apparent to Mr. Cordiner and his committee. It required successfully transforming General Electric from a predominantly centralized organization into one which was highly decentralized. In explanation of why this change was necessary, Mr. Cordiner has said:

> From the beginning of the study, it was apparent that the company was going to require increasingly better planning, greater flexibility, and faster, more informed decisions than was possible under the highly centralized organization structure, which was suited for earlier and different conditions.[5]

The program of implementation developed by Mr. Cordiner and his committee was put into operation eight years later—in 1951. Mr. Cordiner had become president in 1950 and so presided over the change in structure, which was carried out in gradual steps over a period of five years.

The anticipated expansion did in fact take place, as can be seen from the financial data in Exhibit 1. The organizational changes were thus carried out while the company was growing rapidly and enjoying great prosperity.

The company continues optimistic about its prospects for future growth. The long-term forecasts for the use of electricity indicated a doubling within the following eight to ten years. In the past, this measure had proved to be the most reliable gauge of growth prospects.

THE NEW ORGANIZATION STRUCTURE

General Electric's philosophy and implementation of decentralized management was a basic part of its approach to long-range planning. The decentralized organization structure had been developed with specific recognition of the need for "continuing, competent attention to the long-range future."

In Mr. Cordiner's words, the new decentralized organization structure hinged closely on the concept that—

> The "Manager," and especially the Chief Executive (or the General Manager of a Business), must deliberately free up and devote more man-hours of his personal, normal working time to planning and organizing, as distinct from operating.[6]

The new organization structure provided for three basic kinds of responsibility: executive work, services work, and operating work. A

EXECUTIVE OFFICE:
(To advise and assist the
president in the overall
leadership of the company)

SERVICE COMPONENTS:
(To advise and serve the
Executive Office, other
Service Components, and
provide functional service
and appraisal throughout
the company)

OPERATING COMPONENTS:
(To be responsible and
accountable for the successful
conduct of its business within
the framework of the overall
company objectives)

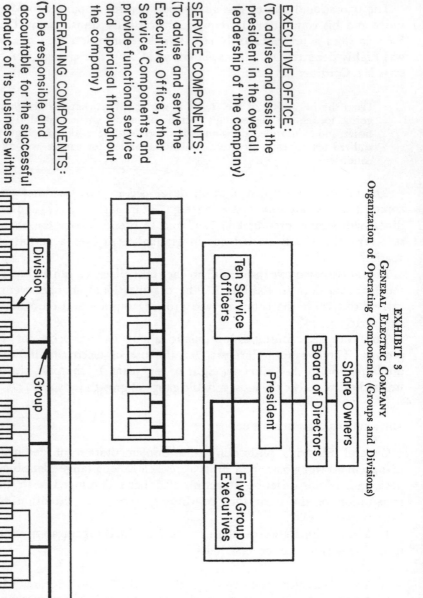

EXHIBIT 3
GENERAL ELECTRIC COMPANY
Organization of Operating Components (Groups and Divisions)

Share Owners

Board of Directors

President

Ten Service
Officers

Five Group
Executives

Departments

Division

Group

schematic organization chart showing these various relationships is reproduced in Exhibit 3.

1. *Executive work.* Executive work in 1962 was organized as the responsibility of members of General Electric's Executive Office, composed of the president, the chairman of the board, the five "group executives," and the ten "service officers."

The responsibility of the members of the Executive Office was to give—

> specific and adequate time and thought to matters concerning company-wide, broad-gauge objectives, policies, and plans of the company as a whole and for appraisal of overall results in the short-term and long-term balanced best interest of customers, share owners, employees, suppliers, and the public.

Under this concept of the Executive Office, each group executive and services officer was required to organize his other work so as to be able to devote about 20 per cent of his time to working as a member of the Executive Office. In his other work the group executive was required to represent the president in business dealings and relationships with the heads of reporting divisions, while the services officer was responsible for managing his particular services component.

The group executives did not constitute a separate layer of management in the General Electric Company. Instead, their role was explained in these terms:

> They are an extension of the mind and arms of the president, working closely with him, familiar with his aims, plans, and organization concepts; and able to speak for him and in his stead in interpreting these to the divisional and departmental operating managers within their respective groups.

The *Position Guide* which outlined the work required of group executives stressed the need for preponderant attention to long-range considerations. An excerpt from this *Position Guide* reads as follows:

> Preponderant attention must be given to long-range rather than short-range factors, plans, problems, and analyses. Normally, therefore, approximately three-quarters of the group executive's work will deal with long-range affairs of both the group components and of similar responsibilities as a member of the Executive Office, in order to attain the goals of the company as a whole.

The purposes of the Executive Office, as stated by the General Electric Company, are set out in Exhibit 4.

2. *Services work.* The services components as of 1961 were established

EXHIBIT 4

GENERAL ELECTRIC COMPANY

Purposes of the Executive Office

1. Provide for adequate companywide, long-range business planning;
2. Provide for adequate thought, research, and discussion leading to wise, long-range company policy formulation and adoption;
3. Effectuate decentralization of operating decision making to the general managers and functional managers of operating components;
4. Provide for adequate measuring and appraisal of performance with thorough study of both favorable and unfavorable deviations of achieved results from plans, forecasts, schedules, and budgets;
5. Promote individual self-development on the part of all employees, and particularly on the part of highly skilled, professional individual contributors and professional managers—making companywide promotional opportunities available to all who prove themselves competent in their present job and who seek and earn promotions;
6. Take full advantage of all resources and of all business opportunities;
7. Achieve "business statesmanship" so that the General Electric Company will be, and will be known to be, a good "corporate citizen" demonstrating outstanding performance in productivity, profitability, service, and leadership.

SOURCE: General Electric Company records.

---

at the corporate level of General Electric in the following major business functional areas:

- Accounting.
- Engineering.
- Legal and Corporate.
- Management Consultation.
- Manufacturing.
- Marketing.
- Public Relations.
- Employee and Plant Community Relations.
- Treasury.
- Research.

These components were charged with "the responsibility, through research and teaching and through acting as a clearinghouse for specialized knowledge, for providing all components with most advanced knowledge of principles and practices in all functional fields; and for doing so better and faster than individual operating departments could do, or could afford to do, each for itself. Thus the relatively small, competitive, hard-hitting teams of managers of distinct departmental businesses can have the advantages of large company know-how in all functional areas."

This General Electric concept of services work was said to be a direct outgrowth of the long and successful progress made by the company with research work in the physical sciences. The conviction was held that an approach similar to that used in uncovering new knowledge about materials and processes would also pay off in learning how to accomplish the work of all basic functions of the business more effectively.

Special attention was also given by executives to the way in which services work was oriented toward the future. This characteristic was contrasted with "other more familiar concepts of so-called 'staff work.'"

The Management Consultation Services component provides an example of the way in which a services component is organized. This division is charged with "the research and teaching of principles of managing and organizing," and was organized into three components, as follows:

> a. *Management Research Service.* This component was established for the investigation and analysis of basic theory with regard to managing and with regard to the nature of the social order in which modern business exists. It thus came into contact with such subjects as "the different phases of industrial evolution," "future value systems," and "the legitimacy of large corporations." Only about one book out of every six in the component's library was concerned specifically with a business topic.
>
> b. *Operations Research and Synthesis Consulting Service.* This component undertook the research and teaching of conceptual approaches to systematic and rational business decision making. The component studied and investigated patterns and situations in business where tools of operations research might be usefully applied.
>
> c. *Organization Consulting Service.* This component was responsible for research and teaching in the areas of organization planning and procedures. It frequently carried out special studies analyzing some aspects of the work of a manager, and in 1960 a senior man in this component was a member of a task force which produced a report on business planning.

3. *Operating work.* According to the General Electric Company, "Operating managers are responsible principally for profitable execution of objectives and policies in their particular component operating business and have complete accountability for performance and profit."

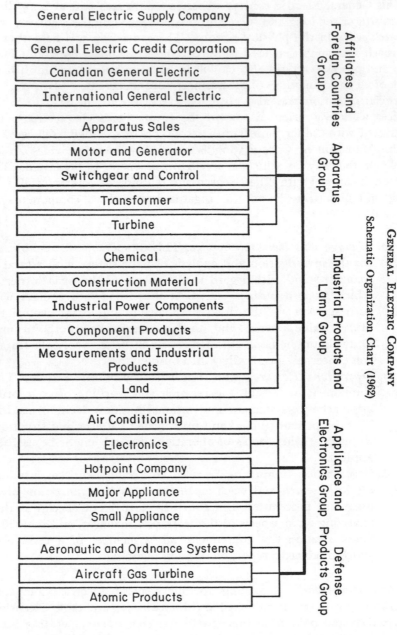

General Electric Supply Company

General Electric Credit Corporation
Canadian General Electric
International General Electric

Apparatus Sales
Motor and Generator
Switchgear and Control
Transformer
Turbine

Chemical
Construction Material
Industrial Power Components
Component Products
Measurements and Industrial Products
Land

Air Conditioning
Electronics
Hotpoint Company
Major Appliance
Small Appliance

Aeronautic and Ordnance Systems
Aircraft Gas Turbine
Atomic Products

Affiliates and Foreign Countries Group

Apparatus Group

Industrial Products and Lamp Group

Appliance and Electronics Group

Defense Products Group

EXHIBIT 5
GENERAL ELECTRIC COMPANY
Schematic Organization Chart (1962)

SOURCE: General Electric Company Records

Approximately 98 per cent of the company's total number of employees worked in the operating components. Organizationally, the five major groups were divided into more than 20 operating divisions and approximately 100 operating departments. The organization structure of operating components is shown in outline form in Exhibit 5.

The individual business components (departments) were established in accordance with these broad requirements:

- Each should represent an identifiable and distinct product, service, or geographic business entity.
- Each should have a foreseeable sales volume sufficient to justify its own physical facilities and to permit and support staffing with competent managers within two or three years of establishment.
- Each should have access to and responsibility for all basic elements essential to its performance and success.
- Each should have its own distinct, identifiable market or markets.

The division general manager was required to think "essentially for the whole family of businesses included in the division to which he is assigned, in terms of *long-range* objectives, policies, plans, budgets, and schedules."

The department general manager had responsibilities of a similar nature within a departmental framework:

> Determine, within company policy, the long-range objectives, policies, plans, programs, schedules, budgets, and other accountability factors for the long-term successful conduct of the business of the department.

The personal responsibility in each case was declared to be something which could not be delegated.

THE CONCEPTUAL APPROACH TO PLANNING

As a direct result of this decentralized organization structure's being implemented, the work of the manager had received detailed analysis and attention in General Electric during the past dozen years. Numerous task force assignments within the services components had investigated phases of the subject, and the company had developed a detailed conceptual approach to the job of managing, which was described as: "[the integration of] the employees, the materials, the machines, and the money which make up the human and material resources from which the objectives of the enterprise may be achieved."

The company viewed the subject of "managing" as including four separate but interdependent elements. In other words, these elements were distinct in concept, but "the successful doing of each is ultimately dependent upon the degree of perfection achieved simultaneously in the others." The work elements are:

1. *Planning*—to determine what objectives should be established to utilize the human and material resources of the enterprise, including policies and plans for the business.
2. *Organizing*—to determine how the human and material resources of the enterprise are to be utilized in a clear, well-classified organization structure, manned by competent individuals with adequate compensation and incentives.
3. *Integrating*—to integrate and synchronize the human resources to obtain most effective utilization of men, materials, machines, and money—the resources of the business.
4. *Measuring*—to evolve standards, to devise measuring mechanisms to analyze progress and performance.

Through various internal publications General Electric also made explicit several underlying assumptions which affected its analysis of "planning" as one of the elements of "managing." In the first place, the true starting point from which managers may plan was said to be a "legitimacy of purpose." This legitimacy was described as flowing from the common purposes of both leaders and followers. The common purposes stemmed from the fact that the economy is built on the framework of a free market, and therefore all members of society have a common status as individual customers in the marketplace.

Second, the idea of planning was described as based on man's assumption that even though the future is uncertain he can do something to make it better than it would otherwise be. The company did not agree with the theory that the future is altogether too unpredictable for long-range planning to be of any use.

Third, the concept of "management by exception" was extended into a broader area of consideration. General Electric was said to hold that the manager's job included the need to match the new complexities which are being brought by unfolding science, with patterns of simplicity among such complexities. The task of planning was essentially to reveal and use such patterns, so that the job of managing in the complex world of today and tomorrow would still be manageable.

Fourth, the company saw planning as a creative concept. "Purposeful managers need to develop the capacity to influence rather than merely adapt to the business environment," said one company paper.

Fifth, effective planning required a long-range point of view. Mr. Cordiner, chairman of the company, had made this point explicit in a speech, saying: "[Business planning's] final validity depends on the long-range viewpoint which today's manager must develop as a habit of mind." [7]

ANALYSIS OF PLANNING

In analyzing its concepts of "planning" in detail, the General Electric Company subdivided the subject into six constituent parts, or elements, as follows:

1. Determining objectives.
2. Establishing policies.
3. Formulating plans.
4. Making known the objectives, policies, plans, and standards.
5. Readjusting continually the work of planning.
6. Effectuating the planning work and progress.

The company also prepared an outline statement which described the major characteristics of these constituent parts; this statement is reproduced in Exhibit 6. Several of the concepts mentioned in this statement have special relevance to a study of long-range planning activities. They are therefore described in more detail below.

1. Objectives. Companywide objectives were described by General Electric as—

> expressions of the long-term goals which are in the balanced best interest of all persons and all groups of persons who contribute to and who benefit from the company's total output of goods and services.

The "persons" and "groups of persons" include:

- Customers.
- Share owners.
- Employees.
- Suppliers and distributors.
- The public.
- Governmental agencies, as representatives of the public.

General Electric formulated and published a statement of its corporate objectives. These objectives were given in ten paragraphs, and they

EXHIBIT 6

GENERAL ELECTRIC COMPANY

The Planning Elements of the Work of a Professional Manager

1. *Determining Objectives*
   - Making sharp, clear analyses of past and present trends.
   - Thinking ahead—making sound, practical forecasts.
   - Anticipating, rather than merely forecasting, so as to make and not simply meet the next situation with perception, imagination, courage, and faith; looking to the future hopefully, constructively, and creatively; combining originality and boldness with capacity for thinking clearly under pressure so as to take full advantage of all opportunities and avoid costly mistakes.
   - Choosing the best from possible alternatives, considering both long- and short-range advantages and disadvantages.
   - Selecting and stating optimistic, difficult goals for the component, or the whole enterprise being managed, in terms both of service to be rendered and profits to be earned and of the inseparable relationship between them.
   - Avoiding confusion, rigidity, stagnation; accepting change, flexibility, and progress; and looking to the future creatively and constructively.
2. *Establishing Policies*
   - Developing, formulating, and affirming sound policies, reflecting broad understanding of human values and keeping good perspective and balance between long- and short-range goals, as well as between each job and component and the whole enterprise being managed.
   - Determining priorities and maintaining realistic balance among specific objectives, recognizing that conflicts among overall interests are normal from time to time.
   - Anticipating obstacles or difficulties to be encountered, and requiring persistence and confidence in selecting the best practical steps to overcome them.
   - Expecting high standards of performance from self and all associates.
   - Expressing policies—and their factual background—so as to secure acceptance loyally within, and understandingly without, the component, or enterprise, being managed.
3. *Formulating Plans (Including Schedules); and Standards of Performance*
   - Finding the right way by orderly research, a factual approach, and by analyzing problems resourcefully, intelligently, and aggressively; assembling and presenting adequate facts so that they may be available to all concerned, in advance, as a basis for making reasoned decisions—coolly, impersonally, objectively.
   - Selecting and stating tasks to accomplish objectives.
   - Determining programs, including time schedules, and developing patterns of objectives and work of the business which are clear enough to facilitate accurate visualization and understanding participation by all employees.
   - Expressing programs in budgets for—
   - Manpower-managerial, other professional, and other.

EXHIBIT 6

Concluded

- Facilities and equipment.
- Operations—sales and income, outgo and expenses, net profit, and return on investments.
- Cash and financing, including new money required.
- Making definite development plans for individual managerial, professional, and other associates.
- Developing and expressing factors, units, and standards for measuring performance, of individuals and of components; establishing valid criteria to assess significance of accomplishment and growth.

4. *Making Known the Objectives, Policies, Plans, and Standards*
   - To all those involved or concerned with their performance.
5. *Using Results of Measuring to Readjust Continually the Work of Planning*
   - Of objectives, policies, plans, schedules, and standards.
6. *Exercising Judgment and Making Reasoned, Objective, and Timely Decisions to Effectuate the Planning Work and Progress*
   - Taking reasonable risks confidently, competitively, courageously, and on own responsibility, on basis of facts available, choosing wisely from among possible alternatives as responsibility and need for decision arise.

SOURCE: General Electric Company records.

---

sought to outline the purpose of the company's existence. The statement is reproduced in Exhibit 7.

The manager of each division, department, and successively smaller component within the company was responsible for seeing that objectives were also established for his component. These objectives had to be consistent with previously established companywide goals and with the goals of larger components of which his component was a part. Explaining this requirement, a company publication declared:

> This stepwise interpretation and detailing of objectives transform the broad-gauge, long-term, companywide objectives into specific objectives for each component, hammered out against the hard facts of the particular competitive business situation in which that component operates.

In addition to this general statement of objectives, General Electric also developed a list of eight "key result areas." These, according to one executive, might be called the "operational exemplification" of the general statement of objectives. Each was considered to be of such importance that—

continued failure in any one area would prevent the attainment of mana-

EXHIBIT 7

GENERAL ELECTRIC COMPANY

Statement of Objectives

1. To carry on a diversified, growing, and profitable worldwide manufacturing business in electrical apparatus, appliances, and supplies, and in related materials, products, systems, and services for industry, commerce, agriculture, government, the community, and the home.
2. To lead in research in all fields of science and in all areas of work relating to the business, including managing as a distinct and a professional kind of work, so as to assure a constant flow of new knowledge and of resultant useful and valuable new products, processes, services, methods and organizational patterns and relationships; and to make real the company theme that "Progress Is Our Most Important Product."
3. To operate each business venture to achieve its own favorable customer acceptance and profitable results; especially by planning the product line or service through decentralized operating management, on the basis of continuing research as to markets, customers, distribution channels, and competition, and as to product or service features, styling, price range, and performance for the end user, taking appropriate business risks to meet changing customer needs and to offer customers timely choice in product and service availability and desirability.
4. To design, make, and market all company products and services with good quality and with inherent customer value, at fair prices for such quality and value.
5. To build public confidence and continuing friendly feeling for products and services bearing the company's name and brands through sound, competitive advertising, promotion, selling, service, and personal contacts.
6. To provide good jobs, wages, working conditions, work satisfactions, and opportunities for advancement conducive of most productive performance and also the stablest possible employment, all in exchange for loyalty, initiative, skill, care, effort, attendance, and teamwork on the part of employees— the contributions of individual employees that result in "value to the company" and for which the employee is being paid.
7. To manage the enterprise for continuity and flow of progress, growth, profit, and public service through systematic selection and development of competent managerial personnel for effective leadership through persuasive managerial planning, organizing, integrating, and measuring for best utilization of both the human and material resources of the business; using a clear and soundly designed organization structure, and clearly expressed objectives and policies, as a vehicle for freeing the abilities, capacities, resourcefulness, and initiative of all managers, other professional workers, and all employees for dynamic individual efforts and teamwork, encouraged by incentives proportionate to responsibilities, risks, and results.
8. To attract and retain investor capital in amounts adequate to finance the enterprise successfully through attractive returns as a continuing incentive for wide investor participation and support; securing such returns through sound business and economic research, forecasting, planning, cost management, and effectively scheduled turnover of all assets of the enterprise.

EXHIBIT 7

Concluded

9. To cooperate both with suppliers and with distributors, contractors, and others facilitating distribution, installation, and servicing of company products, so that company efforts are constructively integrated with theirs for mutually effective public service and competitive, profitable progress.

10. To adapt company policies, products, services, facilities, plans, and schedules to meet continuously, progressively, foresightedly, imaginatively, and voluntarily the social, civic, and economic responsibilities commensurate with the opportunities afforded by the size, success, and nature of the business and of public confidence in it as a corporate enterprise.

SOURCE: General Electric Company records.

---

gerial responsibility for advancing General Electric as a leader in a strong competitive economy, even though the results in all other key result areas are good.

The eight key result areas are listed in Exhibit 8.

2. Policies. Policies were viewed as being expressions of common interests which company (or component) leaders agreed upon as being the best way of reaching the chosen objectives. They were "road maps" which provided subordinate managers and individual contributors with understanding of the thinking behind proposed courses of action.

Policies, like objectives, were required to be set out in writing, to insure the maximum possible clarity.

3. Formulating plans. This was the stage in the planning process where complex objectives and policies needed to be broken down into specific task assignments for individuals or groups. The company held that these plans should be expressed in quantitative terms, and that they should cover:

- Manpower.
- Facilities and equipment.
- Operations.
- Cash and financing.

In formulating plans General Electric placed special stress upon manpower planning. Mr. Cordiner emphasized this in a speech, when he said: "Not customers, not products, not plants, not money, but MANAGERS may be the limit of General Electric's growth."

Harold F. Smiddy, vice president of Management Consultation Services,

EXHIBIT 8

GENERAL ELECTRIC COMPANY

Key Result Areas

1. Profitability.
2. Market position.
3. Productivity, or the effective utilization of human, capital, and material resources.
4. Product leadership.
5. Personnel development.
6. Employee attitudes.
7. Public responsibility.
8. Balance between short-range and long-range goals.

SOURCE: General Electric Company records.

---

described this phase of General Electric's planning as having three distinct, though interlocked, parts:

> *a. Long-range* Manager Manpower Planning; with a time span of anticipation and planning of at least five years, based on the required organization structure for the component, or business, not as it is today but as it will need to be to cope with then-anticipated conditions.
>
> *b. Short-range* Manager Manpower Planning; focusing on specific needs of the particular component for the 18 months next ahead; to provide for orderly filling of vacancies and for proper promotion and placement of men, companywide as well as in each decentralized component.
>
> *c. Planning for Continuity of Managerial Leadership,* in a sound organization structure; the integrating and measuring phase of the whole Manager Manpower Planning process.[8]

4. Communication. Speaking of the importance of communication in the planning process, the company said in one of its publications: "In order for the work of planning to be effective, details must be communicated so that those concerned know how their work fits into the total team operation."

5. Flexibility. General Electric also stressed the need for building flexibility into plans. Plans need to be changeable as occasions demand, said the company, because the conditions affecting the work of managing are dynamic and are themselves always changing. It explained further that continuous feedback could help in making whatever adjustments might be necessary to keep the whole operation in balance and going in the right direction:

In growing businesses, managers will be continually reviewing and reappraising results achieved, and then replanning both in the light of results achieved as shown by the measurements, and of probable future needs as indicated by the social-economic situation.

DEPARTMENTAL PLANNING

"You can see that we don't just accept the notion that 'planning' and 'doing' ought to be separated," said an executive with the Management Consultation Services, as he discussed the planning required at the department level in General Electric. "Planning, both short- and long-range, needs the special skills and knowledge which can only be found at the operating level," he said. "This becomes even more true as business becomes more complex. We think that our experience with decentralized management has shown conclusively that planning is done more effectively at the operating level than at headquarters."

General Electric's spokesman drew attention to two previously unmentioned areas in which the departments were called upon to make long-range plans. First, there was the requirement that each department make explicit, quantitative, long-range planning schedules. These plans involved commitment to five years, and estimates for ten years, and included sales volume and net earnings estimates, product development plans, and plant and equipment plans. The plans took the form of rolling forecasts which were reviewed and extended each year.

Under the company's decentralized management structure, the department's results were measured on ability to reach the goals which it had established itself, with the concurrence of its division general manager and group executive.

Second, each one of the company's individual businesses (departments) was required by company policy to prepare for submission to the Executive Office a written *Business Charter*. Such a Charter needed to be reviewed, and revised as necessary, each year. It was expected to define: (1) The purposes of the particular business in relation to the company as a whole. (2) The scope of operations within the particular business.

By insisting upon written Charters, the company believed it could develop a clear understanding of spheres of responsibility and consequently could minimize waste, overlapping, or gaps in assignment. Furthermore, it helped the Executive Office in ascertaining internal consistency with the broader objectives of the whole company.

General Electric Company

(B)

Department "X"

ARTHUR WOOD AND WILLIAM SCOFIELD WERE DISCUSSING THE progress made on a project which they called the "Integrated Planning Study." This was a study being undertaken in Department X, a decentralized business component of the General Electric Company. The two men were attached to the Operations Research and Synthesis section of this department and had been assigned responsibility for the project.

"We feel we have made quite substantial progress, all things considered," said Mr. Wood. "Of course, this doesn't mean that we have in final form a complete business plan. We are far from that. We have not even reached 'the end of the beginning' in this project. But we have made progress. For example, I can see in our weekly manager meetings that there are some changing features in our discussions. The managers are, by and large, talking about more important things, while bringing up less frivolous and trifling matters."

Mr. Scofield supported this analysis. "We are still banging our heads on a good number of problems," he said, "and for the last four or five months the project has been stalled because of special circumstances. But the planning documents which we have prepared as we have gone along will testify as to the progress made. We are also confident that the project will soon be rolling forward once again."

INFORMATION ABOUT DEPARTMENT X

The General Electric Company was organized into approximately 100 separate departments, each of which was managed along the lines of an independent business enterprise in accordance with the company's philosophy of management decentralization. [See General Electric Company (A) for a description of this approach to management.]

The annual sales volume of Department X has exceeded $50 million in recent years. It manufactured and sold specialized industrial machinery. The products required a high degree of engineering skill and were usually produced on an order basis.

Chief competitive factors were usually price, delivery time, and capability of design. In addition, the customer invariably demanded follow-up service for the life of the equipment. Salesmen were required to be trained engineers, and most sales were the result of continuing contact with potential customers over a period of many months.

226

Historically, cyclical movements in the economy seriously affected the level of production in Department X. The job of planning for these cyclical changes was becoming more difficult each year because of increasingly long production lead times. In 1962 it was taking up to three or four years to convert an idea from the drawing board to a finished product.

Department X was the largest single producer in the industrial area in which it competed. It took 40 per cent of the domestic market in this industrial area, and the department was confident of retaining its share in the market. Its major competitors were several other large electrical companies.

ORGANIZATION

Department X of the General Electric Company was organized functionally in six major sections. A partial organization chart, showing top management echelon of the department, is shown in Exhibit 1.

These six functional managers met with the department's general manager, Martin Adams, once every week for a general staff meeting. Any subject could be brought up for discussion, and the "Integrated Planning Study" was first requested because of dissatisfaction registered in these meetings.

The Operations Research and Synthesis section was the most recent one to be added to the department's organization structure. The work of Operations Research and Synthesis has been defined by the General Electric Company in the following way:

> Operations Research and Synthesis is the work of seeking and finding such patterns that managerial decisions may be based upon more rigorously established information concerning relevant factors and probable consequences which would be likely to result from pursuing various alternatives.[1]

Mr. Wood said that he viewed the work of his section as "the responsibility of applying diverse knowledge to an analysis of the business and its parts in order to understand them better." He went on to explain that currently he had three specialists working for him, each covering a major area of work.

THE SITUATION PRIOR TO 1960

Mr. Scofield observed that the department's planning procedures prior to 1960 were "typical functional planning procedures." He continued:

EXHIBIT 1

DEPARTMENT X, GENERAL ELECTRIC COMPANY

Partial Organization Chart (as of 1962)

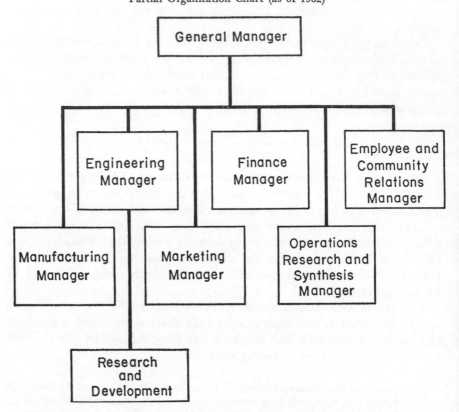

"We did product planning and market forecasting, but generally speaking these things were done without being 'pulled together' properly."

As indicated earlier, the subject of integrated planning first came up at the weekly manager staff meetings. At these meetings special attention was drawn to the requirement of planning further ahead. It was stressed that planning would have to be more and more interdependent if the resultant plans were to be realistic and effective.

Following these discussions, Mr. Adams requested Mr. Wood to have the Operations Research and Synthesis (O.R.&S.) section undertake a major study of integrated planning. The study, he said, would be designed to explore ways in which the department could integrate its planning activities more effectively.

The O.R.&S. section (like any section in an operating component of the General Electric Company) was able to draw upon information and advice provided by the service components. In fact, as the project progressed, the section recruited the aid of an executive from Marketing Services who spent considerable time aiding in the formulation of progressive steps in the analysis. However, the section was able to determine the approaches it might take in the project, and its decisions were subject only to approval by the department's general manager, Mr. Adams.

INITIAL APPROACH TO THE STUDY

Mr. Scofield related that it was not easy to decide where the study would begin. The subject could be looked at from any number of angles, but it quickly became evident to Mr. Wood and himself that there was a deceptive harmony when the subject was couched in general terms. "There is general agreement that planning is desirable," he said, "but when you start looking at a specific situation, the agreement begins to crumble."

It quickly became clear to them that they must determine a basic strategy of approach to the study. They felt that they were faced with two sharply dissimilar alternatives from which to choose. These were:

1. Whether the study should be a search by the O.R.&S. men *personally*, bringing to bear their own ideas and experiences in attempting to develop some possible solutions to the problems of integrating planning activities; or
2. Whether they should seek the cooperation of *section managers*, interviewing them to find out what were the important, meaningful, and constructive aspects of the study to them, in terms of their own job responsibilities.

The second alternative offered the prospect of a more complex study, said Mr. Scofield, but it also offered the best chance for long-term effectiveness. Because of this, they decided that this second alternative would be the underlying factor in the methodology of the study.

Looking back on the decision in retrospect in 1962, Mr. Scofield expressed the firm belief that it had been the wisest move. "The prime prerequisite for success in integrating the planning activities of a business must be *involvement*," he emphasized. "A staff agency, such as our O.R.&S. group, can help in identifying relevant factors and in organizing them for effective use. Basically, however, the elements of any plan must be built up by the top management group itself."

Once they had made this choice, Mr. Wood and Mr. Scofield began scheduling a series of interviews with the general manager, and with each of the functional managers. In these interviews they sought to identify the integrated planning needs of the department as seen by each of these managers. The two O.R.&S. men put a series of 11 questions to each manager and took extensive notes of replies and ideas expressed in each case. (The 11 questions are listed in Exhibit 2.)

Mr. Scofield said that both he and Mr. Wood attempted to be nondirective in all the interviewing procedures of the project. Their job, he said, was to ask probing questions and to reflect the ideas expressed in the interviews as impartially and objectively as possible.

This series of interviews was conducted, and then about four weeks later Mr. Wood submitted a summary statement to Mr. Adams. It represented an accurate reflection of the ideas and beliefs expressed by the managers, and it was prepared after a careful scrutiny of all notes taken in the interviews. (Main points from this summary statement are shown in Exhibit 3.)

Mr. Scofield pointed out that the summary statement used the term "business plan." "One of the basic points agreed upon by the managers," he continued, "was that, if we are to have integrated planning, we need a general business plan. We might just as well have used the term 'long-range plan,' or 'strategic plan'—to us this makes no important difference. The important thing is the principle of needing such a plan."

Upon receipt of this summary statement, Mr. Adams called a special

EXHIBIT 2

DEPARTMENT X, GENERAL ELECTRIC COMPANY

Integrated Planning Study

Series of 11 Questions Asked in Initial Interviews

1. What do you consider to be the planning activities in your section and in the rest of the department?
2. What activities in your section are strongly dependent on, or influenced by, planning activities?
3. What activities in other components are strongly dependent on, or influenced by, planning activities?
4. What is your standard, what test do you use, for including something in the category of planning activities?
5. Do you believe that this thing we call "better integration" is necessary?
6. Can you tell us what you think integrated planning is?
7. How is business planning done now?
8. What is wrong with it
9. Why aren't we doing properly integrated planning now?
10. What activities in other sections should be integrated with activities in your section?
11. Are there some parts of integrated planning activities that are more important than others, that have higher priorities than others? If so, what are they?

EXHIBIT 3

DEPARTMENT X, GENERAL ELECTRIC COMPANY

Integrated Planning Study

Summary Statement (9 Main Points)

1. Planning can be divided into two categories:
   - "Business" planning.
   - "Operational" planning.
2. To operate most effectively it is necessary to integrate certain planning activities; for integration of business planning activities a business plan is necessary.
3. Broad, timely, and accurate communications are essential to sound integration and to profitable business planning.
4. Specific identification and evaluation of alternatives (products, strategies, markets, and the like) are essential for sound business planning.
5. The department's business is large enough and complex enough both to afford and to require continuous and broad attention to be devoted to planning and to the integration of planning activities.
6. Good planning requires a very much larger investment of time and effort than not doing planning.
7. Business planning of the proper scope and effectiveness is practically an unknown activity in much of industry.
8. A strong and acted-upon conviction of the need for business planning is necessary if it is not to be slighted in favor of numerous operational pressures.
9. A sound balance between fixedness and flexibility is critical to good planning.

---

meeting of managers to discuss its conclusions. At this meeting each manager agreed that his views had been accurately expressed in the statement. Each manager also appeared to agree with the assessment that, if these statements could be translated into an operational approach, it would help the department immensely.

However, Mr. Adams noted that the statement and the discussion were still at a generalized and abstract level. While everyone agreed a business plan was desirable, they were still short on any specific details of content. He therefore proposed another meeting of managers to be held two weeks later and suggested that this meeting, and the next phase of the study, should concentrate upon more specific analysis.

ELEMENTS OF THE BUSINESS PLAN

At this ensuing meeting, Mr. Adams took a major part in initiating the discussion. The prime purpose of the meeting was the generation of ideas, and all sorts of thoughts were brought forward for consideration.

Most of them were directed toward providing an operational basis for the proposed business plan: For example, it was proposed that quarterly managers' meetings be held to hear and discuss the latest market conditions as they affected the actions of the various sections of the department.

According to Mr. Scofield, this was a lively meeting and in it the general manager, Mr. Adams, demonstrated his enthusiasm for the project more clearly than he had ever done before. Following the meeting, one of the functional managers commented to Mr. Scofield that "this project is well worthwhile. There were a number of points raised in that meeting that I never would have thought of. My attention was held for two and a half hours, and it is a rare person who can hold my attention for more than 20 minutes at a time!"

This meeting served as a base for the next phase of the study, which included a second series of interviews. The interviews were designed to take a more detailed look at the subject and if possible to isolate major elements which the managers believed should be included in a business plan. As a result of these interviews, Mr. Wood and Mr. Scofield reported that the managers were "unanimous" in identifying seven major elements needed in the business plan. (These seven elements are listed in Exhibit 4.)

Next, the O.R.&S. men sought to find appropriate terms and measurements in which to express these major elements of the business plan. It was at this point that they turned to the work of the service components of the General Electric Company and sought to relate the company's "key result areas" (see General Electric Company *A* case for details) to the elements of the business plan which they had drawn from the interviews with managers in the department. This, they thought, seemed to be a logical step, since the key result areas helped to direct the managers toward the kind of information they would need.

A large matrix was therefore developed, relating the eight areas to the

EXHIBIT 4

DEPARTMENT *X*, GENERAL ELECTRIC COMPANY

Integrated Planning Study

Seven Major Elements of a Business Plan

1. The present situation.
2. Future conditions (forecasts).
3. Assumptions (other than forecasts).
4. Goals (results to be achieved).
5. Plans (actions to be taken).
6. Measurements of actions accomplished and of results achieved.
7. Integration (identifying related activities and associating them).

Key Result Areas / Elements of a Plan	Present Situation	Future Conditions (Forecasts)	Assumptions (Other than Forecasts)	Goals (Results)	Plans (Actions)	Actions Accomplished	Results Achieved	Integration Program
Profitability								
Market Position								
Productivity								
Product Leadership								
Personnel Development								
Employee Attitudes								
Public Responsibility								
Balance Between Short and Long Term Goals								

EXHIBIT 5

DEPARTMENT X, GENERAL ELECTRIC COMPANY

Integrated Planning Study—Large Matrix

seven elements of the plan. Mr. Wood and Mr. Scofield believed that the information required to fill in the matrix would provide all the information necessary for a highly effective business planning structure. (The matrix developed is shown in Exhibit 5.)

It soon became evident, however, that this approach would not be practical. In the first place, it would be very hard to develop satisfactory measurements for many of the relationships in the matrix. Second, and even more fundamentally, it was doubtful whether a large number of these relationships would prove useful in the project at hand.

In these circumstances Mr. Wood and Mr. Scofield reoriented their efforts to thinking in terms of a simplified approach. They talked with members of the Marketing Services component of General Electric and eventually decided to include just the two items of most frequent and most intense concern to the managers: (1) market position and (2) profitability. While preparing this approach, both Mr. Wood and Mr. Scofield engaged in informal discussions with Mr. Adams and the other functional managers. Consequently, when the new approach was decided upon, they felt they had a consensus of agreement on a method which would be the basis upon which a formalized business plan might be built. (The form of the new approach is shown in Exhibit 6.)

POLICY STATEMENT ON BUSINESS PLANNING

Having reached this point, Mr. Wood and Mr. Scofield believed they should develop a policy statement on business planning for the department. Explaining this move, Mr. Scofield drew attention to the importance placed upon recording each phase of the project. "We have considered it very important to get down in writing the findings of each successive step," he said, "even if much of what has been written appears obvious. We feel that we will all gain a better understanding of what we have accomplished, and of what we should do next, if we are explicit and insist on writing things down."

The development of the policy statement was desirable for several reasons, said Mr. Scofield. First, it would draw together a framework for the evolution of a business plan. Second, it would clarify some of the existing fuzziness about the concept of planning. "We wanted to express the basis of our thinking as clearly as possible." Third, it would help to implement the expressed desire of the general manager to establish performance standards for planning. This last aspect indicated the need for:

* Clear and definite procedures.

(text continues on page 237)

Plan Elements	Significant Business Considerations	Market Position	Profitability	
Department Objectives				
Goals				
Primary Influences				
Assumptions and Forecasts				
Alternative Courses to Reach Goals				
Limitations and Alternatives				
Selected Alternatives				
Department Plans				
Responsibilities				

EXHIBIT 6

DEPARTMENT X, GENERAL ELECTRIC COMPANY
Integrated Planning Study—New Approach

EXHIBIT 7

DEPARTMENT X, GENERAL ELECTRIC COMPANY

Integrated Planning Study

Policy Statement on Business Planning (excerpts)

Shifting economic environment, advancing technology, and changing social considerations impose rapid, sometimes sudden, changes upon the conditions under which the department is doing business. As conditions change, it is necessary to reappraise current plans in the light of the conditions for which the plans were made, analyze those plans and current actions stemming from them, and make appropriate revisions in the plans.

Changes in the overall department strategies, which should be reflected in a "department business plan," impose new requirements upon all planned actions within the department. Since a high level of organized performance is dependent upon integrated actions of the department's functional components, it is of utmost importance that the plans for these actions be integrated *with respect to both nature and timing*.

The economic, technological, and social conditions imposed on the business have been observed, at times, to require drastic and abrupt revision of plans of action. In retrospect, there is reason to believe that the drastic and abrupt nature of the revisions could have been avoided, or at least moderated, if the changing conditions and their effect upon current planning had been recognized earlier.

A policy is needed to provide a means whereby the department will generate and maintain a well-understood, documented "Department Business Plan," will make timely reviews of the conditions imposed upon the business of and make appropriate revisions to the "Department Business Plan," and will insure that the revisions are recognized and understood by all of the functional components whose own plans and actions are affected.

DEFINITIONS

Department Business Plan. Within this document the Department Business Plan will be referred to as "the plan." It is defined to be an official document of the department that meets the following general requirements and, later, specific requirements that emerge in the course of developing a Department Business Plan, as provided for in the Policy.

1. It will contain a set of statements that reflect the department's appraisal and interpretation of current economic, technological, and social conditions that are imposed upon the business.
2. It will contain a set of planned departmental actions. These action plans will be in terms of (a) strategies, or general directions, to govern detailed plans and actions of functional components, (b) specific goals, and time of achievement, for functional components, or (c) both.

EXHIBIT 7

Concluded

3. It will contain the current overall business goals, in measurable terms, and the timing of expected achievement.

Planning Process. Within this document, the words "planning process" will be used to encompass the conceptual approach to business planning; the determination of relevant factors to be considered; the methods for analyzing these factors, the selection and definition of imposed conditions, action plans, and goals; and the procedure for accomplishing business planning.

POLICY

It is the policy of Department X to develop a sound business planning process concurrently with, and for the purpose of, the generation and use of a Department Business Plan.

- Methods for early detection of changes.
- Accurate recording of current decisions, to help in future planning.

(Excerpts from the policy statement are included in Exhibit 7.)

AN EMBRYONIC BUSINESS PLAN

At this point Mr. Adams called a meeting of managers to discuss the "Integrated Planning Study," particularly the prepared policy statement. In this meeting it was determined that the next step should involve the preparation of a preliminary document which would develop later into the department's business plan. The document was to bypass discussion of the planning process (this having been done earlier), and to concentrate on operational details of the plan. Specifically it was to include:

1. A list of assumptions being made by the department in appraising the future.
2. A statement of the department's objectives and goals in the areas of (a) market position, and (b) profitability.
3. A procedure designed to keep the plan continuously up to date.

Accordingly, this document was then prepared and submitted to another meeting of managers. Certain modifications in form and content were suggested, following which the preliminary document was officially submitted to Mr. Adams.

Mr. Scofield commented that the document contained no startling innovations. Most of the information was readily available within the department. Much of it, in fact, had been submitted in one form or another to the head office at General Electric. "The things which were new," continued Mr. Scofield, "were the ways in which different pieces of information were drawn together and the systematic effort to bring basic assumptions and premises into a coordinated plan."

Thus the nucleus of a business plan had been constructed. In the words of the O.R.&S. men, "Although this was only a starting point, the managers all appeared pleased that such a start had been made and that things were on the move."

Notes to the Text

Notes to the Text

Foreword

1. D. W. Ewing (editor), *Long-Range Planning for Management,* Harper & Row, Publishers, Inc., New York, 1958.

1. The Nature of Business Planning

1. The validity of this statement is assumed for the present, without supporting evidence. However, later discussion in this chapter and in Chapters 2 and 3 will demonstrate clearly that the assumption is well grounded in fact.

2. The term "orthodox theory of management" is used to refer to the school of thought which is usually associated with such people as Fayol, Mooney, Urwick, and more recently, Newman, Koontz, and O'Donnell. This is a school of thought which, in very general terms, can be characterized as containing two basic spheres of enquiry: (1) analysis of management in terms of functions and as a process of "getting things done through people," and (2) identification of "universal principles" of organization.

Over the years the second of these spheres of enquiry has been sharply attacked. The work done has been criticized as suffering from "superficiality, oversimplification, lack of realism" (H. A. Simon, *Administrative Behavior,* The Macmillan Company, New York, 2nd edition, 1959, p. 38). The result is that there is a growing view today which holds that "these principles no longer represent the heart of our knowledge of management, but instead are a small part of the total body of administrative thought" (W. W. Haynes and J. L. Massie, *Management,* Prentice-Hall, Inc., Englewood Cliffs, New Jersey, 1961, p. 6).

However, these criticisms have generally left the other sphere of enquiry relatively unscathed. It seems fair to conclude, in fact, that there is wide agreement among most writers on management that attempts to classify the job of managing into various task orientations and functions are both important and necessary. This is, of course, the aspect of the "orthodox theory" with which we are concerned here.

For an interesting, though somewhat biased, article which seeks to describe the various approaches to management theory and their participation today in a "kind of confused and destructive jungle warfare," see H. Koontz, "Keeping Informed: Making Sense of Management Theory," *Harvard Business Review,* July-August 1962, pp. 24ff.

3. H. Koontz and C. O'Donnell, *Principles of Management,* McGraw-Hill Book Company, Inc., New York, 1955, p. 42.

4. H. Fayol, *General and Industrial Management,* Sir Isaac Pitman & Sons, Ltd., London, 1949. See Chapter V.

5. For an examination of some of the reasons for these differences, see R. Tannenbaum, "The Manager Concept: A Rational Synthesis," *Journal of Business,* October 1949, pp. 229ff.

6. Some examples of modern-day controversies in this area include:

    • Can "staffing" be considered a function of managing?
    • Is "integrating" a more meaningful concept than "coordinating"?
    • Does "directing" convey one functional concept more accurately than "commanding"?
    • Does "measuring" convey the same meaning as "control"?

7. In actual fact, the word is subject to a great deal of confused thinking— as will be seen later in the chapter.

8. H. Fayol, *op. cit.,* p. 43.

9. *Ibid.*

10. G. R. Terry, *Principles of Management,* Richard D. Irwin, Inc., Homewood, Illinois, 3rd edition, 1960, p. 123.

11. H. Koontz and C. O'Donnell, *op. cit.,* p. 430.

12. R. S. Edwards and H. Townsend, *Business Enterprise, Its Growth and Organization,* Macmillan and Company, Ltd., London, 1958, p. 44.

13. "Groping" does not usually apply to routine day-to-day planning. Neither does it apply in a variety of other situations where the stable characteristics of key factors make planning seem mechanical rather than groping. However, as the future behavior of many different variables becomes involved and as the time span of a plan lengthens, the planning process increasingly becomes a groping activity.

14. M. H. Spencer and L. Siegelman, *Managerial Economics,* Richard D. Irwin, Inc., Homewood, Illinois, 1959, pp. 16-17.

15. M. E. Dimock, *The Executive in Action,* Harper & Row, Publishers, Inc., New York, 1945, p. 123.

16. R. E. Flanders, "Limitations and Possibilities of Economic Planning," *Annals of the American Academy of Political and Social Science,* July 1932, p. 27.

17. "What the Russians Know About Long-Range Planning," *Business Week,* November 1, 1952, p. 116.

18. National Planning Association Special Report No. 56, *More Long-Range Planning,* (A Joint Statement by Members of the Board of Trustees, Agriculture, Business, Labor, and International Committees and the National Council of the National Planning Association), Washington, D. C., 1959, p. 8.

19. J. A. Schumpeter, *Capitalism, Socialism and Democracy,* Harper & Row, Publishers, Inc., New York, 1942, p. 82.

20. It is easy to overlook how significant and how recent is this environment of change. Alfred North Whitehead once noted that the accepted view of

history has always been that each generation would live substantially amid the conditions governing the lives of its fathers. It would transmit those conditions to mold with equal force the lives of its children. Whitehead states that "We are living in the first period of human history for which this assumption is false." (See A. N. Whitehead's "Introduction" to W. B. Donham's *Business Adrift*, McGraw-Hill Book Company, Inc., New York, 1931, p. xviii.)

21. N. Wiener, *The Human Use of Human Beings,* Houghton Mifflin Company, Boston, Massachusetts, 1950, p. 3.

22. Quoted in R. J. Cordiner, *New Frontiers for Professional Managers,* McGraw-Hill Book Company, Inc., New York, 1956, p. 95.

23. There is such a thing as overplanning, but just when that point is reached is very difficult to say. Unfortunately, as A. G. Hart concluded some years ago, "It must remain eternally a matter of guesswork just where the margin of profitable estimation and planning lies. For it is impossible to tell accurately whether assembling more data and planning more carefully will yield enough improvement in income to pay for itself." (*Anticipations, Uncertainty, and Dynamic Planning*, Studies in Business Administration, Volume XI, No. 1, Chicago University School of Business, Chicago, Illinois, 1940, p. 81.) Overplanning can also have a stultifying effect on both the quality of work done by subordinate employees and on their attitudes. However, it is impossible to draw generalized conclusions about the point at which overplanning becomes a problem.

2. The Meaning of Long-Range Planning

1. Sometimes a classification will refer to more than one such variable, as we will see later in this chapter.

2. P. F. Drucker, "Long-Range Planning: Challenge to Management Science," *Management Science*, April 1959, p. 239.

3. In making this distinction between "strategic" and "implementational" long-range planning, terminology is being used which is very similar to that adopted by Walter B. Schaffir. He distinguished between "strategic" and "implementational" long-range planning in an unpublished paper entitled "Corporate Long-Range Planning: Reduction to Practice," Continental Copper and Steel Industries, Inc., New York, 1960.

4. As will be indicated in the section on research scope and aims at the end of this chapter, implementational long-range planning is not analyzed in detail in this study, except insofar as it comes into considerations of organizing for long-range planning in Part III.

5. H. A. Simon, *Administrative Behavior,* The Macmillan Company, New York, 2nd edition, 1959, p. 68.

6. *Ibid.*

7. These two questions are raised in terms of lead time measurements. There

are two main reasons why this is so. First, most management literature purporting to deal with long-range planning is concerned with implementational long-range planning and hence with lead times. And second, lead time is not only a more comprehensible concept, but it is also demonstrably shorter than either direct impact time or epochal time.

8. M. Gainsbrugh *et al.*, "Planning Capital Expenditures—and the Company's Future," *Business Horizons,* Spring 1958, p. 82.

9. W. Clark, *The Gantt Chart,* Sir Isaac Pitman & Sons, Ltd., London, 2nd edition, 1947, p. 1.

10. "The fine art of executive decision consists in not deciding questions that are not pertinent, in not now deciding prematurely, in not making decisions that cannot be made effective, and in not making decisions that others should make." C. I. Barnard, *The Functions of the Executive,* Harvard University Press, Cambridge, Massachusetts, 1938, p. 194.

11. See "Calling the Shots on 19—," *Business Week,* September 20, 1952, p. 84.

3. Historical Evolution of Long-Range Planning

1. National Planning Association, Special Report No. 56, *More Long-Range Planning,* (A Joint Report by Members of the Board of Trustees, Agriculture, Business, Labor and International Committees and the National Council of the National Planning Association), Washington, D. C., 1959, p. 4.

2. Actually there was some activity which might be termed long-range planning as early as the 1870's and 1880's. However, it seems adequate for our purposes here to use the year 1900 as a starting point.

3. E. T. Penrose, *The Theory of the Growth of the Firm,* John Wiley & Sons, Inc., New York, 1959, p. 183 (footnote).

4. Material drawn from J. W. Hammond, *Men and Volts—The Story of General Electric,* J. B. Lippincott Company, Philadelphia, Pennsylvania, 1941, p. 283ff.

5. One might, indeed, take the example of possible use of monorail systems for rapid urban transportation as a modern-day comparison. A General Electric spokesman was recently quoted as saying that his company is not totally sold on monorails for mass transportation. But he added that if the monorail does catch on, "we certainly want to be the foremost producer of monorail propulsion systems." See E. Cony, "Tomorrow's Transit: Cities Ponder Monorail as Facility in Seattle Operates Successfully," *The Wall Street Journal,* November 20, 1962. Since then, in September 1964, Tokyo opened a monorail from its airport to the main downtown area.

6. This is not to imply that there is no place for intuition in modern management. As General Electric executives have themselves said, intuition can have its place, and as a matter of practical fact *does* have its place, in managing a business. This view also receives support from J. S. Bruner in his book *The Process of Education,* Harvard University Press, Cambridge, Massachu-

setts, 1960. Professor Bruner calls for a major research effort to learn more about the nature of intuition and the variables that influence it.

7. C. R. Christensen, unpublished lecture in business policy, Harvard Business School, Cambridge, Massachusetts, May 17, 1960.

8. A review of progress in the practice of management during this period is to be found in *Fifty Years' Progress in Management, 1910-1960,* The American Society of Mechanical Engineers, New York, 1960.

9. This is the phrase used by A. D. Chandler, Jr., in describing the Pennsylvania Railroad's managerial innovation. Chandler gives no other examples of companies which adopted this distinction in activities so early, and he implies that Du Pont (1902) was the next major company he knows of that followed suit. See his *Strategy and Structure: Chapters in the History of the Industrial Enterprise,* The Massachusetts Institute of Technology Press, Cambridge, Massachusetts, 1962, p. 36. Some of the other material in this section is also based upon information contained in this book.

10. Peter Drucker, in a study published in 1946, said that General Motors was the only American company he knew which had for almost 25 years been working at the basic problems of policy. See his *Concept of the Corporation,* The John Day Company, New York, 1946, p. 11. See also Alfred P. Sloan's *My Years with General Motors,* Doubleday and Company, New York, 1964.

11. For further detail, see M. M. Hunt, "Bell Labs' 230 Long-Range Planners," *Fortune,* May 1954, pp. 120ff.

12. J. O. McKinsey, *Budgetary Control,* The Ronald Press Company, New York, 1922, p. iii.

13. H. Fayol, *General and Industrial Management,* Sir Isaac Pitman & Sons, Ltd., London, 1949, p. 72.

14. P. E. Holden, L. S. Fish, and H. L. Smith, *Top Management Organization and Control,* Stanford University Press, Stanford, California, 1941, p. 4.

15. For a concise summation of American planning ideas in the period 1930-1932, see H. Haan, "American Planning in the Words of Its Promoters," *The American Academy of Political and Social Science,* March 1932.

16. D. E. Lilienthal, *TVA—Democracy on the March,* Harper & Row, Publishers, Inc., New York, 1944, p. 58.

17. W. B. Donham, *Business Adrift,* Whittlesey House, McGraw-Hill Book Company, Inc., New York, 1931, pp. 8, 9.

18. A. G. Hart, *Anticipations, Uncertainty, and Dynamic Planning,* Studies in Business Administration, Vol. XI, No. 1, Chicago University School of Business, Chicago, Illinois, 1940.

19. R. J. Cordiner, *New Frontiers for Professional Managers,* McGraw-Hill Book Company, Inc., New York, 1956, p. 45.

20. The problems of wartime planning are well described in E. Devons, *Planning in Practice,* Cambridge University Press, London, 1950.

21. P. F. Drucker, *Concept of the Corporation,* The John Day Company, New York, 1946, pp. 76-78.

22. E. Ginzberg and E. W. Reilley, *Effecting Change in Large Organizations,* Columbia University Press, New York, 1957, p. 27.

23. P. Gustafson, "Plan Tomorrow's Profits," *Nation's Business,* August 1958, p. 29.

24. B. Payne, "Long-Range Planning: Special Report," *Chemical Week,* January 9, 1960, p. 78.

25. See, for example, G. Colm, *The American Economy in 1960,* National Planning Association, Washington, D. C., 1952.

26. For further discussion, see G. Colm, "How Good Are Long-Range Projections of G. N. P. for Business Planning?" *California Management Review,* Winter 1959, pp. 1-10.

27. *The New York Times,* May 22, 1964.

28. Eastman Kodak Company, 1960 Annual Report.

29. This is especially true in Western Europe, as the achievements of the European Common Market indicate.

30. "The Service Economy," *Time,* October 31, 1960, p. 76.

4. Some Basic Tenets of Strategic Long-Range Planning

1. One possible alternative is the word "directional," but it was rejected because it fails to convey a sense of competitive environment, and this omission is too serious to accept. Another possibility is "basic policy." For some people this term would certainly convey the meaning intended, but it was rejected on semantic grounds. The word "policy" has so many different meanings in current management literature that confusion would have been unavoidable.

2. C. I. Barnard, *The Functions of the Executive,* Harvard University Press, Cambridge, Massachusetts, 1938, pp. 202-203.

3. There is always going to be some degree of overlap between strategic and implementational long-range planning.

4. This subject is discussed in greater detail in Chapter 10.

5. Quoted in A. D. Chandler, Jr., *Strategy and Structure: Chapters in the History of the Industrial Enterprise,* Massachusetts Institute of Technology Press, Cambridge, Massachusetts, 1962, p. 235.

6. Quoted in "Calling the Shots on 19—," *Business Week,* September 20, 1952, p. 91.

7. Professor Kenneth E. Boulding has talked about this type of change in terms of a "system boundary." He was quoted as saying: "I think that, in

planning for the long range, the concept of the system boundary is of enormous importance. That is, you can only go so far along certain lines until there is some certain kind of boundary which changes the parameters of your system." See S. Thompson, *How Companies Plan,* Research Study No. 54, American Management Association, Inc., New York, 1962, p. 19.

8. P. F. Drucker, "Long-Range Planning: Challenge to Management Science," *Management Science,* April 1959, p. 238. Drucker was talking particularly about the type of long-range planning which is here termed strategic.

9. It is, of course, entirely possible that the demand for a product may regenerate after reaching a point of maturity, level-off, or perhaps decline. There are many instances of this happening, and it means, from our standpoint, that the product is beginning a second life cycle.

10. For source material, see: C. J. V. Murphy, "The Plane Makers Under Stress: II," *Fortune,* July 1960, pp. 111ff.; E. K. Faltermayer, "Corporate Horizons," *The Wall Street Journal,* October 25, 1961, p. 1f.; and S. Thompson, *op. cit.,* pp. 144-150.

11. Especially noteworthy among the planning abilities displayed by Martin's management are three which receive attention in Part II. First, there is an ability to determine the basic nature and skills of the firm and to relate the findings intelligently to the environmental needs of the time. Second, there is an ability to anticipate the mainstream of technological progress in areas related to the company's present skills. Third, there is an ability to unify the purposes of the company and to make decisions on the basis of systematic analysis and judgment.

12. One conclusion of a Stanford Research Institute study inquiring into "how companies grow" was that—

The exercise of plotting product (or service) life cycles in a time frame has the effect of revealing gaps in a company's future capability, either due to attrition of products or to expected inability to compete.

W. J. Platt, "How Companies Grow: I. Pre-Testing Company Planning," *Proceedings, 3rd Annual Industrial Economics Conference,* Stanford Research Institute, Menlo Park, California, 1958, p. 83.

13. M. E. Salveson, "Planning Business Progress," *Management Science,* April 1959, p. 225.

14. See J. A. Schumpeter, *Business Cycles,* Volume I, McGraw-Hill Book Company, Inc., New York, 1939, especially pp. 91-95.

15. The concept of "distant early warning" is discussed in Chapter 11.

5. Corporate Self-Appraisal

1. W. E. Hill and C. H. Granger, *Long-Range Planning for Company Development,* W. E. Hill and Company, Inc., New York, 1956.

2. P. F. Drucker, *The Practice of Management,* Harper & Row, Publishers,

Inc., New York, 1954, p. 49. Drucker goes on to conclude that perhaps the most important single cause of business failure is that the question, "What is our business?" is so rarely asked and so rarely given adequate study and thought.

3. Some other problems in attempting to classify products were discussed in Chapter 4.

4. Useful comments on this subject are to be found in W. R. Simmons, "The Elements of an Industrial Classification Policy," *Journal of the American Statistical Association,* September 1953, pp. 429ff.

5. W. Maclaurin, "Technological Progress in Some American Industries," *American Economic Review,* May 1954, p. 187.

6. It may be argued, with some degree of justice, that the cotton textile industry was made up mainly of small firms and that therefore it would have been difficult to sponsor research into synthetics. In this sense, the difficulties of strategic planning in dealing with "unmanageable" changes become clear.

7. T. Levitt, "Marketing Myopia," *Harvard Business Review,* July-August 1960, p. 45.

8. Even for the automobile, however, the strategic long-range plan must examine the possibilities of major change. Hear the observation by the president of Chrysler Corporation:

> In the automobile business we must be prepared for change. There is nothing sacred about piston engines or turbine engines, generators or alternators, four wheels or even one wheel. They can be replaced.

> But there is something irreplaceable about the relationship between the people who build and sell automobiles and the people who buy them. And the relationship must be preserved. Whatever changes lie ahead in the field of new products and new service techniques, we should always remind ourselves that the customer must continue to receive the best possible transportation that we can provide for him.

> If that means fuel cell engines, or cars without wheels—fine. . . . Customer satisfaction will never be obsolete.

> L. A. Townsend, quoted in "Notable and Quotable," *The Wall Street Journal,* November 14, 1962.

9. My observations here suggest agreement with a conclusion expressed in an American Management Association study:

> In appraising the capability of a firm, the focus is less and less likely to be solely on the industry in which the firm has traditionally operated. Broad industrial classifications will become less and less meaningful to managers as they seek unique opportunities to exploit the capabilities of their businesses.

> S. Thompson, *How Companies Plan,* Research Study No. 54, American Management Association, Inc., New York, 1962, p. 87.

10. Peter Drucker has drawn attention to a railroad which went beyond this concept of transportation and found that its real business was the development of the region it served rather than the physical movement of freight and people. See P. F. Drucker, *The New Society*, Harper & Row, Publishers, Inc., New York, 1949, p. 204.

11. C. I. Barnard, *The Functions of the Executive*, Harvard University Press, Cambridge, Massachusetts, 1938, especially pp. 227, 231.

12. See "Comments on the Job of the Executive," *Harvard Business Review*, Spring 1940, which was a rejoinder to a critique of *The Functions of the Executive* by M. T. Copeland in the previous issue. An adaptation later appeared as Chapter IV in *Organization and Management*, Harvard University Press, Cambridge, Massachusetts, 1948, pp. 111-133.

13. R. Donham, *His Brother's Keeper*, unpublished thesis, Harvard University Graduate School of Business Administration, Boston, Massachusetts, 1933, p. 101. While Donham was clearly oversimplifying when he talked about this as "the sole reason for a company's existence," he nevertheless was rendering a useful contribution in pointing up the need to give more attention to the customer's viewpoint.

14. H. C. Passer, "Development of Large-Scale Organization: Electrical Manufacturing Around 1900," *Journal of Economic History*, Fall 1952, p. 392.

15. This conclusion seems to be in substantial agreement with that of the Stanford Research Institute's study on growth. See R. W. Smith, "How Companies Grow: II. Management Implications of the S.R.I. Study," *Proceedings, 3rd Annual Industrial Economic Conference*, Stanford Research Institute, Menlo Park, California, 1958, p. 88.

16. E. T. Penrose, *The Theory of the Growth of the Firm*, John Wiley & Sons, Inc., New York, 1959, p. 137.

6. Establishing Objectives

1. General management textbooks, by and large, offer little help in clarifying prevalent problems about objectives. Objectives always receive some discussion in these textbooks, but in general the treatment is superficial and does not grapple with the more difficult conceptual problems. The majority fail to mention semantic fuzziness, and also pay little attention to the interconnected nature of the relationship between this phase (establishing objectives) and the planning process as a whole.

2. Objectives which are implied in this way often seem self-evident, and when spelled out in detail they sometimes appear to be excessive elaborations of the obvious. Nevertheless, making them explicit can be a very illuminating way of examining their validity; this is especially true in the case of strategic long-range planning activities.

3. These preliminary "bedrock" objectives are covered in greater detail later in this chapter.

4. E. H. Hempel, *Top-Management Planning,* Harper & Row, Publishers, Inc., New York, 1945, p. 25.

5. B. Payne, "Steps in Long-Range Planning," *Harvard Business Review,* March-April 1957, p. 95. Also see his *Planning for Company Growth,* McGraw-Hill Book Company, Inc., New York, 1963.

6. As Chester Barnard points out, the maintenance of incentives, particularly those relating to prestige, pride of association, and community satisfaction, all call for growth. "To grow," he writes, "seems to offer opportunity for the realization of all kinds of active incentives." See C. I. Barnard, *The Functions of the Executive,* Harvard University Press, Cambridge, Massachusetts, 1938, p. 159.

7. These terms are adopted from the analysis of E. Devons in *Planning in Practice,* Cambridge University Press, London, 1950, pp. 27ff. As the reader will observe, most of the following analysis is applicable not only to strategic long-range planning but also to planning more generally.

8. E. Devons, *op. cit.,* pp. 38-39.

9. See, for example, E. C. Schleh, *Management by Results,* McGraw-Hill Book Company, Inc., New York, 1961, p. 43.

7. Assumptions About the Future

1. F. H. Knight, *Risk, Uncertainty and Profit,* Houghton Mifflin Company, Boston, Massachusetts, 1921, especially pp. 347-348. On this subject see also M. H. Spencer and L. Siegelman, *Managerial Economics,* Richard D. Irwin, Inc., Homewood, Illinois, 1959, Chapter 1.

2. E. Devons, *Planning in Practice,* Cambridge University Press, London, 1950, pp. 157-158.

3. "The greater part of a complete plan is unexpressed thought (intention), implied or assumed action not stated, and the materials or 'givens' of the situation to which it relates, much of which is also not made explicit." C. I. Barnard, *Organization and Management,* Harvard University Press, Cambridge, Massachusetts, 1948, p. 166.

4. Occasionally the planners in a company will challenge the validity of an assumption that has been imposed and will take the matter back to top management for further discussion.

5. Such assumptions need not always be imposed at the start of the planning process, however. Sometimes planners discover during the course of their analysis that some matter requires the judgment of the top managers, who may say that "for the purpose of this plan you should assume such-and-such." Then this becomes an imposed assumption.

6. The parallel between the administrative considerations of making assumptions and those of setting objectives (described in Chapter 6) is apparent.

7. In actual practice, most of the detailed analysis undertaken by planners in

developing assumptions has revolved around economic considerations as is apparent in subsequent discussion. More recently there has been increasingly greater interest shown in developing assumptions about technology, both in the general and in the industry environment. This subject receives special attention in Chapter 8, "Anticipation of Technological Change."

8. *Looking Ahead With Pacific Telephone,* Chief Statistician's Division, Pacific Telephone and Bell of Nevada, November 1961, p. 1.

9. Although these assumptions are described as "judgmental" by Pacific Telephone, some of them, notably 6 and 7, have been derived directly from quantitative forecasts.

10. For a detailed analysis of this subject, see J. A. Shubin, *Managerial and Industrial Economics, Part IV: Forecasting and Long-Range Business Planning,* The Ronald Press Company, New York, 1961.

11. Industrial environment assumptions (discussed later on) are also present to some extent in this example.

12. A. D. Chandler, Jr., *Strategy and Structure: Chapters in the History of the Industrial Enterprise,* Massachusetts Institute of Technology Press, Cambridge, Massachusetts, 1962, pp. 233-234.

13. These concepts of industry are described in Chapter 5.

14. Quoted in S. Thompson, *How Companies Plan,* Research Study No. 54, American Management Association, Inc., New York, 1962, pp. 33-34.

15. Frequently these assumptions about factors of production are imposed by top management, in some cases because it is unwilling to have planners investigating subjects which are "close to home." This illustrates again a point made in Chapter 5: Most long-range planning concentrates upon the development of company strengths rather than facing up to its weaknesses. At other times the assumptions are imposed so that the planners can spend all their time working on developing ideas about what might be done. The top management frequently takes the attitude, in such cases, that "if the plan is good enough, it's our responsibility to guarantee the resource requirements can be met."

16. L. A. Kimpton, quoted in "Notable and Quotable," *The Wall Street Journal,* October 29, 1962.

8. Anticipation of Technological Change

1. This term was coined by W. E. G. Salter in his *Productivity and Technical Change,* Cambridge University Press, London, 1960. See pp. 26 *et seq.*

2. There are some clear-cut advances in technology which will *never* be incorporated into best-practice techniques because their adoption cannot be justified commercially.

3. For further discussion of this subject, see C. F. Carter and B. R. Williams, *Industry and Technical Progress,* Oxford University Press, London, 1957,

pp. 163 *et seq.* See also W. Maclaurin, "Technological Progress in Some American Industries," *American Economic Review,* May 1954, p. 182.

4. See, for example, J. A. Schumpeter, *Business Cycles,* Volume I, McGraw-Hill Book Company, Inc., New York, especially p. 100.

5. Sometimes the factors of production vary in their price relationships to one another. Take, for example, the case of an agricultural commodity which is produced in different parts of the United States. In one section of the country labor may be relatively expensive while land is relatively cheap, and here the most appropriate kind of technological advance will normally be in the direction of labor-saving machinery. In another section of the country, however, labor may be relatively cheaper and land more expensive. In this case technological advance will normally be oriented toward methods which allow more intensive cultivation of the land. These two different sets of relationships are likely to result in different best-practice techniques applying in different sections of the country.

6. On this subject see G. Terborgh, *Dynamic Equipment Policy,* McGraw-Hill Book Company, Inc., New York, 1949. Also, Y. Brozen, "Adapting to Technological Change," *Journal of Business,* April 1951, pp. 114ff.

7. W. E. G. Salter, *op. cit.,* p. 52.

8. See, for example, J. R. Bright (editor), *Technological Planning on the Corporate Level,* Harvard University Graduate School of Business Administration, Boston, Massachusetts, 1962. This book reports the proceedings of a management conference held at the Harvard Business School in September 1961.

9. Two well-known examples help to clarify further the causative nature of prediction. First, public opinion polls which seek to predict the outcome of a political contest may sometimes have the effect of influencing the actual outcome of such a contest. Prediction of victory by a substantial margin for one candidate, for example, may lead to complacency on the part of his supporters. Second, predictions of economic conditions may directly influence the ensuing cyclical behavior of the economy. Franklin Roosevelt's declaration that "the only thing we have to fear is fear itself" was inferentially referring to the causative nature of prediction.

10. The term is used by S. C. Gilfillan in "The Prediction of Technical Change," *Review of Economics and Statistics,* November 1952, p. 384.

11. The importance of giving attention to peripheral items in making assumptions for strategic long-range planning was also described in some detail in Chapter 7.

12. See S. W. Herwald, "Appraising the Effects of the Technological State of the Art on the Corporate Future," in J. R. Bright (editor), *op. cit.,* pp. 56-58.

13. "Gunpowder destroyed feudalism. Railroads created cities. The steam engine increased divorce. The automobile is moving the department store and the supermarket to the suburbs. The airplane reranked the great military powers." W. F. Ogburn, "How Technology Causes Social Change,"

in F. R. Allen *et al.*, *Technology and Social Change*, Appleton-Century-Crofts, Inc., New York, 1957, p. 12.

14. W. J. Platt and N. R. Maines, "Pretest Your Long-Range Plans," *Harvard Business Review*, January-February 1959, p. 125.

9. *The Choice of a Strategy*

1. On this subject see also Chapter 10.

2. "The present state of microeconomic theory of a firm limits applications of rigorous mathematical methods of analysis. While such methods can be applied to certain suboptimization problems, analysis of the strategic planning problem must, of necessity, proceed along less rigorous lines." H. I. Ansoff, "State of the Art in Making Plans—Some Comments on the Ill-Structured Problem," The Institute of Management Sciences, *First Symposium on Corporate Long-Range Planning*, Chicago, June 6, 1959, T.I.M.S. mimeograph, p. 5. See also: H. A. Simon and A. Newell, "Heuristic Problem-Solving," *Operations Research*, January 1958, p. 1ff.

3. H. A. Simon, *The New Science of Management Decision*, Harper & Row, Publishers, Inc., New York, 1960, p. 13.

4. Simon concludes that "there is now good reason to believe that the processes of nonprogrammed decision making will soon undergo as fundamental a revolution as the one which is currently transforming programmed decision making in business organizations." (*Ibid.*, p. 21) In justifying this view, Simon points to research which has uncovered basic discoveries about the nature of human problem solving.

5. "While business planning emphasizes trends, military planning emphasizes contingencies. To use a crude analogy, a business planner is concerned with planning for continuous, successful, day-to-day operation of a supermarket. If he is progressive, he also buys an insurance policy against fire, but he spends relatively little time in planning for fires. The military is more like the fire engine company. The fire is the thing. Day-to-day operations are of interest only insofar as they can be utilized to improve the readiness and fire-fighting techniques." H. I. Ansoff, "A Model for Diversification," *Management Science*, July 1958, p. 398.

6. Many businessmen speak of "shaping the future," but they are really attempting only to shape a small, though (to them) strategic part of the future.

7. "The fine art of executive decision consists in not deciding questions that are not now pertinent [and] in not deciding prematurely." C. I. Barnard, *The Functions of the Executive*, Harvard University Press, Cambridge, Massachusetts, 1938, p. 195.

8. The importance of growth as a bedrock objective in strategic planning is discussed in Chapter 6.

9. As is seen shortly, the very large corporation is handicapped in acquisition

activities by the difficulty of finding prospective companies which are of substantial size and which are willing to be acquired.

10. "Any entrepreneur who is ambitious to create an extensive firm in his own lifetime will find the opportunity to do so in the acquisition of already existing firms." E. T. Penrose, *The Theory of the Growth of the Firm*, John Wiley & Sons, Inc., New York, 1959, p. 187.

    Also: "We found several situations in which the chief operating executives evidenced dissatisfaction with their companies' current growth rates and notified all key executives that 'favorable consideration will be given to suggestions for desirable acquisitions.' " M. L. Mace and G. G. Montgomery, Jr., *Management Problems of Corporate Acquisitions*, Division of Research, Harvard Business School, Boston, Massachusetts, 1962, p. 66.

11. For further discussion on this point, see M. L. Mace and G. G. Montgomery, Jr., *op. cit.*, Chapter IX: "Some Problems in Integration," pp. 227-276.

12. Of course this statement is not meant to imply that all companies which engage in systematized long-range planning activities are aggressively managed or seek high rates of growth. As we have already noted, there are many companies which give priority to conservative soundness in their long-range planning. This discussion is simply designed to focus attention upon some important considerations which relate to those companies which do have rapid growth objectives.

13. Or perhaps not. It is entirely possible that in some instances companies have formalized their long-range planning activities as a result of dissatisfaction with declining rates of growth. However, we have no definite evidence on this point.

14. Some of the discussion which follows relies in part upon the analysis developed by H. I. Ansoff in two closely related articles: "Strategies for Diversification," *Harvard Business Review*, September-October 1957, especially pp. 113-114, and "A Model for Diversification," *Management Science*, July 1958, pp. 392-414.

15. Not until the 1930's did planned diversification become a widespread policy in business. The Great Depression hurt single-product companies with conspicuous severity, especially those engaged in the production of industrial goods. As a result of this experience, companies more readily saw the wisdom of broadening the product base of their activities. Additional attention to planned diversification was also encouraged by a resurgence of governmental antitrust activity in the late 1930's. Management's viewpoint in this connection was that, "increasing dominance of a single market and aggressive attempts to acquire a larger and larger place in it laid a firm open to prosecution, then the better part of growth was entry into new markets rather than more intensive cultivation of the old one." K. R. Andrews, "Product Diversification and the Public Interest," *Harvard Business Review*, July 1951, p. 102.

    A further fillip came in the years following World War II, when growing prosperity offered many opportunities to would-be diversifiers. There was also the wartime plant capacity provided by the Government, and after 1947 there were many new military needs as well.

In addition there has developed a greater recognition of the inevitability of technological and social change and of the existence of a product life cycle. Management has come to realize that the attainment of a monopolistic position in the marketplace or the establishment of fine research facilities might not be sufficient to stave off long-term adverse trends in demand for existing product lines.

16. One of the contributing factors to the troubles of the movie industry (see Chapter 5) was that some companies had vertically integrated by building and leasing chains of cinemas during the 1930's. This had the effect of increasing their dependence upon the movie as their product, and suggests the long-term dangers of this strategy.

   On the other hand, companies whose product lines have apparently strong long-term prospects do not hesitate to engage in a high degree of vertical integration, such as companies in the automobile, steel, and oil industries.

17. Lord Heyworth, *Capital Investment,* Lever Brothers, Port Sunlight, England, April 26, 1960, pp. 9-10.

18. Material abstracted and interpreted from Hamilton Watch Company case, on file with Intercollegiate Case Clearing House, Harvard Business School, Boston, Massachusetts.

19. The distinction between link diversification and conglomerate diversification is not always clear, especially to an outsider looking at a particular corporate situation. Many diversifications first appear to be unrelated, but upon investigation it is found that some basic skill or resource has logically linked the company's previous activities and its new diversification. Thus when Sears, Roebuck and Company entered the insurance field through Allstate Insurance, it might have appeared at first glance to have embarked upon a conglomerate diversification strategy. However, Sears is a merchandising firm with an important skill in its ability to sell to families of modest means. Seen in this context, the expansion into insurance selling appears to have had something of the character of link diversification.

10. *The Role of Top Management in Long-Range Planning Activities*

1. S. Carlson, *Executive Behavior,* Strombergs, Stockholm, 1951, p. 106. The few studies undertaken in the United States which have a bearing on the subject seem to support Carlson's findings. Dale and Urwick, for example, report the results of an informal survey in which they found chief executives making similar comments. See E. Dale and L. P. Urwick, *Staff in Organization,* McGraw-Hill Book Company, Inc., New York, 1960, especially p. 33.

2. "Putting all the commitments together, we get a work week something like this: forty-five to forty-eight hours of daytime work, one night working late at the office, two nights working at home, one night entertaining—all in all, some fifty-seven to sixty hours. And this evidently is a minimum; come

convention time, a trip, a company emergency, and the week can easily go to seventy or eighty hours." The Editors of *Fortune, The Executive Life,* Doubleday and Co., Inc., Garden City, New York, 1956, p. 65.

3. While this point was not directly examined during the present study and therefore no firm conclusions can be drawn, there appears to be a tendency within many firms to regard top management executives as the busiest unit in the whole organization. To cite one illustration: In two companies the members of staff planning units explained that they spent relatively less time with corporate officers than with key executives within divisions, mainly because of time pressures on the former. One planner observed that "we have to put a lot more in writing for the officers of the corporation."

4. P. F. Drucker, *The Practice of Management,* Harper & Row, Publishers, Inc., New York, 1954, pp. 161-165.

5. S. Carlson, *op. cit.,* p. 52.

6. These observations are not meant as a damning indictment of the way in which most top management executives do their job. First, this study does not include an analysis of top management work patterns, and therefore no definite conclusions can be drawn. Second, and even more important, no one has yet devised an orderly approach to the practice of top management that is really practical. Many general management textbooks enunciate tidy classifications and methodical approaches in trying to describe the work of an executive, but, unfortunately, fail to convey the wide-ranging, varied, and often inevitably disorganized nature of the work pattern of the real-life top management executive. The purpose here is only to point out the difficulties in seeking substantial amounts of time to spend on long-range planning.

7. This subject is covered later in the chapter under the heading "The Desirability of Separating Planning and Doing."

8. P. F. Drucker, *op. cit.,* p. 168. While Drucker was speaking particularly of the chief executive, his ideas are applicable to top managers generally.

9. J. G. March and H. A. Simon, *Organizations,* John Wiley & Sons, Inc., New York, 1958, p. 185.

10. There is little empirical evidence which deals in detail with this hypothesis. March and Simon mention only two studies: one conducted in 1940 within the Department of Agriculture, where the stimulus of deadlines was shown to direct attention to some tasks rather than others, and a 1956 sociological study of a group which was kept out of the stream of day-to-day operating tasks.

11. For another discussion of this subject, see J. E. Janney, "Company Presidents Look at Themselves," *Harvard Business Review,* May-June 1952, especially p. 64.

12. A. D. Chandler, Jr., *Strategy and Structure: Chapters in the History of the Industrial Enterprise,* Massachusetts Institute of Technology Press, Cambridge, Massachusetts, 1962, p. 41.

13. *Idem.*

14. R. J. Cordiner, *Problems of Management in a Large Decentralized Organization,* General Management Series No. 159, American Management Association, Inc., New York, 1952, p. 6.

15. Chandler has observed that the general executive of the large corporation is "as crucial and identifiable a figure in mid-twentieth century economy as Adam Smith's capitalist was in the late eighteenth century, and Jean Baptiste Say's entrepreneur in the early nineteenth." See A. D. Chandler, Jr., *op. cit.,* p. 314.

16. M. T. Copeland and A. R. Towl, *The Board of Directors and Business Management,* Division of Research, Harvard Business School, Boston, Massachusetts, 1947, p. 60.

17. A cynic has unkindly defined long-range planning as "the art of seeing neither the forest nor the trees."

18. J. C. Baker, *Directors and Their Functions,* Division of Research, Harvard Business School, Boston, Massachusetts, 1945, pp. 16-20.

19. These are the subjects with which boards have historically been most closely associated. See J. C. Baker, *op. cit.*

20. M. T. Copeland and A. R. Towl, *op. cit.,* p. 39.

21. Quoted in W. E. Hill and C. H. Granger, *Long-Range Planning for Company Development,* William E. Hill and Company, Inc., New York, 1956.

22. For a firsthand account of the Advisor-Board in use, see L. E. Newman, "Advice for Small Company Presidents," *Harvard Business Review,* November-December 1959, pp. 69ff.

23. L. E. Newman, in the article cited above, refers to a recent canvass of 100 company presidents which, he says, shows that "few chief executives regard their boards of directors either as sources of advice or as desirable checkreins on their own corporate actions."

24. F. W. Taylor, *The Principles of Scientific Management,* Harper & Row, Publishers, Inc., New York, 1911, p. 22.

25. W. E. Hill, "Planning for Profits: A Four-Stage Method," *California Management Review,* Spring 1959, p. 37.

26. W. B. Schaffir, *Corporate Long-Range Planning: Reduction to Practice,* unpublished paper, Continental Copper and Steel Industries, Inc., New York, 1960.

27. P. F. Drucker, *op. cit.,* p. 284.

28. A. Brown, "Some Reflections in Organization," PERSONNEL, July 1954, p. 35.

29. Devons's conclusion, which was based upon extensive observations of military aircraft planning activities in wartime England, was expressed as follows:

Anyone at a meeting who could promptly present in quantitative terms the various alternatives that were open, and the consequences of each, could usually ensure that the course of action which he thought most advisable was adopted.

E. Devons, *Planning in Practice,* Cambridge University Press, London, 1950, p. 188.

30. "It is not enough for top management itself to *awaken* to the need for more formal planning. Someone very near the top must also take the initiative in *pushing* long-range planning of the company-wide kind; otherwise the chances are remote that it will ever be started." H. E. Wrapp, "Organizing for Long-Range Planning," *Harvard Business Review,* January-February 1957, p. 38. (Italics in original.)

31. "No one but the chief executive can assume the final responsibility for approving a program of change that will unsettle established traditions, relationships, and policies and that commit a company to operating in ways with which it has had no prior experience." E. Ginzberg and E. W. Reilley, *Effecting Change in Large Corporations,* Columbia University Press, New York, 1957, p. vi.

32. In no company visited for this study were divisional performances said to be measured solely in terms of yearly profit results. Equally significant, however, was the fact that none of those interviewed expressed themselves as being satisfied with the appraisal criteria so far evolved within their companies.

33. In some large companies, long-range planning activities are carried out under direction of division or department as well as at the corporate level. In the present context "centralization" is construed as implying the headquarters office of the particular unit (that is, division, department) for which the long-range planning is designed.

34. "Centralization" is not synonymous with top management. It implies persons located in corporation headquarters who may be either staff or line executives.

35. E. Devons, *op. cit.,* p. 14.

36. R. J. Ross, "For LRP—Rotating Planners and Doers," *Harvard Business Review,* January-February 1962, pp. 105-115.

37. *Ibid.,* p. 115.

38. M. Smith, "How to Initiate Effective Long-Range Planning," Management Report No. 14, *The Dynamics of Management,* American Management Association, Inc., New York, 1958, p. 76.

39. While the department in the following case is called a "product line planning and control department," the activities for which it was ostensibly responsible come within our concept of long-range planning.

40. Material adapted and interpreted from Hadley Company case, File No. ICH 2M31, Intercollegiate Case Clearing House, Harvard Business School, Boston, Massachusetts.

11. The Staff Planning Unit

1. The fact is (as we shall see) that staff planning units are not nearly so homogeneous in character as the term itself seems to imply.

2. A. D. Chandler, Jr., *Strategy and Structure: Chapters in the History of the Industrial Enterprise,* Massachusetts Institute of Technology Press, Cambridge, Massachusetts, 1962.

3. Cited in American Institute of Management, *Executive Evaluation in the Corporation,* New York, 1959, p. 90.

4. This excludes the special case of the General Electric Company which is difficult to compare because of its various services divisions.

5. Of course, if one were to take into account all those people throughout a company who spend time working on detailed forecasting and fact-finding activities related to long-range planning, then the total number of people would have risen substantially in practically every case. Thus the accountant, the market researcher, the production planner, and many others have become involved increasingly in providing detailed information for long-range planning.

6. E. J. Benge, "The Common Sense of Long-Range Planning," *Advanced Management,* June 1959, p. 26.

7. T. Levitt, "Blue-Skies Approach to Tomorrow's Marketing," *Business Horizons,* Spring 1958, p. 121.

8. This discussion again excludes the case where men are engaged full time as detailed forecasting analysts.

9. Once again the case of men engaged full time in detailed forecasting analysis is excluded here. Sometimes these men are hired straight out of college.

10. Perhaps, since top management often thinks of long-range planning as a pioneering undertaking and one which requires imaginative thinking, it feels that the subject demands youthful vigor and enthusiasm.

12. Implications for Top Management

1. "Numbers tend inordinately to dominate decision making. They do this in two ways: first, by crowding out or pushing aside those intangibles which cannot be quantified but which may exceed in importance that which is measurable and second, by acquiring an aura of accuracy which leads the decision maker to forget that numbers sometimes have dubious validity." R. H. Roy, *The Administrative Process,* The Johns Hopkins Press, Baltimore, Maryland, 1958, p. 85.

2. Among these companies which have established formalized organizational arrangements for long-range planning, the opinion invariably seems to be "approval." No case is known in which a corporate staff planning unit, once having been established, has later been abandoned. Of course, it would

take considerable courage to institute such action, since the subject has been accorded so much publicity and popularity in top management circles during recent years.

3. On this point see the views of a chemical company executive, F. E. Smith, as quoted in *Chemical and Engineering News,* April 22, 1957, p. 47.

4. W. E. Hill and C. H. Granger, *Long-Range Planning for Company Develop-ment,* William E. Hill and Company, Inc., New York, 1956.

5. *The Wall Street Journal,* April 4, 1955, p. 1.

6. *Time* magazine made Harlow Curtis, then President of General Motors, its "Man of the Year" for 1954, chiefly on the basis of this policy decision. It is also worth noting that President Eisenhower reportedly viewed the mildness of the 1954 recession as being attributable to business executives who had become accustomed to think in "ambitious long-range terms" and who, expecting the economy to grow and prosper, did not permit minor variations in sales to divert them from their long-range goals. (Cited in H. Thomassen, *Business Planning for Economic Stability,* Public Affairs Press, Washington, D. C., 1958, p. 4.)

7. In the event that a company is large enough to undertake a variety of "lumpy" investments and seeks to spread them on a noncyclical basis, this may have the effect of evening out its investment pattern and therefore make some contribution toward overall regularization of business invest-ment in the economy.

8. "It has been found that in many instances where the total sales for the in-dustry are accurately estimated, there will nevertheless be substantially overexpanded facilities because most firms in the industry have projected a larger share of the growing market for themselves." A. R. Oxenfeldt, "How to Use Market-Share Measurement," *Harvard Business Review,* January-February 1959, p. 63.

9. The answer is not simply one of unilateral action, because beneficial results for the initiating company in that case would be contingent upon similar actions being taken by many other companies within a given industry. It is significant that in a study of investment regularization, Melvin DeChazeau did not find one firm which had consciously followed a policy of investment regularization. See M. G. DeChazeau, "Regularization of Fixed Capital In-vestment by the Individual Firm," in the National Bureau of Economic Re-search, *Regularization of Business Investment,* Princeton University Press, Princeton, New Jersey, 1954, p. 86.

10. A. N. Whitehead, "Introduction" to W. B. Donham, *Business Adrift,* McGraw-Hill Book Company, Inc., New York, 1931, p. xxvii.

11. N. W. Chamberlain, "The Need for a New Economics Unorthodoxy," *Business Horizons,* Summer 1960, p. 30.

12. See H. C. Metcalfe and L. Urwick (editors), *Dynamic Administration: The Collected Papers of Mary Parker Follett,* Harper & Row, Publishers, Inc., New York, 1940.

13. When a jury dismissed a court action against a cigarette company brought by a lung cancer sufferer, its ruling was that although smoking cigarettes *had* contributed to the man's lung cancer, the cigarette manufacturer could not be held liable. A counsel for the company hailed this verdict as a "great demonstration of the good sense and integrity" of American juries. (See *The Wall Street Journal,* November 12, 1962, p. 6.)

14. P. F. Drucker, *The Practice of Management,* Harper & Row, Publishers, Inc., New York, 1954, p. 373.

Notes to the Appendix

General Electric Company (A)

1. R. J. Cordiner, *New Frontiers for Professional Managers,* McGraw-Hill Book Company, Inc., New York, 1956, p. 33.

2. R. J. Cordiner, *Problems of Management in a Large Decentralized Organization,* General Management Series No. 159, American Management Association, New York, 1952, p. 7.

3. J. W. Hammond, *Men and Volts—The Story of General Electric,* J. B. Lippincott Company, Philadelphia, Pennsylvania, 1941, p. 102.

4. Material drawn from J. W. Hammond, *ibid.,* p. 283f.

5. R. J. Cordiner, *New Frontiers for Professional Managers,* McGraw-Hill Book Company, Inc., New York, 1956, p. 45.

6. R. J. Cordiner, *Problems of Management in a Large Decentralized Organization,* p. 6.

7. R. J. Cordiner, *New Frontiers for Professional Managers,* p. 91.

8. H. F. Smiddy, *General Electric's Philosophy and Approach for Manager Development,* General Management Series No. 174, American Management Association, Inc., New York, 1955, p. 21.

General Electric Company (B)

1. General Electric Company records.

Bibliography

Bibliography

Books

Albers, H. H., *Organized Executive Action*, John Wiley & Sons, Inc., New York, 1961.

Alderson, W., *Marketing Behavior and Executive Action*, Richard D. Irwin, Inc., Homewood, Illinois, 1957.

Allen, F. R., *et al.*, *Technology and Social Change*, Appleton-Century-Crofts, Inc., New York, 1957.

Allen, L. A., *Management and Organization*, McGraw-Hill Book Company, Inc., New York, 1958.

Anshen, M., and G. L. Bach, *Management and Corporations, 1985*, McGraw-Hill Book Company, Inc., New York, 1960.

Assuring the Company's Future Today, General Management Series No. 175, American Management Association, Inc., New York, 1955.

Baker, R. L. (editor), *Business Leadership in a Changing World*, McGraw-Hill Book Company, Inc., New York, 1962.

Barnard, C. I., *The Functions of the Executive*, Harvard University Press, Cambridge, Massachusetts, 1938.

———, *Organization and Management*, Harvard University Press, Cambridge, Massachusetts, 1948.

Baumgartner, J. S., *Project Management*, Richard D. Irwin, Inc., Homewood, Illinois, 1963.

Beichline, J. R., *Military Management for National Defense*, Prentice-Hall, Inc., Englewood Cliffs, New Jersey, 1950.

Branch, M. C., *The Corporate Planning Process*, American Management Association, Inc., New York, 1962.

Bright, J. R. (editor), *Technological Planning on the Corporate Level*, Harvard University Graduate School of Business Administration, Boston, Massachusetts, 1962.

Brookings Lectures, 1958-9, *Economics and the Policy-Maker*, The Brookings Institution, Washington, D. C., 1959.

Burns, T., and G. M. Stalker, *The Management of Innovation*, Tavistock Publications, London, 1961.

Bursk, E. C., and D. H. Fenn (editors), *Planning the Future Strategy of Your Business*, McGraw-Hill Book Company, Inc., New York, 1956.

Burton, W. W., "Forecasting Manpower Needs: A Tested Formula," in *Labor and Management Face the Future*, Personnel Series No. 172, American Management Association, Inc., New York, 1957.

Business Planning in a Changing World, General Management Series No. 167, American Management Association, Inc., New York, 1953.

Carpenter, R. N., *Guidelist for Marketing Research and Economic Forecasting*, Research Study No. 50, American Management Association, Inc., New York, 1961.

Carter, C. F., and B. R. Williams, *Industry and Technical Progress*, Oxford University Press, London, 1957.

————, *Investment in Innovation,* Oxford University Press, London, 1958.

The Challenge of a Buyer's Market, General Management Series No. 168, American Management Association, Inc., New York, 1954.

Chamberlain, N. W., *The Firm: Micro-Economic Planning and Action,* McGraw-Hill Book Company, Inc., New York, 1962.

Chandler, A. D., Jr., *Strategy and Structure: Chapters in the History of the Industrial Enterprise,* Massachusetts Institute of Technology Press, Cambridge, Massachusetts, 1962.

Charting the Company's Future, Financial Management Series No. 108, American Management Association, Inc., New York, 1954.

Clark, J. M., *Competition as a Dynamic Process,* The Brookings Institution, Washington, D. C., 1961.

Company Organization for Economic Forecasting, Research Report No. 28, American Management Association, Inc., New York, 1957.

Copeman, G., *The Role of the Managing Director,* Business Publications Ltd., London, 1959.

Dale, E., *Planning and Developing the Company's Organization Structure,* American Management Association, Inc., New York, 1952.

Dale, E., and L. F. Urwick, *Staff in Management,* McGraw-Hill Book Company, Inc., New York, 1960.

Davis, R. C., *The Fundamentals of Top Management,* Harper & Row, Publishers, Inc., New York, 1951.

DeArmond, F., *Executive Thinking and Action,* Loyd R. Wolfe, Chicago, Illinois, revised edition, 1952.

Devons, E., *Planning in Practice,* Cambridge University Press, London, 1950.

Dimock, M. E., *The Executive in Action,* Harper & Row, Publishers, Inc., New York, 1945.

Donham, R., *His Brother's Keeper,* (unpublished doctoral thesis), Harvard Business School, Boston, Massachusetts, 1933.

Donham, W. B., *Business Adrift,* McGraw-Hill Book Company, Inc., New York, 1931.

————, *Business Looks at the Unforeseen,* McGraw-Hill Book Company, Inc., New York, 1932.

Doob, L. W., *The Plans of Men,* Yale University Press, New Haven, Connecticut, 1940.

Drucker, P. F., *America's Next Twenty Years,* Harper & Row, Publishers, Inc., New York, 1955.

————, *Concept of the Corporation,* The John Day Company, New York, 1946.

————, *Landmarks of Tomorrow,* Harper & Row, Publishers, Inc., New York, 1959.

————, *Managing for Results,* Harper & Row, Publishers, Inc., New York, 1964.

————, *The New Society,* Harper & Row, Publishers, Inc., New York, 1949.

————, *The Practice of Management,* Harper & Row, Publishers, Inc., New York, 1954.

Edwards, R. S., and H. Townsend, *Business Enterprise, Its Growth and Organization,* Macmillan and Company, Ltd., London, 1958.

Ends and Means of Modern Management: Guides for Top Management Planning and Action, Management Report No. 30, American Management Association, Inc., New York, 1959.

Ewing, D. W. (editor), *Long-Range Planning for Management*, Harper & Row, Publishers, Inc., New York, revised edition, 1964.

Fayol, H., *General and Industrial Management*, Pitman Publishing Corporation, New York, 1949.

Fenn, D. H. (editor), *Management in a Rapidly Changing Economy*, McGraw-Hill Book Company, Inc., New York, 1958.

Ferrell, Robert W., *Customer-Oriented Planning*, American Management Association, Inc., New York, 1964.

Financial Planning for Greater Profits, Management Report No. 44, American Management Association, Inc., New York, 1960.

Folsom, M. B., *Executive Decision-Making: Observations and Experience in Business and Government*, McGraw-Hill Book Company, Inc., New York, 1962.

Ginzberg, E., and E. W. Reilley, *Effecting Change in Large Organizations*, Columbia University Press, New York, 1957.

Goetz, B. E., *Management Planning and Control*, McGraw-Hill Book Company, Inc., New York, 1949.

Gordon, R., *Business Leadership in the Large Corporation*, The Brookings Institution, Washington, D. C., 1945.

Gort, M., *Diversification and Integration in American Industry*, Princeton University Press, Princeton, New Jersey, 1962.

Hardwick, C. T., and B. F. Landery, *Administrative Strategy*, Simmons-Boardman Publishing Corp., New York, 1961.

Hart, A. G., *Anticipations, Uncertainty, and Dynamic Planning*, Chicago University School of Business, Studies in Business Administration, Vol. XI, No. 1, Chicago, Illinois, 1940.

Hempel, E. H., *Top-Management Planning*, Harper & Row, Publishers, Inc., New York, 1945.

Heyel, C., *Appraising Executive Performance*, American Management Association, Inc., New York, 1958.

Hodges, H., *Management*, Houghton Mifflin Company, Boston, Massachusetts, 1956.

Holden, P. E., *et al.*, *Top-Management Organization and Control*, Stanford University Press, Stanford, California, 1941.

Holland, M., *et al.*, *Management's Stake in Research*, Harper & Row, Publishers, Inc., New York, 1958.

Ingersoll, R., *Setting Policies and Operating Objectives in a Decentralized Organization*, Michigan Business Papers No. 29, Bureau of Business Research, School of Business Administration, University of Michigan, Ann Arbor, Michigan, 1954.

International Congress of Scientific Management, *Management Methods in the Next Decade* (Proceedings, 12th Congress), Sydney, Australia, 1960.

Jones, M. H., *Executive Decision Making*, Richard D. Irwin, Inc., Homewood, Illinois, revised edition, 1962.

Jurgensen, C. A., "A 12-Point Program for Effective Planning," in *Planning for Growth: Three Company Programs*, General Management Series No. 185, American Management Association, Inc., New York, 1957.

Kaplan, A. D. H., *Big Business in a Competitive System*, The Brookings Institution, Washington, D. C., 1954.

Keezer, D. M., *et al., Making Capitalism Work,* McGraw-Hill Book Company, Inc., New York, 1950.

Knight, F. H., *Risk, Uncertainty and Profit,* Houghton Mifflin Company, Boston, Massachusetts, 1921.

Koontz, H., and C. O'Donnell, *Principles of Management,* McGraw-Hill Book Company, Inc., New York, revised edition, 1959.

Koontz, H., and C. O'Donnell (editors), *Readings in Management,* McGraw-Hill Book Company, Inc., New York, 1959.

LeBreton, P. P., and D. A. Henning, *Planning Theory,* Prentice-Hall, Inc., Englewood Cliffs, New Jersey, 1961.

Lepowsky, A., *Administration,* Alfred A. Knopf, Inc., New York, 1949.

Levitt, T., *Innovation in Marketing,* McGraw-Hill Book Company, Inc., New York, 1962.

Lilienthal, D. E., *TVA—Democracy on the March,* Harper & Row, Publishers, Inc., New York, 1944.

Long-Range Economic Projection Studies in Income and Wealth, Vol. XVI, The Conference on Research in Income and Wealth, National Bureau of Economic Research, Princeton University Press, Princeton, New Jersey, 1954.

Long-Range Planning in an Expanding Economy, General Management Series No. 179, American Management Association, Inc., New York, 1956.

Long-Range Projections for Economic Growth: The American Economy in 1970: A Staff Report, National Planning Association, Washington, D. C., October 1959.

Lorwin, L. L., *Time for Planning,* Harper & Row, Publishers, Inc., New York, 1945.

Lucas, A. W., and W. G. Livingston, "Long-Range Planning and the Capital Appropriations Program," in *Financial Planning for Greater Profits,* Management Report No. 44, American Management Association, Inc., New York, 1960.

Mace, M. L., and G. G. Montgomery, Jr., *Management Problems of Corporate Acquisitions,* Division of Research, Graduate School of Business Administration, Harvard University, Boston, Massachusetts, 1962.

MacGowan, T. G., "Marketing Research—Vital Advance Planning Tool," in *Proceedings, Twentieth Annual Institute on Accounting,* Ohio State University, Columbus, Ohio, May 1958.

Management Planning and Control: The H. J. Heinz Approach, Financial Executives Research Foundation, Inc., New York, 1957.

Management Takes the Long View: Master Planning in a Growth Economy, General Management Series No. 171, American Management Association, Inc., New York, 1954.

March, J. G., and H. A. Simon, *Organizations,* John Wiley & Sons, Inc., New York, 1958.

Massachusetts Institute of Technology, *Management in an Era of Dynamic Technology,* Massachusetts Institute of Technology, Cambridge, Massachusetts, 1959.

Maurer, H., *Great Enterprise: Growth and Behavior of the Big Corporation,* The Macmillan Company, New York, 1955.

McFarland, D. E., *Management Principles and Practices,* The Macmillan Company, New York, 1958.

McHugh, K. S., "Long-Range Business Policies: A Case Study," in *Progressive Policies for Business Leadership,* General Management Series No. 156, American Management Association, Inc., New York, 1953.

"Men, Markets, Machines and Money: Long-Range Planning," in *Management Planning and Manpower Development*, General Management Series No. 173, American Management Association, Inc., New York, 1954.

Monaco, R., *Long-Range Planning for Business Growth*, (unpublished master's thesis), New York University Graduate School of Business, New York, 1959.

Monsaroff, B., *Economics, Science and Production*, Vantage Press, New York, 1958.

National Bureau of Economic Research, *Regularization of Business Investment*, Princeton University Press, Princeton, New Jersey, 1954.

National Planning Association Special Report No. 56, *More Long-Range Planning*, (A Joint Report by Members of the Board of Trustees, Agriculture, Business, Labor and International Committees and the National Council of the National Planning Association), Washington, D. C., 1959.

National Society for Business Budgeting, *Annals for 1953*, Cincinnati, Ohio.

————, *The Road Ahead*, Cincinnati, Ohio, 1952.

Newman, W. H., *Administrative Action*, Prentice-Hall, Inc., Englewood Cliffs, New Jersey, 1951.

Newman, W. H., and J. P. Logan, *Business Policies and Management*, South-Western Publishing Company, Cincinnati, Ohio, 4th edition, 1959.

————, *Management of Expanding Enterprises*, Columbia University Press, New York, 1955.

Owen, W. V., *Modern Management*, The Ronald Press Company, New York, 1958.

Payne, B., *Planning for Company Growth*, McGraw-Hill Book Company, Inc., New York, 1963.

Penrose, E. T., *The Theory of the Growth of the Firm*, John Wiley & Sons, Inc., New York, 1959.

Planning Ahead for Profits, Management Report No. 3, American Management Association, Inc., New York, 1958.

Planning for Profit, The 3rd Conference on Controllership, sponsored by the School of Business, University of Chicago and Controllers Institute of America, Chicago, Illinois, 1954.

Planning, Managing and Measuring the Business, A Case Study of Management Planning and Control at General Electric Company, Series II, Business Planning and Control Report No. 3, Financial Executives Research Foundation, Inc., New York, 1959.

Pritchard, C. W., "Launching a Company Expansion Program: III. Long-Range Planning Procedures and Organization," in *Launching a Company Expansion Program*, Financial Management Series No. 112, American Management Association, Inc., New York, 1955.

Riencke, J. O., "Planning and Screening for Products That Sell," in *The Dynamics of Management*, Management Report No. 14, American Management Association, Inc., New York, 1958.

Royal Institute of Public Administration, *Vitality in Administration*, George Allen and Unwin, Ltd., London, 1957.

Salter, W. E. G., *Productivity and Technical Change*, Cambridge University Press, London, 1960.

Sampson, R. C., *The Staff Role in Management*, Harper & Row, Publishers, Inc., New York, 1955.

Scaff, H. H., "Financial Planning—Long Term Forecasting," in *Corporate Treasurer's and Controller's Handbook,* edited by Lillian 'Doris, Prentice-Hall, Inc., Englewood Cliffs, New Jersey, 1958.

Schaffir, W. B., *Corporate Long-Range Planning: Reduction to Practice,* (unpublished paper), Continental Copper and Steel Industries, Inc., New York, 1960.

Schelling, T. C., *The Strategy of Conflict,* Harvard University Press, Cambridge, Massachusetts, 1960.

Schleh, E. C., *Management by Results,* McGraw-Hill Book Company, Inc., New York, 1961.

Schumpeter, J. A., *Business Cycles,* Vol. I, McGraw-Hill Book Company, Inc., New York, 1939.

——, *Capitalism, Socialism and Democracy,* Harper & Row, Publishers, Inc., New York, 1942.

——, *The Theory of Economic Development,* (translated from the German by Redvers Opie), Harvard University Press, Cambridge, Massachusetts, 1949.

Shubin, J. A., *Managerial and Industrial Economics,* The Ronald Press Company, New York, 1961.

Simon, H. A., *Administrative Behavior,* The Macmillan Company, New York, 2nd edition, New York, 1959.

——, *The New Science of Management Decision,* Harper & Row, Publishers, Inc., New York, 1960.

Smith, M., "How to Initiate Effective Long-Range Planning," in *The Dynamics of Management,* Management Report No. 14, American Management Association, Inc., New York, 1958.

Songer, W. A., "Organizing for Growth and Change," in *Management Takes the Long View,* General Management Series No. 171, American Management Association, Inc., New York, 1954.

Spencer, M. H., and L. Siegelman, *Managerial Economics—Decision-Making and Forward Planning,* Richard D. Irwin, Inc., Homewood, Illinois, 1959.

Spriegel, W. R., *Principles of Business Organization and Operation,* Prentice-Hall, Inc., Englewood Cliffs, New Jersey, 3rd edition, 1960.

Stanford Research Institute, *Implementing Long-Range Company Planning,* Menlo Park, California, 1957.

——, *Proceedings, Industrial Economics Conference,* Menlo Park, California, 1956.

——, *Proceedings, Long-Range Planning Service Client Conference,* Menlo Park, California, 1962.

——, *Proceedings, 3rd Annual Industrial Economics Conference: How Companies Grow,* Menlo Park, California, 1958.

Steiner, G. A. (editor), *Managerial Long-Range Planning,* McGraw-Hill Book Company, Inc., New York, 1963.

Stryker, P., and the Editors of *Fortune, A Guide to Modern Management Methods,* McGraw-Hill Book Company, Inc., New York, 1954.

Tait, R. C., "Long-Range Planning: New Dimensions and Established Principles," in *Targets for Management,* General Management Series No. 177, American Management Association, Inc., New York, 1955.

Taylor, F. W., *The Principles of Scientific Management,* Harper & Row, Publishers, Inc., New York, 1911.

Technical Planning in the Defense Industry, Management Bulletin No. 25, American Management Association, Inc., New York, 1963.

Techniques of Long-Range Company Planning, National Industrial Conference Board, Round Table Panel, New York, May 15, 1952.

Terborgh, G., *Dynamic Equipment Policy*, McGraw-Hill Book Company, Inc., New York, 1949.

Terry, G. R., *Principles of Management*, Richard D. Irwin, Inc., Homewood, Illinois, 3rd edition, 1960.

The Institute of Management Sciences, *First Symposium on Corporate Long-Range Planning*, Baltimore, Maryland, mimeographed, 1959.

Thole, H. C., and C. C. Gibbons (editors), *Business Action in a Changing World*, Public Administration Service, Chicago, Illinois, 1956.

Thomassen, H., *Business Planning for Economic Stability*, Public Affairs Press, Washington, D. C., 1958.

Thompson, S., *How Companies Plan*, Research Study No. 54, American Management Association, Inc., New York, 1962.

Urwick, L., *The Elements of Administration*, Harper & Row, Publishers, Inc., New York, 1943.

Villers, R., *Dynamic Management in Industry*, Prentice-Hall, Inc., Englewood Cliffs, New Jersey, 1960.

———, *The Dynamics of Industrial Management*, Funk and Wagnalls Company, New York, 1954.

Articles

Acheson, D., "Thoughts About Thought in High Places," *The New York Times Magazine*, October 11, 1959.

"Adjusting to Changing Business Conditions," MANAGEMENT REVIEW, April-June 1958.

Alderson, W., "Perspectives on the Planning Process," *The Journal of the Academy of Management*, December 1959.

Anderson, R. C., "Organization of the Planning Process," *Advanced Management*, May 1958.

Anderson, T. A., *et al.*, "Planning for Diversification Through Merger," *California Management Review*, Summer 1959.

Andrews, K. R., "Product Diversification and the Public Interest," *Harvard Business Review*, July 1951.

Anshen, M., "Businessmen, Lawyers, and Economists," *Harvard Business Review*, March-April 1957.

Ansoff, H. I., "Company Objectives: Blueprint—or Blue Sky?" MANAGEMENT REVIEW, September 1962.

———, "A Model for Diversification," *Management Science*, July 1958.

———, "Strategies for Diversification," *Harvard Business Review*, September-October 1957.

Applebaum, W., and D. Carson, "Supermarkets Face the Future," *Harvard Business Review*, March-April 1957.

Ardner, J. W., "Sales Forecasting Methods and Their Place in Long-Range Planning,' *N.A.A. Bulletin,* August 1958.

Atkinson, D. S., "Short-Term Controls Keep Long-Term Plans on Target," *Iron Age,* December 20, 1962.

Bachofer, J. B., "Short- and Long-Term Forward Planning Based on Contribution Margin," *N.A.A. Bulletin,* March 1964.

Bartlett, R. H., "Line Managers Play New Planning Role," *Iron Age,* May 30, 1963.

Benge, E. J., "The Common Sense of Long-Range Planning," *Advanced Management,* June 1959.

Bennion, E. G., "Capital Budgeting and Game Theory," *Harvard Business Review,* November-December 1956.

Besse, R. M., "Company Planning Must Be Planned," *Dun's Review and Modern Industry,* April 1957.

Blass, W. P., "Economic Planning, European-Style," *Harvard Business Review,* November-December 1956.

Bolin, R. L., and R. F. Messing, "A Better Way to Plan Your Company's Growth," *Chemical Week,* May 19, 1956.

Branch, M. C., "A Missing Link in Planning," *California Management Review,* Fall 1963.

Bronner, S. Z., "Reconciling Short-Term Profit Prospects with Long-Term Goals," *N.A.A. Bulletin,* July 1959 (section 2).

Brozen, Y., "Adapting to Technological Change," *Journal of Business,* April 1951.

Buckley, N., "How Sears, Roebuck Plans for the Future," *Dun's Review and Modern Industry,* October 1963.

Burck, G., and S. Parker, "Productivity: The Great Age of 3%," *Fortune,* November 1955.

"Businessman of the Future: Special Report," *Nation's Business,* January 1964.

Cady, E. L., "Departments Without Names," *Scientific American,* October 1956.

"Calling the Shots on 19—," *Business Week,* September 24, 1952.

Capan, F. S., "Essentials of Corporate Planning," *The Controller,* May 1960.

Chamberlain, N. W., "The Need for a New Economics Unorthodoxy," *Business Horizons,* Summer 1960.

"Chart Future Expansion Now," *Nation's Business,* November 1958.

Clamp, J. C., "Total Concept of Company Growth Planning," *Industrial Development and Manufacturing Record,* September 1963.

Clee, G. H., and F. A. Lindsay, "New Patterns for Overseas Operations," *Harvard Business Review,* January-February 1961.

Colm, G., "Economic Projections: New Tool for Top Management," *Sales Management,* November 10, 1955.

———, "How Good Are Long-Range Projections of G.N.P. for Business Planning?" *California Management Review,* Winter 1959.

"Coming: Revolution in Management," *Nation's Business,* August 1958.

"Company Organization for Expansion Planning," *Industrial Development and Manufacturing Record,* May 1959.

Cordiner, R. J., "Long-Range Planning—New Dimension in Our Economy," General Electric Company, New York, 1956.

Cornell, F. S., "How to Plan Products and Profits for the Future," *Management Methods,* November 1958.

Cowan, D. R., "Management and Business Forecasting," *Journal of Marketing,* October 1950.

Cresap, M. W., Jr., "Long Term Planning," *Advanced Management,* January 1953.

Danielson, C. A., "How We Took Hold of Long-Range Planning," *N.A.A. Bulletin,* March 1962.

Dauton, P. M., Jr., "Management Philosophy: The Time Dimensions of Planning," *The Journal of the Academy of Management,* April 1958.

De Pace, P., "Planning Ahead for Profits," *Advanced Management,* March 1959.

"Distant Planning Formula Wanted," *Chemical Week,* February 2, 1956.

Dowd, J., "Board of Directors Looks at Long-Range Planning," *The Controller,* November 1962.

Drucker, P. F., "How to Make a Business Decision," *Nation's Business,* April 1956.

———, "Integration of People and Planning," *Harvard Business Review,* November-December 1955.

———, "Long-Range Planning: Challenge to Management Science," *Management Science,* April 1959.

———, "Management and Automation," MANAGEMENT REVIEW, September 1955.

———, "The Management Horizon," *Journal of Business,* July 1955.

———, "Managing for Business Effectiveness," *Harvard Business Review,* May-June 1963.

———, "Population Trends and Management Policy," *Harvard Business Review,* May-June 1951.

Dufty, N. F., "The Planning Function in the Business Enterprise," *Journal of the Academy of Management,* April 1961.

Eaton, W. W., "Technological Insurance: A Must for Industry," MANAGEMENT REVIEW, June 1954.

"Economics and the Manager," *Business Week,* January 1, 1956.

Eppert, R. R. (interview), "Intelligent Program for Management Must Score Meaning of Facts for Forward Thinking," *Credit and Financial Management,* November 1956.

Evans, M. K., "Accountant's Role in Long-Term Profit Planning," *N.A.A. Bulletin,* July 1959 (section 2).

Evans, M. K., and L. R. Hague, "Master Plan for Information Systems," *Harvard Business Review,* January-February 1962.

Ewing, D. W., "Looking Around: Long-Range Business Planning," *Harvard Business Review,* July-August 1956.

"Executives Find Long-Range Planning Pays Off," *N.I.C.B. Business Record,* November 1956.

"Extra Dividends from LRP," MANAGEMENT REVIEW, October 1957.

Fair, W. W., "Long-Range Planning Is Only Effective When It Too Is Planned," *Office Management,* January 1958.

"Faster Rate of Business Change Puts Heat on Planning," *Iron Age*, June 28, 1962.

Fisch, G. G., and D. L. Jacoby, "Long-Range Planning—An Approach to Leadership," *Cost and Management*, April 1959.

"Focussing Farther and Sharper," *Business Week*, June 1, 1963.

"Forecasting," *Journal of Business*, January 1954 (entire issue).

Forrester, J. W., "Industrial Dynamics," *Harvard Business Review*, July-August 1958.

Freeman, W. M., "Big Job Is Open: 'Looking Ahead,'" *The New York Times*, August 7, 1960, section III.

Fredman, J. J., "Long-Range Planning and Cloudy Horizons," *Dun's Review and Modern Industry*, January 1963.

Gilfillan, S. C., "The Prediction of Technical Change," *Review of Economics and Statistics*, November 1952.

Gilmore, F. F., "Anatomy of Corporate Planning," *Harvard Business Review*, November-December 1962.

Gooking, R. B., "Profit Planning and Control at Heinz," *American Business*, September 1959.

Granger, C. H., "Best-Laid Plans," *The Controller*, August 1962.

———, "The Hierarchy of Objectives," *Harvard Business Review*, May-June 1964.

Grant, G. P., and R. E. Sellers, "Effective Systems Through Long-Range Planning," *Systems and Procedures*, August 1954.

Gustafson, P.,, "Planning Tomorrow's Profits," *Nation's Business*, August 1958.

Haan, H., "American Planning in the Words of Its Promoters," *The American Academy of Political and Social Science*, March 1932.

Harris, H., "How to Plan Profits Five Years Ahead," *Nation's Business*, October 1955.

———, "Three Year Study Shows How Managers Are Made," *Nation's Business*, March 1956.

Heimann, E., "Planning and the Market System," *Social Research*, November 1934.

"Help for Planners," *Business Week*, September 12, 1953.

Heyworth, Lord, "Captain Investment," Lever Brothers, England, 1960.

Hill, W. E., "The Planned Approach to Product Diversification," MANAGEMENT REVIEW, April 1954.

———, "Planning for Profits: A Four-Stage Method," *California Management Review*, Spring 1959.

Hill, W. E., and C. H. Granger, "Charting Your Company's Future Growth," *Dun's Review and Modern Industry*, August 1957.

———, "Long-Range Planning for Company Development," William E. Hill & Co., Inc., New York, 1956.

———, "LRP for Company Growth," MANAGEMENT REVIEW, December 1956.

Hitch, C. J., "The New Approach to Management in the U. S. Defense Department," *Management Science*, October 1962.

Hoadley, W. E., "Business Implications of Expected Population and Income Changes," *Commercial and Financial Chronicle*, June 13, 1957.

———, "Economist's Contribution to Management Planning," *Financial Executive*, December 1963.

Hogan, W. J., "Management Needs in Tomorrow's World," *N.A.A. Bulletin,* July 1959 (section 2).

Hoopes, T., "The Corporate Planner," *Business Horizons,* Winter 1962.

"How Management Tackles Advanced Planning," *Management Methods,* January 1958.

Hunt, M. M., "Bell Labs' 230 Long-Range Planners," *Fortune,* May 1954.

Hurni, M. L., "Decision Making in the Age of Automation," *Harvard Business Review,* September-October 1955.

"In Business, Everyone's Looking Ahead," *Business Week,* June 5, 1957.

"Is This the Coming Thing?" *Business Week,* June 23, 1956.

Jackson, H. M., "To Forge a Strategy for Survival," *Public Administration Review,* Summer 1959.

Janney, J. E., "Company Presidents Look at Themselves," *Harvard Business Review,* May-June 1952.

Juran, J. M., "Universals in Management Planning and Controlling," Management Review, November 1954.

Kami, M., "Electronic Data Processing: Promise and Problems," *California Management Review,* Fall 1958.

Kast, F., and J. Rosenzweig, "Minimizing the Planning Gap," *Advanced Management,* October 1960.

Kline, C. H., "The Strategy of Product Policy," *Harvard Business Review,* July-August 1955.

Koch, E. G., "A Practical Approach to Management Planning and Control," *Advanced Management,* July 1959.

Koontz, H., "Make Your Plans Succeed," *Nation's Business,* October 1958.

———, "A Preliminary Statement of Principles of Planning and Control," *The Journal of the Academy of Management,* April 1958.

Lester, D. R., and M. L. Owen, "How to Conduct a Manpower Audit," Personnel, May-June 1959.

Levitt, T., "Blue Skies Approach to Tomorrow's Marketing," *Business Horizons,* Spring 1958.

———, "Marketing Myopia," *Harvard Business Review,* July-August 1960.

Lindsey, F. D., "Statistics Frame the Future," *Nation's Business,* July 1955.

Long, N. E., "Businessmen's Stake in Regional Planning," *Harvard Business Review,* July-August 1958.

"Long-Range Planning," *Business Week,* June 23, 1956.

"Long-Range Planning: A Survey of Company Procedures," Management Review, October 1952.

"Long-Range Planning Becomes a Must," *Steel,* June 25, 1962.

"Long-Range Planning: Business Raises the Sights," Management Review, July 1961.

"Long-Range Planning in the Chemical Industry," *Chemical and Engineering News,* March 12, 1956.

Maclaurin, W. R., "Sequence from Invention to Innovation and Its Relation to Economic Growth," *Quarterly Journal of Economics,* February 1953.

———, "Technological Progress in Some American Industries," *American Economic Review,* May 1954.

Maines, N. R., "Meaning of Change," *Sales Management,* April 3, 1959.

"Management in the Future—Symposium," *Nation's Business,* July 1963.

"Marketing Planned 5 Years Ahead," *Sales Management,* May 19, 1961.

Marvin, P., "Management Strategy for Product Engineering," *Business Horizons,* Spring 1958.

McEachron, W. D., "By Long-Range Planning Shape Your Company's Future," *American Business,* February 1958.

Miles, S. B., Jr., and T. E. Vail, "Thinking Ahead: Dual Management," *Harvard Business Review,* January-February 1960.

"National and World Planning," *The Annals of the American Academy of Political and Social Science,* July 1932.

Neuschel, R. P., "How Flexible Shall We Make Our Plant and Facilities," *Advanced Management,* January 1951.

Newman, L. E., "Advice for Small Company Presidents," *Harvard Business Review,* November-December 1959.

Newman, R. W., *et al.,* "Toward a Communicable Understanding of Planning: Creeds and Objectives," *Management Technology,* December 1960.

"1960's: A Forecast of Technology," *Fortune,* January 1959.

Osborn, R., "G.E. and UNIVAC: Harnessing the High Speed Computer," *Harvard Business Review,* July-August 1954.

Ostpow, P. B., "Budgeting, Forcasting—and Planning," *N.A.A. Bulletin,* April 1963.

Oxenfeldt, A. R., "How to Use Market-Share Measurement," *Harvard Business Review,* January-February 1959.

Paley, W. S., "Materials: A Curb on Expansion?" MANAGEMENT REVIEW, March 1953.

Patterson, B., "How to Prepare for Future Company Growth," *Iron Age,* October 15, 1959.

Payne, B., "Corporate Planning: All Dressed Up and No Place to Go?" MANAGEMENT REVIEW, April 1963.

————, "How to Set Realistic Profit Goals," *Harvard Business Review,* September-October 1958.

————, "Long-Range Planning: Dynamic Discipline for Your Company's Future," address given at MacKay-Shields Associates, Inc., New York, 1960.

————, "Steps in Long-Range Planning," *Harvard Business Review,* March-April 1957.

Payne, B., and J. H. Kennedy, "Making Long-Range Planning Work," MANAGEMENT REVIEW, February 1958.

Pearson, A. E., "An Approach to Successful Marketing Planning," *Business Horizons,* Winter 1959.

Phillips, C., "'Subtle Spectacular' on Capitol Hill," *The New York Times Magazine,* May 29, 1960.

"Plan Tomorrow's Profits," *Nation's Business,* August 1958.

"Planning Capital Expenditures—and the Company's Future," *Business Horizons,* Spring 1958.

"Planning Inside Business: Thinking Big and Small," *The Economist,* July 13, 1963.

Platt, J. R., "Can We Foresee the Future?" *The New Republic,* December 8, 1959.

Platt, W. J., and N. R. Maines, "Pretest Your Long-Range Plans," *Harvard Business Review*, January-February 1959.

Prentice, H. W., "Industrial Progress of the Future," MANAGEMENT REVIEW, January 1955.

"The President's Panel: Corporate Size," *Dun's Review and Modern Industry*, May 1959.

"Push-Button Planning: In Sight for Businessmen," *Business Week*, December 15, 1951.

Rapoport, L. A., and W. P. Drews, "Mathematical Approach to Long-Range Planning," *Harvard Business Review*, May-June 1962.

Read, R. B., "Planning in the Larger Company," MANAGEMENT REVIEW, April 1958.

Reilley, E. W., "Planning the Strategy of Your Business," *Advanced Management*, May 1956.

Richardson, W. W., "Significance of Company Forward Planning," *N.A.A. Bulletin*, January 1960.

Rickard, E. B., "Past is History, Future is Planning," *The Controller*, October 1962.

Roberts, W. E., "Planning in the Medium-Size Company," MANAGEMENT REVIEW, April 1958.

Rockwell, W. F., Jr., "Planned Diversification of Industrial Concerns," *Advanced Management*, May 1956.

Ross, R. J., "For LRP—Rotating Planners and Doers," *Harvard Business Review*, January-February 1962.

Roy, H. J. H., "Operations Research in Action," *Harvard Business Review*, September-October 1958.

Royce, W. S., "Research as a Tool in Company Planning," *The Controller*, November 1958.

Salveson, M. E., "High-Speed Operations Research," *Harvard Business Review*, July-August 1957.

———, "Long-Range Planning in Technical Industries," *Journal of Industrial Engineering*, September-October 1959.

———, "Planning Business Progress," *Management Science*, April 1959.

Sanderson, J. P., "Draft Long-Range Plans That Get Results," *Business Management*, November 1963.

Schisgall, O., "How to Stay in Business 100 Years," *Nation's Business*, August 1954.

Seney, W. T., "Management Faces the Challenge of Change: How Long-Term Trends Are Affecting Planning and Control Practices," MANAGEMENT REVIEW, November 1958.

Shelley, T., Jr., and A. E. Pearson, "A Blueprint of Long-Range Planning," *Business Horizons*, Winter 1958-59.

Siegel, I. H., "Conditions of American Technological Progress," *Journal of Business*. May 1954.

———, "Technological Change and Long-Run Forecasting," *Journal of Business*, July 1953.

"The Significant Aspects of Profit Planning," *N.A.A. Bulletin*, January 1962.

Silberman, C. E., and S. S. Parker, "Economy's Scouts: Business and Government Economists," *Fortune*, December 1955.

Simmons, W. R., "The Elements of an Industrial Classification Policy," *Journal of the American Statistical Association,* September 1953.

Sims, R., Jr., "Industrial Intelligence," *Advanced Management,* July 1959.

Slichter, S., "Industry of Discovery," *Science,* December 26, 1958.

Spencer, M. H., "Uncertainty, Expectations, and Foundations of the Theory of Planning," *Journal of the Academy of Management,* December 1962.

Spooner, P., "Long-Range Planning: How Firms Decide Where They Want to Go," *Business,* July 1958.

"Splurge of Research Is Piling New Problems for Management," *Business Week,* January 4, 1958.

Staudt, T. A., "Program for Product Diversification," *Harvard Business Review,* November-December 1954.

Steiner, G. A., "Making Long-Range Company Planning Pay Off," *California Management Review,* No. 2, 1962.

————, "What Do We Know About Using Long-Range Plans," *California Management Review,* Summer 1959.

Stoltz, R. K., "Planning—Key to Research Success," *Harvard Business Review,* May-June 1957.

Strong, L., "Every Day Is Doomsday: The Ordeal of Executive Decision," MANAGEMENT REVIEW, November 1955.

Summer, C. E., Jr., "The Future Role of the Corporation Planner," *California Management Review,* Winter 1961.

"Symposium on Corporate Planning," *Operations Research,* July-August 1958.

Tait, R. C., "Long-Range Planning," *The Controller,* July 1956.

Teitsworth, C. S., "Growing Role of the Company Economist," *Harvard Business Review,* January-February 1959.

Thompson, K. L., "Long-Range Planning for a Growing Firm," *Journal of Accountancy,* March 1960.

Thompson, S., "How Top Companies Plan Success," *Nation's Business,* May 1962.

————, "New Dimensions in Creative Planning," *The Business Quarterly,* Summer 1959.

Thornton, F. O., "Planning and Aircraft Development," *Journal of the Royal Aeronautical Society,* May 1951.

Tilles, S., "How to Evaluate Corporate Strategy," *Harvard Business Review,* July-August 1963.

Tillman, R., Jr., "Problems in Review: Committees on Trial," *Harvard Business Review,* May-June 1960.

"Time to Worry," *Business Week,* April 7, 1951.

Tomb, J. O., "A New Way to Manage—Integrated Planning and Control," *California Management Review,* Fall 1962.

Trace, L., "How to Arrange the Future Today," *Business,* January 1963.

Trundle, R. C., "Planning Profits 10 Years Ahead," *Factory Management and Maintenance,* July 1958

Upgren, A. R., "What's Ahead for Business in the Next Ten Years?" *Commercial and Financial Chronicle,* November 15, 1956.

"Utilities Get a New Way to Plan," *Business Week,* November 28, 1959.

Waring, M. E., and P. W. Demarest, "The Follow Through—Necessity in Planning," *N.A.A. Bulletin,* August 1962.

Warren, E. K., "Where Long-Range Planning Goes Wrong," MANAGEMENT REVIEW, May 1962.

Weiland, P. E., "Long-Range Planning for Public Utilities," *Public Utilities Fortnightly,* December 17, 1959.

"What About Ten Years Hence? Leaders Bank on Huge Gains," *Credit and Financial Management,* April 1954.

"What Business Might Be Like 10 Years from Today," *Business Week,* May 24, 1952.

"What the Russians Know About Long-Range Planning," *Business Week,* November 1, 1952.

"Why Companies Grow," *Nation's Business,* November 1957.

Wolozin, H., "New Guides Help You Plan," *Nation's Business,* August 1963.

Wrapp, H. E., "Organization for Long-Range Planning," *Harvard Business Review,* January-February 1957.

"Year of the Planner," *Chemical Week,* March 7, 1964.

Bibliographies

Olmstead, B. E., *et al.* (editors), *Bibliography on Planning,* College on Planning of the Institute of Management Sciences, The Institute of Management Sciences, Pleasantville, New York, 1960.

United States Bureau of the Budget—Executive Office of the President, *Comprehensive Planning: A Bibliography of Current Publications,* Government Printing Office, Washington D. C., 1962.

Index

Index